EXPERIENCES OF CRIMINAL JUSTICE

Perspectives From Wales on a System in Crisis

Daniel Newman and Roxanna Dehaghani

With a Foreword by
The Right Honourable Carwyn Jones

Afterword by
Baron Thomas of Cwmgiedd, Kt, PC

I0222892

BRISTOL
UNIVERSITY
PRESS

First published in Great Britain in 2023 by

Bristol University Press
University of Bristol
1-9 Old Park Hill
Bristol
BS2 8BB
UK
t: +44 (0)117 374 6645
e: bup-info@bristol.ac.uk

Details of international sales and distribution partners are available at bristoluniversitypress.co.uk

© Bristol University Press 2023

British Library Cataloguing in Publication Data
A catalogue record for this book is available from the British Library

ISBN 978-1-5292-1422-2 hardcover
ISBN 978-1-5292-1423-9 paperback
ISBN 978-1-5292-1424-6 ePub
ISBN 978-1-5292-1425-3 ePdf

The right of Daniel Newman and Roxanna Dehaghani to be identified as authors of this work has been asserted by them in accordance with the Copyright, Designs and Patents Act 1988.

Cover design: blu inc, Bristol
Front cover image: gbimages / Alamy Stock Photo

Contents

List of Figures and Tables

Figures

Tables

Foreword

The Right Honourable Carwyn Jones

England and Wales is a strange legal jurisdiction. It encompasses two countries, one of which is far larger than the other and is often assumed to speak for the other. It is the only jurisdiction in the common law world with two parliaments that make laws within it, but only one parliament has the ability to enforce not just its own laws, but the laws of the other parliament as well. Legislatures in England, Scotland and Northern Ireland control their countries' legal systems. Not Wales.

Whenever new parliaments are established, it is almost universally the case that they are given legal jurisdiction over their own laws. Wales is the exception; it has the only parliament that has no right to enforce its own laws, that right having been held on to by Westminster. We still have the imaginary country of 'Englandandwales' when it comes to the law. We have 'national' organizations such as the 'National Probation Service', which covers this imaginary country. Too often 'andwales' is forgotten. Little attention is given to effects of justice policy by decision makers in London who are not familiar with Wales and its needs.

I practised law throughout the 1990s and remember Crown Courts at Haverfordwest, Carmarthen and even Lampeter (although this only sat for a fortnight every year and was kept open by the efforts of the late Judge Dewi Watkin Powell). There were Magistrates' Courts at Gowerton, Ystradgynlais, Fishguard and Bridgend, to name a few. Not long before I started to practise there had been courts in smaller settlements such as Mathry and Eglwyswrw. All these courts have gone and the centuries-old practice of justice coming to the people has been discarded by successive governments in favour of forcing people to travel many miles to attend court.

Nowhere is this more obvious than in rural Wales. Courts can be more than 30 miles away from people's homes, in areas where public transport, away from the main arteries, is infrequent. One court seems to do for entire rural counties. In addition, the legal aid reforms of recent years have led to 'advice deserts' in much of the country where people cannot even access legal advice locally. No justice system can claim to be effective if people have to travel significant distances to get to court and get no representation when they get there.

Much of the blame for this state of affairs lies to my mind in successive London-based civil servants simply looking at a map of an area about which they know little and applying urban solutions to rural problems. Ten miles is no distance in a big city; it is a fair way in a rural area far from public transport.

Wales cannot be forgotten, nor can it be assumed that what works in England will work in Wales. Accessing legal advice in the Welsh language together with the ability to conduct trials in Welsh is a service that is only required in Wales, yet it is not clear that this has ever been a factor in Whitehall thinking.

That is why it is so important to commission and conduct research on the justice system in Wales; to understand how changes in the system impact on Wales. Is there proper access to advice in both languages? Can people get to the courts? What are the challenges of providing a working rural justice system in an urban-based UK government department? What is the impact of not having a women's prison in Wales so that all women have to serve their sentences in England away from family?

All these questions are important, and Wales cannot be ignored. This, after all, is the nation of Wales, not the annex of 'andwales'.

Acknowledgements

This research would not have been possible without the support of the participants – who so generously shared their time and their experiences – and the funders (British Academy and Cardiff University) – who provided us with the resources required to conduct this research. We are also grateful to Bristol University Press – particularly Helen Davis, Rebecca Tomlinson and Freya Trand – and the reviewers for their patience and feedback.

We owe a debt of gratitude to colleagues (and, by extension, friends) who have supported us along the way. Particular thanks are owed to Fred Cram, Marianne Doherty, Sophie Doherty, Holly Greenwood, Faith Gordon and Rob Jones for providing feedback on the draft manuscript. As always, any errors and omissions remain our own. Thanks also to those who supported us in gaining access – including Niki Harris, Rob Jones, Ruth Payne and Huw Pritchard.

We are lucky to have worked with fantastic research assistants during this project – Antonia Needham, Samantha O'Rourke, Danielle O'Shea and Rachel Seddon. We have also been fortunate to have had Zara Bain and the team at Academic Audio Transcription transcribe our interview data to such an excellent standard.

Dan would like to thank his wife Rhian for supporting and encouraging this work throughout (and for providing such useful input across the project). He wants to dedicate the work to his children Betsi and Iolo, always his inspiration for trying to do work that makes a difference.

Roxanna would like to express her deepest gratitude to friends (some aforementioned) and family for providing their love and support, and – crucially – for their frequent reminders to take time off! Particular thanks are owed to her partner Matt, who is phased by little and who has made the most difficult academic year (and most difficult year, full stop) liveable and, indeed, enjoyable. A special shout-out to her nieces – Amätise, Beaux and Nöa – for bringing joy to her life this year and always.

1

Why Wales?

Introduction

This book is about criminal justice under austerity. It tells the stories of how those who work in or go through the criminal justice system experience criminal justice. In telling these stories, we focus on voices from Wales. Wales is the site of this research and the book provides a snapshot of how criminal justice is experienced in Wales at a time of austerity. Wales has been too often ignored in consideration of the criminal justice system of England and Wales, so we offer the insights of those with whom we spoke in south Wales to provoke fresh dialogue about criminal justice in the country. We hope the experiences we present will inform discussions about criminal justice in Wales, and across England and Wales.

We began this research at an event listening to heartfelt accounts regarding police racial profiling and the frustrations of the working class community in the heart of Cardiff's former docks area, once known as Tiger Bay (one of the UK's first multicultural communities). The event was the first public meeting of the Commission on Justice in Wales,[1] and was held at the Butetown Community Centre, a location resolutely part of the local community and thus challenging some received notions of the justice system having become detached from the people it serves. The meeting was billed as an equality and engagement event for the first review in over 200 years into the operation of the justice system in Wales. It provided an opportunity to understand the everyday experiences of justice in Wales within the communities who most suffer injustice. During this event we heard enlivening but sobering reflections on how locals felt let down by the criminal justice system; it allowed us to hear first hand the realities of those engaging with the system, particularly how the community felt ignored – and discriminated against – by the police and the broader criminal justice system.

---

[1]   See Welsh Government (2018a).

Most importantly, it reminded us of why we undertake research on the criminal justice system, highlighting the need for empirical study to engage with on-the-ground lived experiences, whether as practitioner, accused or indeed the wider community.[2] It further highlighted the deep and long-lasting impact of criminal justice on families and communities, and the wrongfully accused and/or convicted.[3] As such, we offer this book as a work of critical social research and, in so doing, seek to follow Scraton (2007: 10) by '[setting] out an oppositional agenda ... [seeking out, recording, and championing] the "view from below", ensuring the voices and experiences of those marginalised by institutionalised state practices are heard and represented'.

As Hillyard, Sim et al (2004: 385) have suggested, academic research on criminal justice should 'ask awkward questions of power and the existent social order'. By including marginalized voices, our view from below speaks to the reality of how the system presently functions and offers such a challenge. With sizeable cuts to the criminal justice system and increased poverty, disadvantage and marginalization, it is likely that the individuals and communities are suffering yet further under austerity. By providing detail on these often neglected perspectives, we can challenge the hegemonic narratives of criminal justice under austerity.

There is an additional, pressing need to add the voices from our study to wider discussions. Wales is facing the momentous prospect of devolving criminal justice and having its own legal institutions for the first time in nearly 500 years, yet little is known about the operation of the justice system in Wales specifically. While England and Wales form one jurisdiction, there are significant differences in terms of the historical, cultural, geographic, socio-economic and, indeed, legal landscapes. Often, England and Wales are treated as one entity, with research conducted in England claiming to speak for the whole of the England and Wales jurisdiction. Although our previous research highlighted the undermining of access to criminal justice and the circumventing of procedural safeguards for the accused (Newman, 2013a;

---

[2] We use *practitioners* to cover solicitors, barristers and police officers, although we accept that police officers are not necessarily considered criminal practitioners. We are only using this descriptor as a shorthand to easily communicate the section of our sample that work in and around the criminal justice system. We are using *accused* as a generic term in this book to help provide easily identifiable labelling, a clear narrative and a consistent analysis. This is offered as a simple catch-all term that will refer to those suspected, accused or even convicted of crimes; that is, the part of our sample who have gone through the criminal justice system as suspects/defendants.

[3] Such as the Cardiff Three, who were wrongfully convicted of the murder of Lynette White in Butetown in 1998. Also from Butetown was the wrongfully convicted Mahmood Mattan, the last person to be hanged at HMP in Cardiff in 1952.

Dehaghani, 2019), both pieces of research were conducted in England with little consideration for the specificities in and of Wales.

Further, we saw the need to adopt a holistic approach that brought practitioner and accused experiences into dialogue with one another. Importantly, our aim was also to feature the often marginalized voices of the accused within discussions of the criminal process, providing contemporary detail of criminal justice as it is experienced. To provide 'thick description' (Geertz, 1973), we focused on one locale, interviewing a range of individuals. Seeking to address the marginalization of Wales within criminal justice scholarship (see Jones, 2013; Jones and Wyn Jones, 2019),[4] we provide a place-based account of how criminal justice is experienced during austerity. In so doing, we explore similarities and differences between two countries within one jurisdiction, thus informing the potentially new and emerging Welsh legal jurisdiction while also providing key insights into criminal justice as experienced under a single unitary jurisdiction, thereby informing discussion and debate in relation to the existing jurisdiction as a whole. In particular, we provide a unique contribution to the Welsh debate: research often focuses on technical points of jurisdiction and process, but in doing so has neglected important voices. This research seeks to address this absence. In this chapter we will examine the broad differences and similarities between England and Wales. We also offer background on how justice in general, and criminal justice in particular, operate in the smaller half of this jurisdiction, before returning to this in greater detail in Chapter 2.

In the sections that follow we provide detail on the historical and contemporary legislative and governmental context within Wales, examining the ramifications of being subject to the Westminster parliamentary system under the royal sovereign and being part of the joint legal jurisdiction of England and Wales. We thereafter explore similarities and differences between England and Wales, setting out why criminal justice in Wales, and the experiences thereof, should be considered and examined within criminal justice research. Importantly, we acknowledge and explore the promise of criminal justice devolution and its significance to how justice is experienced and achieved. Wales has been neglected for far too long, and our research, following the Commission on Justice in Wales, seeks to rectify this problem by highlighting new areas for discussion. Towards the end of this chapter, we provide detail on our methods and methodology, and thereafter a chapter outline for the remainder of this book.

---

[4] See also Nason and Pritchard (2020) on administrative justice in Wales, and Winckler (2009) on equality issues in Wales.

Similarity, assimilation and difference

Wales has not always been part of the joint England and Wales jurisdiction. Prior to annexation by England in the 13th century and incorporation into the Kingdom of England under the Laws in Wales Acts 1535–1542, Wales was independent, governed by a variety of kingdoms across different regions of the country, and had its own set of progressive and liberal indigenous laws known as Cyfraith Hywel.[5] In the 16th century Wales became part of the single unitary jurisdiction following the passing of two separate Acts of Union. These Acts of Union aimed to politically unite the two countries, remove the indigenous Welsh laws and any other 'customs and usages', and, in doing so, 'vandalised and replaced indigenous legal practices' with the aim of assimilation and eradication of difference (Evans et al, 2017: 2). A distinctly Welsh 'legal identity' was retained through the separate court system – the Court of Great Sessions – from 1542 to 1830 and although English became the official language in Wales, Welsh was still widely used in the Court. The unitary system of England and Wales remained 'firmly intact' until 1998, following the Government of Wales Act 1998 (Evans et al, 2017: 3).[6] It was not until the Government of Wales Act 2006 that the Welsh Assembly, recently renamed Senedd Cymru,[7] was conferred primary legislative powers in 21 fields such as education, the environment and housing.[8] Yet, all justice matters – including criminal justice – are still reserved to the UK Parliament in Westminster.[9] The appetite for devolution of justice has, however, been steadily increasing, following the Silk Commission (2014) – which concluded that aspects of policing and justice should be transferred to the then Welsh Assembly[10] – and, more recently, the Thomas Commission (2019).[11] Despite

---

[5] Wales under Cyfaith Hywel – named after Hywel Dda (Hywel the Good) – was considered more liberal than its contemporary English counterparts (Davies, 2007), and especially progressive relative to the period (Howells, 2019).

[6] There were plans for a National Assembly in Wales by the 1970s, but these were defeated by referendum in 1979.

[7] During the course of this research, the Welsh Assembly was renamed in recognition of the greater law-making powers of the institution compared to those at its formation. It is now Senedd Cymru (in Welsh) and the Welsh Parliament (in English).

[8] Until this point, the Assembly had only the power to pass secondary legislation.

[9] The Commission on Justice in Wales (2019) notes that, despite further devolution, none of the functions relating to justice were transferred and were instead retained by the Home Office and (the now) Ministry of Justice.

[10] Yet, as Evans et al (2017: 3) highlight, there was a failure, within the Silk Commission, to take account of the fact that the Welsh government, while having no formal responsibility for criminal justice, 'is in fact developing strategies within policy areas that deal directly with the needs of adult and young offenders in Wales'.

[11] Known as the Commission on Justice in Wales (2019). Also referred to herein as 'the Commission'.

such progression, Westminster has appeared resistant to change (see Evans et al, 2017).

The current devolution arrangements, while not formally altering the England and Wales jurisdiction, have allowed Wales to be spoken of as both like and different from England. The similarities are important to acknowledge but so too are the points of divergence, as we will discuss throughout this book. The arrangements are, however, rather different from those in the other UK devolved nations of Scotland and Northern Ireland, whose constitutional architecture has the *trias politica* of legislature, executive and judiciary (Jones and Wyn Jones, 2019). The Welsh arrangements, by contrast, can be viewed as a one- or two-legged stool, initially 'a single "body corporate" with a cabinet grafted onto it' (Jones and Wyn Jones, 2019: 13). The absence of justice devolution has been inherently problematic. As Jones and Wyn Jones (2019) highlight, the 'umbilical link' between, for example, justice and social policy results in significant devolved activity in a non-devolved area, with government departments *beyond* the specific remit of the criminal justice system playing an important role in the administration of justice (Jones and Wyn Jones, 2019).[12] For Hodgetts and MacPartholán (2021: 35–6), 'there is no denying that the Welsh criminal legislation to date has been constructive' with 'the current devolved legislative powers in Wales ... used in a socially-oriented manner'. Yet, devolved activity is 'closely monitored and constrained', despite this 'distinct policy space' (Jones and Wyn Jones, 2019: 14). The establishment of a set of de facto Welsh criminal justice institutions represents an attempt, by the UK government, to overcome the complex policing and criminal justice arrangements in Wales (see Jones and Wyn Jones, 2019). Further, despite policing being 'reserved' to Westminster, the Welsh government has made considerable progress, particularly in relation to crime prevention, youth offending, and domestic abuse (see Evans et al, 2017; Jones and Wyn Jones, 2019). Yet, power, at least for criminal justice and justice more generally, is still firmly in the hands of Westminster, with Wales often viewed as the 'minor partner' in the England and Wales system. The Welsh government often has little influence over the trajectory of UK criminal justice policy,[13] its influence on criminal justice spending or improvements in – or to – the system has been stifled by the devolution arrangements, and Welsh government achievements have

---

[12] One such example is the Crime and Disorder Act 1998, which requires local authorities to work in partnership with voluntary and community organizations to reduce crime and offending (Jones and Wyn Jones, 2019).

[13] Although the Welsh government has not, for example, challenged Whitehall on legal aid cuts or the age of criminal responsibility, despite the Welsh government's purported progressiveness. Evans et al (2021) have questioned the progressiveness of criminal justice policy in Wales, suggesting that it may be a case of style over substance.

been curtailed by budget cuts for Wales pursued by London in the name of austerity (Evans et al, 2017; Jones and Wyn Jones, 2019). The current arrangements frustrate and disaffect Welsh practitioners and policymakers who must constantly remind UK officials to have due regard to the Welsh context (Jones and Wyn Jones, 2019). Indeed, UK policy documents often fail to reflect how policies will work in Wales. Anglocentrism remains rife, Wales is neglected and progress is stifled.

Despite these attempts at assimilation, Wales has retained its unique identity, with the Welsh language serving as the most obvious example. The oldest in Britain, at an estimated 4,000 years old, it suffered immensely under English sovereignty[14] but has experienced a formal revival in the past 25 years, promoted by Welsh government initiatives and measures,[15] with the aim of 1 million Welsh speakers by 2050. Under the Welsh Language Act 1993, Welsh language speakers throughout Wales have the right to conduct their case through the Welsh medium; in police custody, detainees can be provided with the Welsh language version of the Police and Criminal Evidence Act (PACE) Codes of Practice and are entitled to conduct their interview in Welsh or otherwise be provided access to a simultaneous translation service. Currently, one fifth of the population speaks Welsh in addition to English (Welsh Government, 2019d), with the highest proportion of Welsh speakers – over 50 per cent of the population in Anglesey, Ceredigion and Gwynedd – in the north and west, and around 20 per cent of those living in the south (Welsh Government, 2019d). There are also a significant number of lawyers and judges who can conduct cases in the Welsh language.[16]

While the linguistic differences between England and Wales are to be celebrated, there are some disconcerting differences that demand consideration. The first is that of endemic poverty. All regions in Wales contain both areas of affluence and high levels of poverty (Commission on Justice in Wales, 2019); the rate of those living below the poverty line is higher in Wales – at 21 per cent – than the rest of the UK – by 3 per cent – second only to London in the official breakdown of figures (Davies et al, 2011; Welsh Government, 2013), and in 2017/18, Wales was the only

---

[14] Children were, for example, prevented from, and indeed punished for, speaking Welsh at school. English and Welsh were not legally equal languages until the Welsh Language Act 1967 and Welsh Language Act 1993. References to England in legislation also did not include Wales until 1967.

[15] For example, Welsh language standards set by the Welsh Language Commissioner mean that public organizations in Wales should provide correspondence in Welsh and deal with complaints made in Welsh without any delay.

[16] According to the Commission on Justice in Wales (2019) around 30 per cent of solicitors, 20 per cent of barristers and 30 per cent of judges in Wales speak Welsh. They note that, in 2018/19, the Welsh language was used in around 1,000 court and tribunal hearings.

country in the UK to experience a rise – to around one third – in child poverty (Pollock, 2019).[17] Further, the ageing population in Wales is the highest across the UK, social mobility remains low, economic inequalities are significant, and there is higher state welfare reliance than anywhere else in the UK, including London (Equality and Human Rights Commission, 2011; CONDEM, 2014; Social Mobility Commission, 2019).[18] Wales was much harder hit than the rest of the UK by austerity, with the non-devolved nature of welfare provision a significant contributory factor (Welsh Government, 2013).[19] In-work poverty is also higher in Wales than the rest of the UK at 13 per cent, second only to London at 17 per cent (Joseph Rowntree Foundation, 2020); compared with the remainder of the UK, Wales has the lowest pay for every sector (Joseph Rowntree Foundation, 2020) and the lowest mean weekly income (Welsh Government, 2018b), with 28 per cent of the population in Wales being paid low wages compared with the UK-wide figure of just 2 per cent (Davies et al, 2011). Poverty can result in susceptibility to debt and can, inter alia, exacerbate poor mental health (Pleasence et al, 2013; Organ and Sigafoos, 2018).

Disability is also higher in Wales than in England, at 22.7 per cent compared with 17.6 per cent across England (ONS, 2015). The south Wales Valleys – which stretch across the south of the country from Carmarthenshire to Monmouthshire – have 'substantially higher levels of disability and long-term illness than the rest of Wales' (Winckler, 2009: 7). While systemic problems may impede a disabled person's ability to participate in the workforce, those who *are* 'economically active' are typically paid less than those without a disability (Davies et al, 2011; Welsh Government, 2013). Low wages can compound the negative effects of austerity and can render individuals more susceptible to legal issues (Pleasence et al, 2013; Organ and Sigafoos, 2018; Owens, 2020). These issues are yet further compounded by an absence of advice provision (see Robins and Newman, 2021): the number of firms providing legal services has declined by 29 per cent in Wales as compared with 20 per cent in England (Robins, 2019). Individuals who are self-represented – or, more accurately, unrepresented – experience yet further stress, ill-health and social exclusion (Winckler, 2009; Pleasence et al, 2013; Robins and Newman, 2021), thus compounding disadvantage further again. That disabled people in Wales are three times more likely to have no qualifications than non-disabled people (Davies et al, 2011) may serve to further reduce the equality of arms between the state and the individual.

---

[17] Wales had the highest levels of child poverty in the UK (Save the Children, 2012).

[18] See also Statistics for Wales (2019).

[19] For example, 'pensioner poverty' in Wales has been on the rise during the period of austerity (Joseph Rowntree Foundation, 2020).

Inequality, deprivation and disadvantage can therefore affect not only *how* individuals access justice, but also *whether* they are able to do so.

Despite the bleak picture painted earlier, hope may be found in the form of progressive government. Wales has often been proclaimed as more progressive than England. For example, for Wyn Jones and Learner (2020: 236), 'The particular trajectory of Welsh social and political history has served to intertwine national and class narratives in ways that have underpinned perhaps the longest period of progressive/centre-left electoral dominance ever seen: a hundred and fifty years plus and counting'.

Labour has experienced the largest share of the vote at every Westminster election since 1922 and every Welsh Parliament election since 1999, Welsh Labour is purportedly more left leaning than the UK parliamentary party, and governments in Wales are supposedly more progressive than their Westminster counterparts.[20] The progressiveness of Welsh Labour's approach to social policy stands in marked contrast to the 'neo-liberal orthodoxies and right-wing critiques of "big government"' (Evans et al, 2017: 5). Rather, Welsh Labour have committed to 'good government' and the concept of community, with 'the role of the state in supporting communities ... generally accepted' within Welsh political culture (Evans et al, 2017: 5). The Welsh government, under Labour, have committed to universal provision,[21] such as free prescriptions, while also acknowledging that those most in need may require additional services (Evans et al, 2017). Universalism – in addition to reducing stigmatization of public service users and raising standards of service through middle class advocacy – can engender 'a sense of social solidarity and ... of common citizenship' thus binding 'together the more affluent classes with working-class service users in a community of interest' (Evans et al, 2017: 5). The notion of citizenship is also key to the state–citizen relationship in Wales, with guaranteed rights and entitlements, standing in marked contrast to the English consumerist model that emphasizes 'opportunities' (Evans et al, 2017). In addition, the Welsh government seeks to ensure equality of opportunity *and* outcome and

---

[20] It has been said that there is 'clear red water' between Wales and England, which derives from a speech by the then First Minister Rhodri Morgan. This speech set out ideological fault lines between Cardiff and Westminster around social policy issues. For Morgan (2002) 'The actions of the Welsh Assembly government clearly owe more to the traditions of Titmus, Tawney, Beveridge and Bevan than those of Hayek and Friedman. The creation of a new set of citizenship rights has been a key theme in the first four years of the Assembly – and a set of rights, which are, as far as possible: free at the point of use; universal; and unconditional.'

[21] With the rationale that 'any possible savings derived from means-testing or identifying target populations are insignificant and do not often outweigh the benefits of universalism' (Evans et al, 2017: 5).

promote pluralism and diversity. Of particular note is the ' "distinct equality agenda" pursued by the National Assembly for Wales post-devolution' (Owens, 2020: 3) – targeted at limiting the disadvantages faced by vulnerable groups in Wales (see Chaney, 2009; Davies et al, 2011; EHRC, 2011).[22] Such may have indirectly promoted access to justice, thus potentially mitigating some of the impacts of austerity through, for example, the *access to advice* initiative (Owens, 2020). There has also been significant legislative activity to promote human rights, equality and well-being. The Welsh government has committed to its human rights obligations under the United Nations Convention on the Rights of the Child (UNCRC) and the United Nations Principles for Older Persons in the Social Services and Well-being (Wales) Act 2014. It introduced the *Socio-Economic Duty* to ensure that public bodies under their remit worked to promote social equality.[23] And it was the first in the UK to provide an overarching framework for decision making by all (Welsh) public bodies, imposing duties to protect the well-being of Welsh citizens through the Well-being of Future Generations (Wales) Act 2015.[24]

Yet, progression within the legislative sphere, particularly regarding equality and human rights, has been impeded by the neoliberal policies pursued by Westminster (Davies et al, 2011. See also Winckler, 2009). The absence of criminal justice devolution has stymied the equality agenda further again: Her Majesty's Prison and Probation Service (HMPPS) and the police are guided by specific duties under the Equality Act 2010 (Specific Duties) Regulations 2011, but as non-devolved agencies they are outside of the duties set by the Welsh government (Jones and Wyn Jones, 2019). The UK government continues to hold the all-important legislative levers and has thus stifled the introduction of progressive policies such as the establishment of drug consumption rooms (Jones and Wyn Jones, 2019; Wyn Jones and Learner, 2020).[25] Wales also suffers financially as a result of the current devolution arrangements: it loses out on fiscal support when compared with England,[26] yet the Welsh government also provides support to the UK government in

---

[22] There is also a focus on early intervention in Wales, such as reducing adverse childhood experiences.

[23] The duty 'places a legal responsibility on relevant bodies when they are taking strategic decisions to have due regard to the need to reduce the inequalities of outcome resulting from socio-economic disadvantage', illustrating an explicit concern here for using their powers in 'supporting the most vulnerable in our society' (Welsh Government, 2020: 1).

[24] This Act provided the inspiration for a bill of the same name proposed by Lord John Bird in the UK Parliament (Bird, 2021).

[25] See also Brewster and Jones (2019).

[26] On the issue of funding, the Commission on Justice in Wales (2019) criticized the Barnett formula – which awards funds to devolved administrations – for not considering the higher rate of relative need for Welsh public services.

delivering policing and criminal justice services in Wales (Jones and Wyn Jones, 2019). Adding insult to injury, savings generated from the Welsh government's *spend to save* policy are largely being captured by the UK Treasury (Jones and Wyn Jones, 2019). The Welsh government is therefore unable to financially support the policies that would undoubtedly benefit the people of Wales but must also channel funds back to the state that holds them captive. The balance of power thus is firmly tilted towards Whitehall and UK policy departments at the expense of the Welsh legislature (Jones and Wyn Jones, 2019). The policing budget is one such area to suffer tremendously from the current devolution arrangements. The Commission on Justice in Wales (2019) noted that the Home Office has failed to consider the demands of policing Cardiff in the same way as other capitals such as London and Edinburgh; funding decisions more generally fail to account for the 'unique circumstances' of policing in Wales such as the vast expanses of rural areas (Commission on Justice in Wales, 2019: 165). The House of Commons, through Inspectorates such as Her Majesty's Inspectorate of Constabulary and Fire and Rescue Services (HMICFRS), have failed to recognize the distinct legislative and policy contexts in Wales (Jones and Wyn Jones, 2019). The position in which Wales finds itself is unacceptable; devolution of justice is likely the only remedy to the myriad of problems.

While these legislative, political, socio-economic and linguistic differences should be considered, it is worth acknowledging that much of Wales shares some similarities with England, particularly the post-industrial nature of, and large rural expanses within, Yorkshire, the Potteries and the north-east of England.[27] Indeed, the landscape and characteristics of large parts of the north of England may be more similar to parts of Wales such as the south Wales Valleys when compared with the south-east of England and areas with large metropolitan centres as in London, Birmingham and Manchester. A failure to acknowledge and engage with these differences within a country may render invisible the on-the-ground realities within these areas; greater effort should be made, within socio-legal and criminological research and by policymakers, to recognize and shed light on the similarities and differences within countries and regions (as well as between them). Importantly, a southern England- and London-centric frame may serve to exacerbate pre-existing inequalities in England.[28] The effects of neoliberal and austerity policies must be brought to light through greater and meaningful engagement with communities beyond southern England, London and other large metropolitan areas; it should not simply be assumed that budget cuts or policy change manifest in

---

[27] Wales recently replaced the north-east of England as the 'poorest part of the UK' (Jones-Evans and Barry, 2019).

[28] One such example is declining advice provision in rural areas (see Law Society, 2018).

reality or are experienced in the same way across the jurisdiction or across a country, nor should each country be homogenized. Applying such logic to our own example, in the following section we explore the similarities and differences *within* Wales.

Within Wales: similarity, divergence and sites of criminal justice

Wales is often treated and referred to as a single region of the UK or England and Wales, yet this country is one with significant diversity across its regions. While the specific nature of the regional divides within Wales are sometimes contested, the country can be said to be split into north, west, mid and south, with the south further divided between east and west.[29] With a population of 3.14 million, Wales is the third-largest of the four UK countries in population terms (ONS, 2019) and has 22 local authorities. Based in south Wales, this book focuses on the 12 south Wales local authorities of Blaenau Gwent, Bridgend, Caerphilly, Cardiff, Merthyr Tydfil, Monmouthshire, Neath-Port Talbot, Newport, Rhondda Cynon Taff, Swansea, Torfaen, and the Vale of Glamorgan (as in Figure 1.1). Also included is Carmarthenshire, an area sometimes claimed to be part of south Wales but similarly contended as a local authority within west Wales.[30] While we have not examined experiences across every Welsh region and therefore cannot speak for the whole of Wales, given the dearth of socio-legal and criminological research in and on Wales, our south Wales exploration takes the first step in interrogating how Wales is both different from and similar to England.

Even within the south Wales area, there is significant socio-economic and demographic divergence, and this too may have a bearing on experiences of criminal justice. Linguistically, there are differences within Wales generally, as noted earlier, and differences within south Wales specifically. In the south, the highest overall number of Welsh speakers are in Cardiff, whereas the Swansea area has the highest number of first-language Welsh speakers. The experience of criminal justice may differ depending on Welsh language usage; in the north and west investigations and hearings may be more likely to be conducted through the Welsh language. Economic development also differs across Wales, with most activity being centred around Cardiff and along the M4 corridor including other southern cities

---

[29] To complicate matters – and highlight the debatable nature of such divisions – Wales will sometimes be divided into three (north, south and west, with what we understand as mid Wales placed in any of these categories).

[30] For example, the higher levels of Welsh language in Carmarthenshire do distinguish it from many of the other authorities included here as south Wales. The solicitors working in Carmarthenshire also often work in Swansea and Neath-Port Talbot.

Figure 1.1: South Wales local authorities

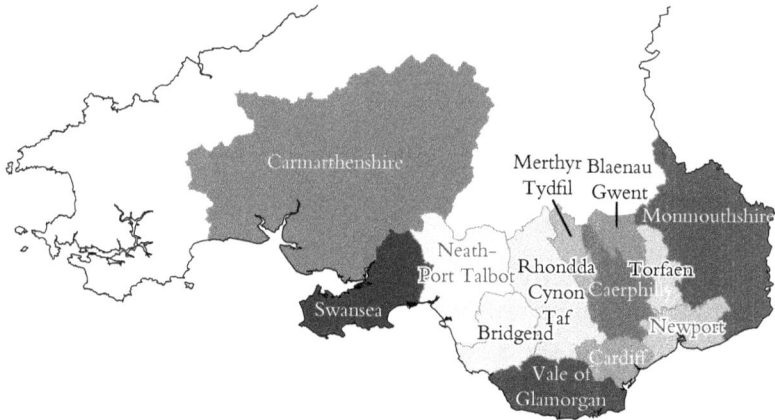

such as Swansea in the west and Newport in the east of south Wales. Along this southern coastal belt, employment and earnings have increased, yet parts of the south Wales Valleys, particularly Blaenau Gwent, Merthyr Tydfil and Torfaen, experience the highest levels of economic inactivity in the country (Welsh Government, 2019c).[31] The fallout from the 2008 financial crisis is thus more pronounced in these areas. Shifts in industries must also be acknowledged: historically, the Welsh economy (especially in areas such as the Valleys) relied on heavy industry and, thereafter, factory production; the economy now relies heavily on the service industry and – to an extent – public sector employment. Cardiff, with its status as a capital city, has a much larger population size relative to other urban areas in Wales and benefits from strong transport links with large English cities such as London. The capital has also dominated service sector employment in Wales and hosts a large proportion of public sector opportunities. The north also benefits from links with and proximity to north-west England, particularly Cheshire and Merseyside, with employment at the highest rate, and unemployment and economic activity at the lowest rate across the country (Welsh Government, 2019a). The lowest levels of employment, as in parts of west Wales, are symptomatic of the ongoing impact of mining industry decline (Welsh Government, 2019b).[32]

---

[31] The Valleys qualified for three rounds of European Union Objective One funding over the first two decades of the 21st century, to promote the development of regions whose economic development is considered lagging behind (Dickins, 2017).

[32] West Wales also received Objective One funding and is rated as one of the poorest regions in Europe, with 72 per cent of the EU average GDP per head (Inman, 2019).

The geography of Wales is also significant in respect of criminal justice experiences, particularly the marked issues with travel and transport, as we will explore in Chapter 4. The expansive areas of valleys, hills and mountains, and the large agricultural areas pose notable obstacles for transport and travel. From north to south, there is no motorway and often train journeys require travel through England. The cities in the south are reasonably well served by public transport, yet expansive mountains, such as in the Valleys, can impede travel and thus access to key sites of criminal justice, such as the courts (see Simson-Caird, 2016). 'Advice deserts' – where advice is not available through legal aid or where there is only one provider locally – are more common in rural than in urban areas (see Newman, 2016a; Robins and Newman, 2021). Gaps in advice provision are experienced in the largely rural Vale of Glamorgan, as well as in mid Wales and parts of the north (Robins, 2019).[33] Per thousand of the population, more affluent areas in Wales seem to have retained more advice provision than poorer areas: in Monmouthshire this was 3,000 people per law firm in 2019 compared with 10,000 people per law firm in Merthyr Tydfil; Ebbw Vale has no legal aid lawyers, no Citizens Advice Bureau and no law centre (Robins, 2019).

Across Wales, there are 89 firms and 126 offices offering legally aided criminal defence.[34] Solicitors working in Wales are generally older than those across England and Wales, with 47 per cent over the age of 45 compared with the combined England and Wales age of 41 (Commission on Justice in Wales, 2019). There are six sets of chambers in Cardiff, three in Swansea and one in Newport; most barristers in Wales practise from chambers in south Wales, with practice predominantly in the fields of criminal law and family law. Across Wales there are 360 barristers, 293 of whom are self-employed (Commission on Justice in Wales, 2019: 377). The average practising age of barristers is similar across Wales as in England and Wales, with 70 and 69.2 per cent of barristers aged 54 and under, respectively (Commission on Justice in Wales, 2019). Wales has seven of the 77 Crown Courts across England and Wales, with only two – Mold and Caernarfon – in the north and only 14 of the remaining 161 Magistrates' Courts across England and Wales (Bowcott and Duncan, 2019), with only two – Haverfordwest and Llanelli – in the west. Wales has five male prisons, holding convicted and unconvicted prisoners and those who have been and have yet to be sentenced, one

---

[33] For example, prior to the introduction of the Legal Aid, Sentencing and Punishment of Offenders Act (LASPO) 2012, there were 31 providers of publicly funded benefits advice in Wales, now reduced to three.
[34] Accurate as of March 2019. This is likely to have declined during the pandemic.

Figure 1.2: Welsh police forces

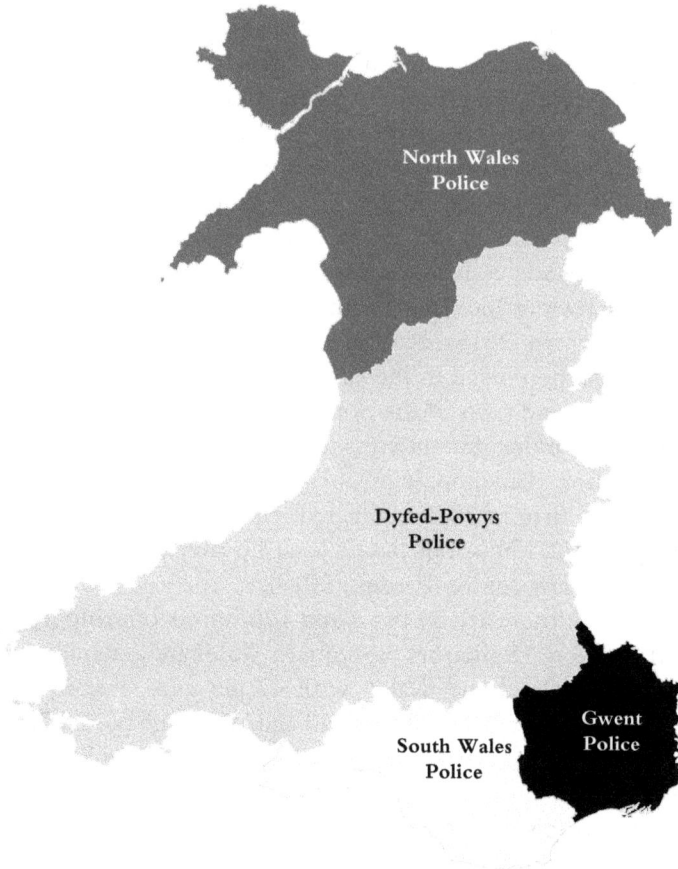

in the north – HMP Berwyn – and the remaining four in the south – HMP Cardiff, HMP/YOI Parc, HMP Swansea and HMP Usk/Prescoed. In November 2019 there were 4,977 people imprisoned in Wales, although 37 per cent of all Welsh prisoners were held in English prisons in December 2018 (Jones et al, 2019). There is no women's prison in Wales; instead, Welsh women prisoners are held in England.[35] The police in Wales are organized across four territorial policing areas: Dyfed-Powys Police, Gwent Police, North Wales Police and South Wales Police (as in Figure 1.2); our research was conducted largely in the South Wales force area but also in Gwent and Dyfed-Powys.

---

[35] In 2018, 74 per cent of Welsh women were held across HMP Eastwood Park in Gloucestershire and HMP Styal in Cheshire (Jones et al, 2019).

The Commission on Justice in Wales

Wales constitutes a distinctive policy space within the shared system due to the division of power and responsibility between the UK and Wales and the inevitable links between justice and wider social policy (Jones and Wyn Jones, 2019). To manage the challenges of working across the 'jagged edge', a number of de facto Welsh criminal justice institutions have been established (Jones and Wyn Jones, 2019), yet the arrangements remain problematic. Beginning at the inception of the Commission on Justice in Wales, our research addresses the distinct problem of which we were aware, but then further alerted to by the Commission's research team: a dearth of research and data with an explicit focus on Wales. Indeed, the Commission on Justice in Wales (2019) findings highlight the importance of understanding justice in Wales and the shortage of scholarship on justice in Wales. The Commission on Justice in Wales was established to address whether – and how – justice could be better served in Wales, with a particular focus on the impacts on people according to characteristics and circumstances, and the fairness of outcome, irrespective of difference.[36]

Their report addressed a range of issues such as access to justice, criminal justice, family law, civil and administrative justice, and the Welsh language. Across criminal justice, they examined the role of victims, BAME[37] experiences, youth justice, criminal legal aid, and the roles of the police, the Crown Prosecution Service (CPS) and the courts. Their recommendations spanned the justice system in Wales and broadly called for greater accountability, a new strategic approach to issues of justice in Wales, and improved funding and legislative arrangements to better serve the people of Wales. They also recommended that criminal legal aid policy and delivery be designed in Wales – to meet needs across Wales – based on the Nordic approach (a public defender service for criminal cases, administered by the court and provided by private practitioners). The Commission proposed the creation of a new Wales Criminal Justice Board that would establish a general justice strategy for Wales, ensure accountability within Wales, uphold victims' rights and guarantee the proper delivery of victims' services. It was further proposed that the police, CPS, judiciary and HMPPS publish a strategy for BAME people in Wales, reporting annually to the (then) Welsh Assembly.

---

[36] Commissioners were drawn from across the public, private and third sectors, that is academia, the legal profession, the judiciary, government, and policy, advice and advocacy services.

[37] Black, Asian and Minority Ethnic. Our use of the acronym represents the language predominantly used by official agencies operating within the criminal justice system although we are aware of the homogenizing effect of this label and the way it potentially hides variations in discrimination and brutalization.

Also recommended was the establishment of a problem-solving approach – akin to the model used in Northern Ireland – with a focus on collaboration and rehabilitation, and with judicial oversight, the devolution of policing and crime reduction policies, and an integrated and whole-systems approach to offender management underpinned by rehabilitation. In making their recommendations, it seems that the Commission on Justice in Wales were influenced by the Welsh government's ethos of prevention, problem solving and long-term well-being. We reflect on some of these recommendations in Chapter 8 when we offer our suggestions for how justice can be better served in – and, crucially, for – Wales.

Methods and methodology

The research explored in Chapters 3–7 builds upon our previous co-authored and single-authored work (Newman, 2013a; Dehaghani and Newman, 2017; Dehaghani, 2019). Our aim was to ground our understanding of criminal justice in key events and relationships, with a focus on communicating the narratives of those with whom we spoke, relaying these stories to facilitate understanding of criminal justice on the ground.

To recruit, we approached law firms and chambers, introducing ourselves and our proposed research to solicitors and barristers, extending our sample using the snowball method.[38] Despite the overwork faced, solicitors and barristers were receptive to taking part in the research; they were pleased to see Wales represented in socio-legal research and were grateful for the opportunity to have their voices heard when they often felt practitioners were ignored in policy debates and by a generally critical wider public. There was a greater reluctance among serving police officers, who wanted approval from their superiors before taking part. We therefore made use of existing contacts and recruited the – albeit small number of – police officer participants through a local retired police officers' association, which kindly placed a call on their website. Retired officers seemed more willing to discuss their experiences than those currently serving. Access to the CPS proved yet more difficult: an initial contact with a CPS manager appeared promising but approval was not forthcoming. Our suspicion was that cuts to the CPS were placing prosecutors and case workers under significant pressure, and the CPS were reluctant for the extent of this pressure to be known.

Contact with the accused and their families was achieved in various ways: by making contact through lawyers[39] (making clear that there was

---

[38] This is where further participants are recruited via existing participants.

[39] Throughout this book, we will use the term *lawyers* to refer to both solicitors and barristers but will distinguish where appropriate. As noted earlier, we will also refer to *practitioners*, which may, unless otherwise stated, include the police, solicitors or barristers.

no obligation to take part and many chose not to do so), by speaking to individuals at court (although many were, understandably, keen to put their ordeal behind them), by making use of social media (Facebook) and classified ads (Gumtree), and by engaging with local support and campaign groups for the convicted (where members were keen to share their stories). We also worked with a charity providing support to Welsh prisoners, through which we spoke to those in prison. While it was more difficult for us to know where to find this part of our sample, once we did talk to people we found a great eagerness to share their stories as the accused often felt overlooked and looked down upon by wider society. We also were advised that many family members were keen to speak with us, thus adding to the family sample in this work. Perhaps more so again than the accused themselves, family members expressed their gratitude as they saw themselves as being somehow invisible as regards their experiences. As our focus was initially on access to justice for the accused, we chose not to include victims in our sample. Although victims' voices may be marginalized, political discourse has, in our view, done more to ostracize the accused – and the 'lefty liberal lawyers' who represent them – than any others within the criminal process. For example, there is a Victims Commissioner in England and Wales but no similar role to articulate concerns for the accused. In hindsight it would have been interesting to explore how victims of crime – and their families – experience criminal justice and how they view the experiences of the accused. We also did not include probation or youth justice, both of which are part of the criminal justice system, but which we judged would have spread our remit too broadly.[40]

Throughout 2018/19 we interviewed 69 individuals: 20 solicitors including practice managers and those with Higher Rights of Audience across 16 firms (DS1–DS20); 16 barristers including Queen's Council across five chambers (BS1–BS16); six currently serving or retired South Wales police officers of various ranks (PO1–PO6); ten individuals accused of crimes who were or had been based in south Wales (AC1–AC10); 12 family members of those accused of crimes who were or had been based in south Wales (FM1–FM12); two prison workers (PW1–PW3); and three individuals who had complaints about being drawn into the criminal justice system but had not approached us on the basis of their being accused of crimes (SC1–SC3). There was a breadth of experience from across the region, with participants drawn from nine of the 13 local authorities noted earlier, and with solicitors and barristers who had either practised solely in Wales or had also worked in England.

---

[40] For greater discussion on these two matters in Wales see Commission on Justice in Wales (2019).

We conducted semi-structured interviews – anonymized to protect the identity of those who took part – in a variety of venues: ours or the participants' offices, at court and in prison. Interviews ranged from ten minutes to two and a half hours, with an average length of around an hour. Interviews were transcribed and then coded using thematic analysis – a method for identifying, analysing and reporting patterns across a data set (Braun and Clarke, 2006). Our lens was one of social constructivism (Denscombe, 2002), a methodology that sits between positivism – which views reality as an objective to be discovered – and interpretivism – which is based upon the recognition that objective knowledge of the social world is impossible to achieve and instead focuses on the socially constructed nature of knowledge. We view reality as not 'out there' to be discovered but instead produced through interaction with others (see Blumer, 1969). Our research also took an integrated approach, resting somewhere between structuralism – an outlook premised upon the development of largely politically motivated, theoretical frameworks that allow the attainment of privileged understanding – and interpretivism – which emphasizes the truth as something which is constructed by individuals, thus leading to multiple realities (Newman, 2013a). Crucially, having not conducted observations to complement these interviews, we were not able to readily contradict or discredit the accounts. As such, while we highlight alternative perspectives or explanations at various points, we do not make it our mission to disprove what we were told. It is in this way, by combining structuralist engagement with the literature and an interpretivist commitment to placing the voices of participants at centre stage, that we have, we hope, provided a holistic analysis.

Our aim was to draw out themes that were representative of the views, experiences and understandings of the participants as recounted to us. Within these experiences there were both commonalities and points of divergence, and we have highlighted these where appropriate. We recognize, however, the limitations in doing so, particularly that while the words may suggest commonalities, the lived realities may be quite different. We acknowledge our position as researchers: we have a role in deciding the questions asked (although using a semi-structured approach to interviews mitigates against this somewhat) and the themes selected. Our aim was to foreground the data although we have offered critical engagement throughout, pointing towards empirical and theoretical literature as relevant for contextualization. In doing so, we arguably add our own interpretation, yet we also hope that in so doing we can connect this research with ongoing and future debate. We have similarly made significant efforts to avoid reductionism or caricatures. There may be those who would wish that certain narratives were challenged or that our stance was more critical. As academics, we often have a platform, yet not everyone has such an opportunity and we aim to use this opportunity – this platform – to make visible the often ignored voices.[41] We recognize our analytical role in organizing these narratives; we hope that we have done so in a manner that is authentic to the speaker and comprehensible for the reader.

Through our focus on those who had experience of the criminal process in one region, we can provide a 'thick description' of how aspects of the criminal process – the police, criminal legal aid and the courts – are working in practice,[42] and thus facilitate an understanding of what has changed and where the problems play out. With the aim of letting those we interviewed 'speak for themselves', we focus largely on participants' voices in Chapters 3–7, dedicating significant space to their stories. Our aim is not generalizability (although this may be possible at certain junctures) but instead to set the *particular* within the *wider* understanding of criminal justice in England and Wales, paying close attention to the rich account offered within this specific locality – something that is not often offered in criminal justice studies. The dearth of research on Wales has necessitated such an approach: our foremost concern was to present an account that is true to those who have experienced criminal justice such that we can provide insight into the specificities of Wales and the synergies with England.

Chapter outline

In Chapter 1, we have provided detail on the specific Welsh context(s). The Anglocentric nature of much criminal justice and socio-legal research and the relative neglect of Wales within policymaking has caused us to provide more detail on the specificities than would perhaps otherwise

---

[41]   It is important to note that our interviews with accused and families, while significant, focused almost exclusively on their specific experiences and frustrations. Practitioners undoubtedly have more day-to-day experience of the criminal process. For accused and family members, there may be limited or significant experience with the criminal justice system but, regardless of the amount of experience, they are only seeing their own experience. In the interviews with the accused and family members we wanted to let them be heard with regard to their own traumatic experiences; they were often uninterested in the (sometimes abstract) questions that did not relate to their own experiences. Because they are often ignored and marginalized within the criminal justice system, we did not want to force them to answer our questions at the expense of being able to get their stories across. We acknowledge that this is a limitation in that we do not always have comparable data for practitioners, and the accused and family members, but we thought that a greater error would be to force these participants to follow our line and thus exacerbate latent feelings of having been ignored. The result is that, at times, some chapters that focus on the criminal justice system more broadly (such as how it functions in south Wales in Chapter 4) may have a preponderance of practitioner voices rather than the accused and their families.

[42]   For thick description in general sociological theory, see Geertz (1973); on socio-legal criminal justice research, see Travers (1997b).

be included within such a monograph. In doing so, we have provided a considerable level of detail regarding the Welsh context, which we extend into the legal context in Chapter 2; this acts to ground the data explored across Chapters 3–7.

We expand further upon the theoretical aspects of the research in Chapter 2, where we explore access to justice, neoliberalism and austerity, and the developments that have impacted upon criminal justice in England and Wales, such as cuts to the police, the CPS, the courts and criminal legal aid, as well as providing detail on the court modernization programme. Specifically, we explore the disproportionate impact on Wales of austerity and neoliberal measures pursued by Whitehall. Chapter 2 thus broadens and deepens the discussion from Chapter 1, upon which we further build in Chapters 3 and 4. Towards the end of Chapter 2, we introduce vulnerability theory, the theoretical framework that underpins our exploration of the experiences of criminal justice, and upon which we reflect in the conclusions of Chapters 3–7, providing yet more detailed consideration in the concluding Chapter 8.

Within Chapter 3, we explore some of the stories about the way our participants came to be involved in the criminal justice system. Initially, we investigate why and how practitioners started in legally aided criminal defence, examining also some of the values that define their approach to this work. We also examine how and why the accused became a subject of – and subjected to – the criminal process, also interrogating their attitudes to the criminal process and those working within it. In doing so, we contextualize the data explored across the subsequent chapters (4–7), thus providing the reader with further detail to fully understand the examination of these experiences. From these stories, two key themes emerge, namely practitioners' strong belief that the criminal justice system is underfunded (Chapters 4 and 5), and the significance of previous experience of the criminal process for the accused (Chapters 6 and 7).

With the background stories of our participants established, in Chapter 4 we examine the importance of geography and place to our research by probing the character of south Wales as both a setting and a subject for this book. We explore the space and time elements of studying south Wales under austerity, drawing out the key differences between England and Wales, with a focus on practitioners' accounts of the distinctive scale of criminal justice in south Wales. We explore the issue of court closures and the resultant travel problems in more detail. This, we posit, is a distinctive feature of criminal justice in an age of austerity both across the England and Wales jurisdiction generally, but with disproportionate impacts on Wales in particular. We additionally explore the uniqueness of the absence of a women's prison in Wales and its impact upon how criminal justice is experienced. We also question the extent to which these issues are distinct from what occurs in England and/or whether they may reflect regional or rural–urban divides. By providing further empirical detail on south Wales, in addition to the background detail in Chapter 2, we ground the broader experiences under examination in the following three chapters setting up the pressures practitioners face (Chapter 5), the way in which relationships function – or fail to function – in the system (Chapter 6), and the experience of being an accused person or a family member of the accused (Chapter 7).

Chapter 5 examines in detail the pressures that neoliberal austerity has placed on the criminal justice system and those working within it. We examine the problems with criminal legal aid funding, thus building on the broader austerity discussions from Chapters 1 and 2 (as contextualized in Chapters 3 and 4). We interrogate the related issue of time pressures on legally aided criminal practice, in addition to the broader pressures of criminal defence work. We explore the precarious future of criminal defence, before questioning whether those outside of the system appreciate the challenges and pressures of practice. In doing so, we outline and examine the fundamental problems underpinning the criminal justice system as relayed by those on the frontline, thus developing our account of how austerity has adversely impacted upon criminal justice (Chapter 2), the practitioner view that criminal justice is underfunded (Chapter 3), and the particularities within south Wales in the context of a system in crisis (Chapter 4). Chapter 5 also provides necessary grounding to understand the nature of the relationships as explored in Chapter 6, and the difficulty of navigating the criminal process as discussed in Chapter 7.

Within Chapter 6 we explore the relationships within the system, providing an insight into the day-to-day realities of criminal justice, and thus explicating further the narratives from Chapter 3, the importance of place as in Chapter 4, and the significance of practice pressures as in Chapter 5. Commencing through a consideration of the working relationships between solicitors, barristers and other practitioners in the criminal process, we subsequently explore practitioner views and perceptions of the accused. We delve deeper into the functioning of the lawyer–client relationship, exploring both the reality and the perception. Finally, we identify and examine the impact of the sentence discount for early guilty pleas as a key factor frustrating the lawyer–client relationship. The challenges of the current legal aid system and underfunding issues presented in Chapters 2 and 3 and drawn out in the work of these practitioners in Chapter 5 are thus used to inform a more thorough examination of the interactions between the various interviewees that were introduced in Chapter 3. In so doing, we develop an understanding of these key relationships that both shape and constitute the experiences of criminal justice, allowing for further grounding of the accounts of the accused and their families, as is the focus of Chapter 7.

In Chapter 7 we amplify the voices of those most often ignored in discussions about the workings of the criminal justice system: the accused and their families. We thus extend the relational component of Chapter 6 and balance out the practitioner dominance of Chapters 4, 5 and 6. Beginning with an examination of the problems faced by the accused, we explore whether and how these issues were acknowledged and understood by lawyers before examining the legacy of criminal justice beyond the police station or courtroom. We also consider the impact of criminal justice on the families of those who have been accused. We thus build upon the narratives of criminal justice involvement from Chapter 3 and, in so doing, highlight the need for a broader understanding of how – and by whom – criminal justice is experienced. Drawing upon these voices allows us to further ponder the possibilities of doing criminal justice differently, as we explore in Chapter 8.

We conclude our examination of the experiences of criminal justice in Wales in Chapter 8 where we reflect on the importance of vulnerability theory (explored in Chapter 2) to the reframing of the state–citizen/defendant relationship. We argue that state responsiveness – and specifically a commitment to improved funding of criminal justice institutions, informed by ethics and justice – is required to address our inherent human vulnerability. We also highlight the implications for policy and practice – to include broader criminal justice recommendations and specific profession-focused recommendations – across England and Wales, and specific to Wales. We reflect upon the Commission on Justice in Wales as discussed in Chapter 1 and what their findings – considering our research across Chapters 3–7 – mean for criminal justice, and specifically a devolved criminal justice system, in Wales. Finally, we assess the need for future research and make a call for further study into criminal justice as affected by austerity, *and* criminal justice in and across Wales.

2

A System in Crisis

Introduction

The criminal justice system of England and Wales has long been in decline. According to the solicitors' professional body – the Law Society – the system is now 'crumbling' (Law Society, 2019), and The Secret Barrister (2018) – an anonymous, best-selling legal blogger – has deemed the law to be 'broken'. In recent times, budget cuts have also been made to the police service, the courts, the CPS and other criminal justice institutions such as prisons. Criminal defence lawyers have seen their fees stagnate or reduce. Defendants have been both compelled to participate in the criminal process and prevented from doing so (Owusu-Bempah, 2017). Some accused have been left to face the criminal process unaided (see Gibbs, 2016). Within the frame of neoliberalism, the criminal process has also become more managerialist and more punitive, adding further to the challenges.

In this chapter we examine the impact of austerity and neoliberalism on the criminal process, also examining some of the policies affecting criminal justice in England and Wales. Neoliberalism, in particular, has resulted in punitive excess and responsibilization, aimed particularly towards the poor and disenfranchised (Garland, 2001; Wacquant, 2009; Bell, 2011). Austerity has forced 'violence' upon marginalized groups such as asylum seekers and the street-homeless (Cooper and Whyte, 2017). We contribute further to these debates by examining how the state has failed – or has deliberately decided not – to properly support those within the criminal process, namely those who require – and are thus denied – access to justice. Within this frame, we address Home Office budget cuts to policing, Ministry of Justice budget cuts to (criminal) legal aid funding, the challenges facing the CPS, and court closures pursued in the name of 'modernization'. Criminal legal aid cuts will form a significant focus of our discussion: how lawyers have been torn, through practice restraints necessitated by financial limitations, from their 'zealous advocate' ideal type (Smith, 2013; Smith and Cape, 2017), which in turn undermines their clients' proper access to justice (Gibbs and Ratcliffe, 2019). In doing so, we will draw out both the effects upon England and Wales and the disproportionate impact on Wales.

Building upon our earlier work (Dehaghani and Newman, 2017; Dehaghani and White, 2020; Dehaghani, 2021), towards the end of this chapter we introduce vulnerability theory. This theoretical framework loosely underpins our exploration of the criminal process in this book, upon which we later reflect in Chapter 8. We posit that vulnerability theory holds powerful potential in reframing the criminal justice process away from austerity-driven neoliberalist agendas and towards a state–citizen relationship that is founded on our inherent human fragility and interconnectedness.

Access to justice, neoliberalism and austerity

Our research into criminal justice in Wales was conducted under the shadow of austerity, the UK government deficit reduction programme that, from 2010, entailed sustained cuts in public spending and a marked reduction in the role of the welfare state. Between 2010 and 2019 more than £30 billion in spending reductions were made to welfare payments, housing subsidies and social services (Mueller, 2019). Farnsworth and Irving (2015: 1) contend that 'the global financial crisis of 2008 was unprecedented in living memory' for the way it transformed capitalism and ushered in what they call the 'age of austerity … the biggest challenge yet to the future of the welfare state'. For Rushton and Donovan (2018: 1):

> The reduction of the state since 2010 is not just a financial retrenchment, the product of the collapse of tax revenues after the banking collapse of 2008. It is also a shrinking of the state in terms of both the scope and the level of public support available across many areas of social policy. Austerity is everywhere and nowhere: in those parts of society where the cuts are falling and living standards static or still declining, there are many problems, both personal and, for those working in public services, professional.

One of the areas where the state is being cut back after austerity is access to justice (see Palmer et al, 2016). Access to justice is central to the state–citizen relationship (Rhode, 2004), providing citizens with the ability and opportunity to be heard, exercise their rights and hold the state to account regardless of financial resources. Within criminal justice, access to justice requires that suspects and defendants can effectively participate in the case against them, enforce their fair trial rights, and ensure that they are able to mount an effective defence against the state. At a European level, access to justice is in part facilitated through the right to a fair trial under Article 6 of the European Convention on Human Rights (ECHR). The criminal limb of the ECHR includes the right of the individual – here, the criminal accused – to adequate time and facilities for the preparation of the defence and the right to defend themself. While Article 6 includes a provision for state assistance, this is based on the individual's means (or otherwise) and where the interests of justice so require. The right – which applies to pretrial as well as trial procedures (see *Teixeira de Castro v Portugal*; *Salduz v Turkey*) – when set against the backdrop of neoliberalism and austerity, is merely a lofty principle rather than a reflection of reality, with rights curtailed and undermined in the criminal courts (McConville and Marsh, 2014) and within legally aided criminal defence (see Newman, 2013a).

While the explicit adoption of austerity policies may formally follow on from the shock of the financial crisis, the roots are to be found in the ideology of neoliberalism (Blyth, 2013). Neoliberalism – a political philosophy founded upon laissez-faire economics and the ideology of free-market capitalism – is fast becoming (or has now become) the dominant ideology of our age (Plehwe et al, 2006). An economic variant of liberalism (W. Brown, 2015), it was, according to Hall (2011), introduced in the UK, during Margaret Thatcher's Conservative government (1979–90), where it continued to thrive during Conservative rule under John Major and, again, from 1997 with New Labour. Within this philosophy, various aspects of the state should function with the purpose of prioritizing economic calculations; the success of social institutions is derived from assessments of economic cost-value (W. Brown, 2015). Neoliberalism – associated with liberal policies such as privatization, marketization, deregulation and globalization – has initiated the rise of liberalism, self-fulfilment, reductions in government and, consequently, a reduction in social welfare and retraction of state welfare. Harvey (2006) suggested that the wealth redistribution generated by neoliberalism – capital accumulation by dispossession – has funnelled wealth and power towards the top and away from those reliant on the welfare state. Austerity has simply accelerated such pre-existing trends and processes across society (Farnsworth and Irving, 2018), as well as specifically in regard to criminal justice (see Welsh, 2016).

The retraction of state welfare has extended into legal aid to include criminal defence. Indeed, the clutches of neoliberalism have grasped the criminal justice system in its entirety. While initially claimed as *the* Conservative issue, populist punitiveness (Bottoms, 1995) was also adopted during Tony Blair's New Labour government.[1] Adopting this stance as their

---

[1] Blair claimed to be 'tough on crime, tough on the causes of crime' (see New Statesman, 2015).

own, New Labour introduced one new offence for every day in office, equating to 3,600 offences in 11 years. They also placed greater emphasis on the victim, provided a fast track for suspects through, for example, the Criminal Procedure Rules, and introduced targets for the police. During this time, lawyers were viewed as 'fat cats' trying to 'milk the system' (Hynes and Robins, 2009) and their clients were an underclass that could be distinguished from the good, law-abiding citizens of the general population.[2] During the second half of Blair's administration, criminal legal aid expenditure witnessed a reduction of 12 per cent in real terms (National Audit Office, 2009).[3]

The Conservative-Liberal Democrat coalition government – explicitly focused on cutting state spending to 'balance the budget' – made a fee cut of 8.75 per cent under their austerity programme (Bowcott, 2015).[4] The Ministry of Justice during the period of austerity suffered the most significant cuts to any Whitehall department: a real terms cut of 40 per cent from £9.3 billion in 2010/11 to £5.6 billion by 2019/20. Legal aid spending (to include both civil and criminal legal aid) from 2012/13 to 2017/18 was significantly reduced, from £2.2 billion to £1.6 billion (see Bowcott, 2018). In addition to cutting legal aid budgets, politicians – specifically those who are right leaning – have continued to attack the legal profession: Theresa May (2016) launched an attack on 'left-wing human rights lawyers' in her first Conservative Party Conference speech as Prime Minister, and more recently her successor Boris Johnson, following comments to the same effect from the Home Secretary Priti Patel (Grant, 2020), claimed that 'the whole criminal justice system [was] being hamstrung by what the Home Secretary would doubtless – and rightly – call the lefty human rights lawyers, and other do-gooders' (Bowcott, 2020). Such portrayals of – particularly defence – lawyers and their clients have allowed neoliberal governments to degrade publicly funded legal assistance for criminal matters without offending the vast majority of the electorate, who are largely unsympathetic to the plight of those facing the criminal process (see Bottoms, 1995; Pratt, 2007).

Neoliberalism has affected every part of the English and Welsh criminal justice system through, for example, the privatization and marketization of aspects of policing, probation, prison, youth justice and criminal legal aid (see Phillips et al, 2020). Victims and defendants are purportedly empowered to make decisions and take action, but are often surveiled and may become

---

[2] New Labour have been applauded for their introduction of a national minimum wage and the Human Rights Act 1998. Our view is that these developments do not excuse or lessen their wrongdoing. See also Robins and Newman (2021).

[3] This approach was lambasted by the National Audit Office (2009) and has led to the former Lord Chancellor expressing regret (Fouzder, 2019).

[4] This was intended as the first of two fee reductions but the other 8.75 per cent cut was not made.

punished for failing to self-govern.[5] Individuals have become responsibilized (Garland, 2001) and sentences are becoming harsher (Welsh, 2013). Under neoliberalism, the need for assistance is framed as an individual problem instead of a social issue.[6]

The period of austerity saw a further retraction of the welfare state and cuts to public spending, with the justification of debt and deficit. The over- and mis-use of state provision was provided by elites as the reason for the 2008 financial crash; they failed to mention the internal problems with capitalism and weak regulation. Austerity, a particularly prominent aspect of neoliberalism (Farnsworth and Irving, 2018), paints the poor – as public service users – as burdens on the state (Blyth, 2013; Tyler, 2013). Austerity has also resulted in the sale of public assets to the private sector, the degradation of public services and the redistribution of income from the poor to the rich. Despite being presented as an attempt to save prudently for the future, the problems austerity has caused are so significant that there may not be a future to speak of, at least for criminal justice and, specifically, criminal legal aid (Dehaghani and Newman, 2021a).

The demise of criminal justice

The neoliberal and managerialist agendas have been the key driver of many developments within criminal justice. Full trials have, for example, been avoided by use of negotiated settlement through the sentence discount for an early guilty plea, formally introduced through the Criminal Justice Act 2003. The sentence discount provides the accused – if entering a guilty plea – with a reduction in sentence; the reduction is based on the stage of proceedings at which the plea was entered and the circumstances under which the indication was given. Thus, an accused entering a guilty plea at the plea hearing – the first available opportunity – may avail themself of a one-third reduction in sentence, reduced to one quarter after the trial date is set, and to one tenth if the plea is given at the door of the court or after the trial date has been set. This enters the accused into a process that McConville and Mirsky (2005) label 'plea bargaining' in their normative and critical account, or which Flynn and Freiberg (2018) identify as 'plea negotiation' in their more supportive reading of the practice. The difference

---

[5]   See for example: Duggan and Grace (2018), and Duggan (2018) on the Domestic Violence Disclosure Scheme and responsibilization; Phoenix and Kelly (2013) and Muncie (2006) on youth justice and responsibilization; and Munro and Scoular (2012), and Scoular and O'Neill (2007) on sex work and responsibilization.

[6]   As we will discuss later in this chapter (and further in Chapter 8), vulnerability theory seeks to counter neoliberal, responsibilizing discourse and instead urges for a responsive state, in recognition of our shared human vulnerability.

in reduction can be stark when the defendant is facing a long prison sentence: on a ten-year sentence, one third would reduce the sentence by three years and almost four months, whereas one tenth would reduce the sentence by one year only. There are various benefits to the sentence discount: it can reduce time on bail or remand and can reduce or alter the type of sentence; it can spare victims and witnesses time and stress; and – perhaps most importantly for the neoliberal agenda – it can reduce pressure on the police, prosecution, courts and – arguably – the defence, thus saving time and money. However, Darbyshire (2000) has argued that sentence discount amounts to a punishment of the innocent; those who refuse to enter a guilty plea may be handed down a harsher sentence than those who decide to enter one. The sentence discount may undermine a defendant's right to a fair trial and may pressurize those with a valid defence in law to plead guilty (Helm, 2019). Moreover, defendants do not have a statutory entitlement to a sentence reduction,[7] and the court is not required to declare the amount of sentence to be given. Guilty pleas have become the norm (Alge, 2013; McConville and Marsh, 2014) and feature heavily in our discussions of experiences, as will be further examined in Chapter 6.

Efficiency has also emerged through the Criminal Procedure Rules and their imposition of case management duties on the defence (see Ministry of Justice, 2012). The Criminal Procedure Rules require the defence to identify the 'real issues' at an early stage and provide information about written evidence, witnesses and points of law to the prosecution. However, this runs counter to the 'zealous advocacy' required of defence lawyers and poses a significant challenge to the traditional primacy of client interests that the defence lawyer should ensure (Smith, 2013).[8] It also undermines the ability of the defence to properly balance the crime control values of prosecuting agencies (Young and Sanders, 2004) and has forced the defence to, in essence, work *for* the prosecution (McConville and Marsh, 2014). Efficiency has been prioritized above all else (see Johnston and Smith, 2017) and appeared yet again in Leveson's (2015) review of the courts. The result was the Better Case Management initiative (and resulting Early Guilty Plea Scheme of 2017), with heightened compliance with the Criminal Procedure Rules, thus 'improving' the processing of cases to reduce their length. The defence position is further undermined by failures in disclosure (although these, too, can create problems for the prosecution). Designed 'to address the inequality of arms between the prosecution and

---

[7] Instead, detail can be found in the Sentencing Council Guidelines (2017).

[8] Smith (2013) defines 'zealous advocacy' as (i) duty to the client (partisanship, detachment, confidentiality), (ii) duty to the court (procedural justice and truth seeking), and (iii) duty to the public (fairness).

the defence', the prosecution – as a state-funded agency – must disclose to the defence the facts of the prosecution case so as to address the 'imbalance of resource' between the two opposing parties (Johnston, 2020: 38).[9] However, disclosure is often 'incomplete, not forthcoming or it is served at a late stage' (Johnston, 2020: 52). Adding the problems of disclosure to the increase in case management duties of the defence noted earlier means the defence's position as a 'gladiator of the accused' is seriously undermined (Johnston, 2020: 52).[10]

Policing has also suffered (see Brogden and Ellison, 2013). Between September 2010 and September 2016 police numbers reduced by 13 per cent for officers, 22 per cent for police staff, and 36 per cent for Police and Community Support Officers (UNISON, 2017). Policing budgets have been estimated to have reduced by 19 per cent in real terms since 2010, with a 30 per cent real-terms reduction of funding from the Home Office (Commission on Justice in Wales, 2019: 166).[11] Criticized by the National Audit Office (2015: 6), cuts to police funds were said to have left the police unable to address 'more complex risks'. By 2017, it was feared that the police in England and Wales would have £700 million less per year to address crime, with the amount available to forces projected to fall by 6 per cent from £12.3 billion in 2017/18 to £11.6 billion in 2020/21, a projected further decline in the number of officers by just under 3,000 to a total of 120,217, and an added 2 per cent cut to the police workforce (Dodd, 2017). A reduced headcount may impair the police's ability to perform their duties but can also impact negatively upon officer welfare (Elliott-Davies et al, 2016), with increasing injuries, stress and sickness rates further reducing staffing levels. Civilianization and privatization have been common within policing, affecting the numbers of police officers and altering staffing types (Skinns, 2011; Skinns, Sprawson et al, 2017; Skinns, Woof et al, 2017).[12] There has been the closure of more than 600 police stations across England and Wales, the largest police station closure programme in the history of policing (Ungoed-Thomas et al, 2018). The closures seemingly stem from cuts to the policing budget as police forces sold their assets to raise funds (Pratt, 2019). In October 2019, however, the Home Office (2019) confirmed that over three years from 2020, there

---

9   Quirk (2006) argues that the adversarial culture of the English and Welsh criminal justice system in part means that the disclosure regime was destined for failure.

10 For discussion of a 'near-miss', see Smith (2018).

11 The policing budget is comprised of central government funding made available through the Home Office and local funding (that is through Council Tax). Local funding has made up for the reduction through increases in Council Tax. See National Audit Office (2018a).

12 See also White, 2014a; White, 2014b.

would be an increase of 20,000 in police numbers across England and Wales. The UK government declared support for the recruitment of up to 6,000 additional officers by the end of 2020 to 2021 by pledging £750 million (Home Office, 2019), an investment that was, according to National Chair of the Police Federation of England and Wales, John Apter, 'long overdue' (BBC, 2019).[13]

The situation in Wales paints a slightly different picture. 'The Welsh government provided further funds and allowed council tax rises to provide extra funds' such that police officer numbers in Wales were not reduced to the extent that they were in England (Commission on Justice in Wales, 2019: 4). Police grant funding per person is, however, on average £17.11 higher in England than in Wales (Commission on Justice in Wales, 2019). Under the new programme of recruitment support described earlier, Wales would witness an increase in officers by 302 in 2020 to 2021, equating to 5 per cent of the total in England and Wales in this period. Most of these officers will be recruited in South Wales (136), followed by Gwent and North Wales (62 each), and finally Dyfed-Powys (42). Police station closures have occurred in Wales as in England. We submitted a freedom of information (FOI) request which illustrates that there were 22 police station closures in South Wales Police between 2010 and 2020, with 65 stations remaining (Figure 2.1a).[14] The effect for south Wales is a loss of a quarter of its police stations (25.29 per cent). Over the same period, there were 14 front desk closures, with 21 remaining, a loss of 40 per cent (Figure 2.1b). Such closures restrict an individual's ability to attend a police station and may also impact upon perceptions of the police within the community, although the rationale for closures was the decrease in footfall. Indeed, South Wales Police (2015) contended that fewer members of the public were attending the police station and this was because of advances in technology.

The CPS has also not escaped funding cuts. In 2018 it was reported that the CPS had lost one third (2,400) of its England and Wales workforce as a budget reduction of 25 per cent (Dearden, 2018). Funding for the CPS reduced from £615.5 million in 2010–11 to £504 million in 2018–19 (Commission on Justice in Wales, 2019). In August 2019, however, it was announced that the CPS would receive an extra £85 million over two years. Prior to CPS budget cuts, the CPS witnessed the introduction in 2008 of a neoliberal mechanism – the Optimum Business Model – which sought 'to improve the efficiency and effectiveness of the Magistrates' Courts systems

---

[13] Concerns were also raised by Dave Thompson, the Chief Constable of West Midlands police, who argued that the police were being pushed to 'tipping point' (Dodd, 2018).

[14] FOI request dated 21 April 2020. Figures accurate as of 12 May 2020.

Figure 2.1a: South Wales police stations

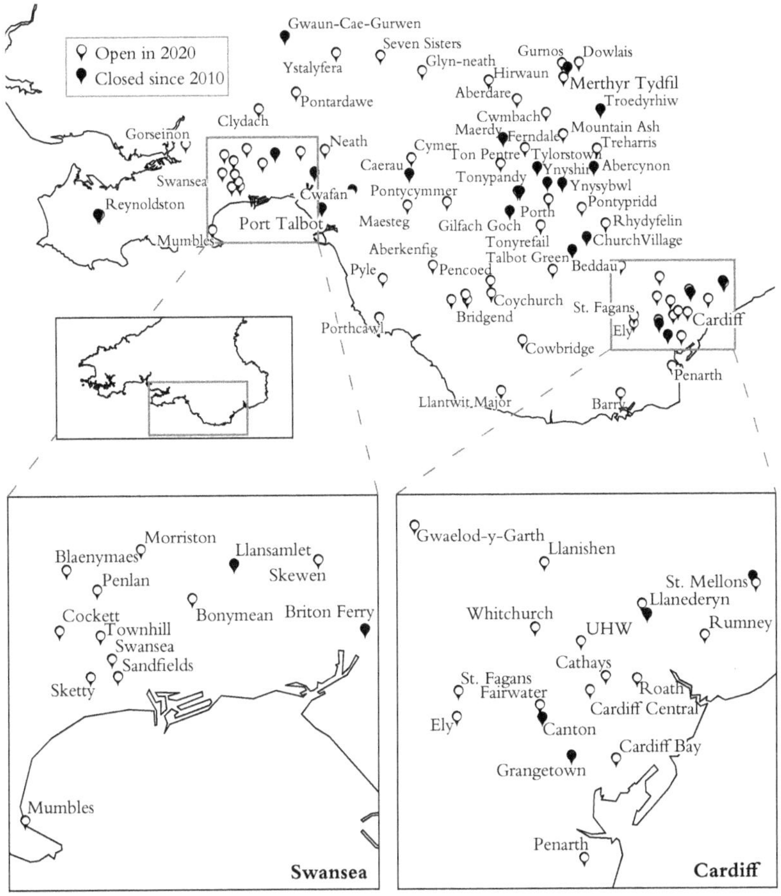

and processes' but has instead 'resulted in fragmentation of the prosecution process, as cases are no longer allocated to individual Crown Prosecutors, but to teams' (Soubise, 2017: 850). This fragmentation has resulted in a loss of ownership over cases, like the 'discontinuous representation' seen among criminal defence solicitors (Newman, 2013a). The use of often less-qualified lawyers, namely paralegals, within the CPS raises questions of prosecution ability, suitability and accountability (Soubise, 2017). Yet, not only is the CPS dependent upon the work of paralegals, it also remains reliant upon the police for constructing the prosecution case (McConville et al, 1991), despite the fact that there have been problems noted with the police's role in disclosing evidence. Liam Allen's recent case was the most publicized disclosure failure in recent memory: the police had failed to disclose text messages to the prosecution and defence, and it was not until three days

Figure 2.1b: South Wales police stations with front desks

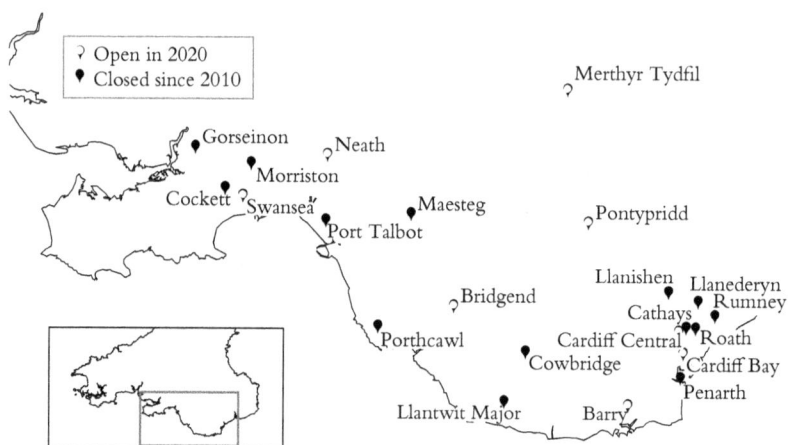

prior to Allen's appearance at Croydon Crown Court that this vital evidence materialized (BBC, 2017; see also Smith, 2018).[15]

Accompanied by a surge in the amount of evidence made available due to smartphone technology, the aforementioned budget cuts have placed the CPS under significant pressure when reviewing evidence, resulting in cases being dropped (Dearden, 2018). While the number of cases not reaching full trial in Wales due to CPS–related reasons rose from 16.5 per cent to 19.6 per cent between 2009 and 2014 (Johnson and Heaney, 2015), Wales has fared better in prosecutions than England, with Wales having 'marginally but consistently higher' prosecution rates than the other half of the jurisdiction (Commission on Justice in Wales, 2019: 188).

Significant cuts have also been levied on the courts. As part of Her Majesty's Courts and Tribunal Service's (HMCTS) 'court modernisation' programme, a total of around half of Magistrates' Courts – 164 out of 320 courts – in England and Wales have been closed (Bowcott and Duncan, 2019), with the money raised from the sale of court buildings purportedly being reinvested to improve the justice system (Simson Caird, 2016). In 2018 the UK government invested £1 billion to modernize the courts, yet in May 2018 HMCTS aimed to reduce staff numbers by 5,000, physical courtroom use by 2.4 million cases per year, and overall spending by £265 million (National Audit Office, 2018b). As of March 2018, it was reported that £108 million was being spent on improving the existing court estate, with £115 million

---

[15] The text messages significantly undermined the complainant's allegation that she did not consent to intercourse and thus also significantly undermined the prosecution's case to the point that the case was dropped.

raised from the sale of buildings being used to invest in the reform programme (Ministry of Justice, 2018). Despite such closures, communities have been reassured that they will have access to alternative courts if affected by closures (Ministry of Justice, 2018). Of course, the nature, extent and quality of such access is not assured.

As will be explored further in Chapter 4, the official optimistic account has not been borne out in Wales. While official accounts place the figure of Magistrates' Court closures at 50 per cent across England and Wales, Wales has experienced a higher reduction in Magistrates' Courts compared with England (59 per cent as compared with 49 per cent).[16] The result is that Wales has lost 22 out of its 36 Magistrates' Courts; nine out of 22 local authorities in Wales operate without a Magistrates' Court, including the third-, fourth-, sixth-, eighth- and tenth-largest towns in Wales, all of which are in south Wales.[17] Of the 22 Magistrates' Court closures, 12 have been in our south Wales sample area; the region has been left with six Magistrates' Courts. Although these six are in the main population centres, the Valleys – following closures in Aberdare, Abertillery, Caerphilly, Llwynypia and Pontypridd – has been left with only two courts – Merthyr and Cwmbran – to serve the population, thus taking these important sites of criminal justice away from local communities and potentially restricting the ability of residents in these communities to access justice. Issues with access may be compounded by limits on travel and may further disadvantage those with a disability, caring responsibilities, limited income or lack of access to their own transport. While court closures – as with police station closures – were rationalized by the UK government based on lack of court usage, the reduced usage may be a result of court avoidance through neoliberal measures, with the police station more readily becoming the site of the trial (Jackson, 2016), and with serious and significant cuts to criminal legal aid, rather than an unwillingness of individuals to attend court. The amount of Magistrates' Court work has also declined in Wales: while 90 per cent of cases in England and Wales are completed in the Magistrates' Court, the decline in Magistrates' work is approximately 35 per cent, materially greater in Wales than in England (Commission on Justice in Wales, 2019). Crown Court work has also suffered a more disproportionate decline in Wales than in England: 24.5 per cent as compared with 16 per cent (Commission on Justice in Wales, 2019). The

---

[16] The greatest travel distance to the nearest criminal court is also found in Wales: residents of Staylittle in Powys (mid Wales) have a 74-mile journey, taking one hour and 50 minutes by car, to Caernarfon criminal justice centre (the designated 'receiving site' for Dolgellau Magistrates' Court, which closed in 2017–18). The journey is almost impossible via public transport.

[17] Barry (population 54,673), Neath (population 50,658), Bridgend (population 46,7575), Caerphilly (population 41,402) and Pontypridd (population 33,457), respectively.

Figure 2.2: South Wales Magistrates' Courts

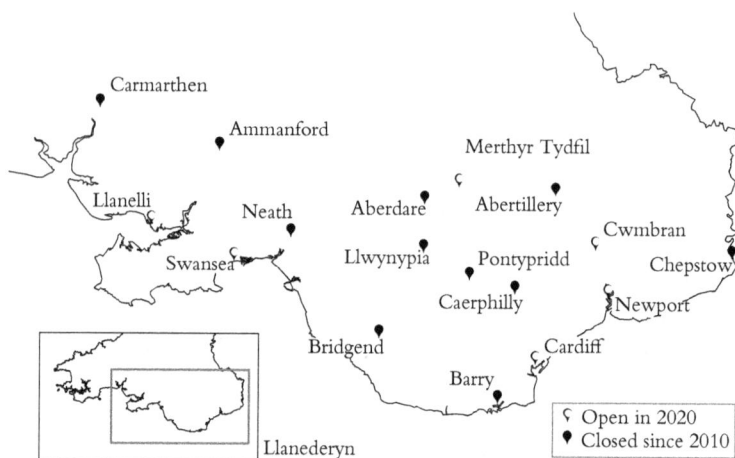

Commission on Justice in Wales (2019) linked this decline – from 2012/13 to 2017/18 – with the reduction in prosecutions. However, it is possible that the court closure programme has had some impact upon an individual's willingness to proceed with their case. Figure 2.2 reveals the extent of closures in south Wales between 2010 and 2020.

Criminal legal aid: restrictions on obtaining access to justice

Criminal legal aid is a means-tested entitlement to state-funded legal representation available for police stations and, depending on the nature of the offence, courts in England and Wales.[18] The necessity for criminal legal aid stems from the complexity of the courts, the higher resource available to police and prosecution, the potentially devastating impact of a conviction upon the accused, and the principle that the ability to defend oneself should not depend on financial resources (Ashworth, 1996). Criminal legal aid is thus vital to secure access to criminal justice for those who cannot afford it. Such is the importance of legally aided criminal defence that we have chosen to dedicate significant space to it. Given that most of the work within criminal justice occurs at the police station and

---

[18] The means test for criminal legal aid was reintroduced via the Criminal Defence Service Act 2006, which amended the Access to Justice Act 1999, amid concerns that the abolition of a means test had caused an increase in criminal legal aid expenditure. See Cape and Moorhead (2005).

Magistrates' Courts, we are dedicating more attention here to solicitors and legal representatives, but – as we will discuss later – the criminal Bar is also facing significant constraints.

At the police station, criminal defence practitioners – criminal solicitors or accredited or probationary police station representatives – can provide advice to suspects who are attending a police station voluntarily or have been detained by the police – usually in police custody – for questioning. The role of police station legal advice was viewed as vitally important during the introduction of PACE because it could 'balance' the vast powers provided to the police under the 1984 Act (Dixon, 1997). At the police station, access to legal advice and assistance is free regardless of the suspect's means, although for some minor offences legal advice may be offered over the telephone. At the courts, a defendant must obtain a representation order and satisfy both the merits and means tests. The merits test – whereby the court must consider the case serious enough for full legal representation, in the interests of justice – is satisfied in all indictable only cases (that is those triable at Crown Court only), but is not always satisfied for those charged with summary (that is Magistrates' Court only) or either way (that is either court) offences. Non-imprisonable offences, in practice, automatically fail the merits test (Gibbs, 2016). The means test is outlined in Table 2.1 (Legal Aid Agency, 2020).

At the Magistrates' Court and for committal for sentence, the accused will automatically be entitled to legal aid if on means-tested state benefits or if, for example, single and on a gross yearly income of below £12,475.

Table 2.1: How the results work depending on case type

Adjusted income	Magistrates' Court	Committal for sentence	Appeal to the Crown Court	Crown Court trial
£12,475 or less	funded	funded	funded	funded, no income contribution
More than £12,475, less than £22,325	depends on full means test	depends on full means test	possible fee, depends on full means test and outcome of appeal	possible income contribution, depends on full means test
£22,325 or more	not funded	not funded	depends on full means test and outcome of appeal	possibly not funded or possible income contribution, depends on full means test
£37,500 or more household income	not funded	not funded	not funded	not funded

For those with a gross yearly income of above £12,475 and below £22,325 entitlement to legal aid will depend upon disposable income; those earning £22,325 or more per year are not entitled to legal aid (Legal Aid Agency, 2020). There are further differences in access to legal aid between the Crown Court and the Magistrates' Court: in the former, the defendant may have to make a contribution to the cost of the case while it is ongoing and will be refunded with interest if found not guilty; in the Magistrates' Court the full cost is initially covered if the defendant passes both tests, although if found guilty may be asked to pay towards prosecution costs. These restrictions may incentivize – or force – some defendants to plead guilty.

Restrictions on access to criminal justice for suspects and defendants also appear in the form of low fees paid to criminal defence practitioners. As noted earlier, the criminal legal aid budget was reduced following austerity. Yet, cost cutting appeared as early as the 1990s, with 'government policy towards legal aid [seemingly] driven solely by the exigency of cost control' (Goriely, 1996: 51). In 1993 the introduction of summary criminal legal aid claims through standard fees increased the number of claims (Cape and Moorhead, 2005). The government then introduced a franchising system to limit the number of firms that could offer legally aided criminal defence, with firms wishing to provide publicly funded advice in legal proceedings required to hold a contract, issued by the Legal Aid Board (replaced by the Legal Services Commission in 1999). This signalled a 'new public management' approach (Sommerlad, 1999), emblematic of neoliberalism. There were later attempts to introduce price-competitive tendering through the Carter Report (Lord Chancellor's Department, 1998), a reverse auction for contracts with the lowest bidder winning, which for Newman (2013a) was a race to the bottom, setting the tone for the devaluation of criminal defence work. This devaluation has continued, as we will discuss in Chapters 3 and 5, and has adversely impacted how criminal defence practitioners manage their work and how – and whether – they interact with clients.

At the police station, fees vary depending on geographic location but are fixed regardless of the number of police station visits, the amount of work required on the case, the seriousness and complexity of the case, and the length of time spent dealing with the case. The fee remains the same regardless of whether the practitioner is requested to attend the police station during the night, in the early hours of the morning, over the weekend or on a Bank Holiday. At the Magistrates' Court, payment is typically a standard fee and based upon the category to which the case is deemed to belong. The categories cover guilty pleas and other uncontested or discontinued matters, trials and other contested matters (including those that are fully prepared but do not go ahead), and committals to the Crown Court which are subsequently discontinued (see Welsh, 2017). At the Crown Court, there are two legal aid fee schemes – the Advocates' Graduated Fee Scheme and the Litigators' Graduated Fee Scheme – with the fee payable depending upon the type of work performed. These cover different types of work such as trial, guilty pleas (although where there are multiple hearings, only the last hearing is paid), cracked trials, the hearing of an appeal (against conviction or sentence), and sentence hearing (where there are proceedings arising out of a committal for sentence). There are fees payable for review of evidence such as witness statements, documentary and pictorial evidence, prosecution summaries and/or transcript of the accused's interview, Achieving Best Evidence interviews, and streamlined forensic reports. However, fees are not payable for CCTV, video evidence or audio evidence, defence-generated evidence, pre-sentence and psychiatric reports, and applications to adduce hearsay or bad character evidence.[19]

There has been no increase in fees for criminal defence solicitors since 1998 (Law Society, 2018) and so the cuts in 2014 have been particularly damaging to the criminal defence sector.[20] Given the – in some cases, steep – rise in the cost of living, the fee paid to criminal defence practitioners is worth less today than in 1998. By way of example in Wales, the average house price has risen from £48,294 to £162,374, thus more than trebling in the time since the last fee increase (Lawthom, 2018). Fee reduction and stagnation can breed disincentivization, which affects the quality of advice and representation being offered to the accused (Fenn et al, 2007). While individuals may enter the criminal defence professions out of commitment to public service and the rule of law, they may inevitably be placed in a position that forces them to compromise their principles to meet the needs of the business (Johnson, 1980; Tata, 2007). Deciding not to do so may result in firms failing to break even. Thus, the surviving businesses are those that focus on volume 'sausage factory' work (Sommerlad, 2001; Newman, 2013a). Yet, such an approach may not mean providing the advice, assistance and representation that the client requires (see Dehaghani and Newman, 2017). This raises concerns about a willingness to engage with poorly paid work, practitioner morale, the future of the criminal defence professions (Dehaghani and Newman, 2021a) and, more generally, access to criminal justice for citizens. The on-the-ground implications of these trends will be examined in Chapters 5 and 6.

Table 2.2 illustrates a decline in the number of criminal defence firms in England and Wales from 2010/11 to 2018/19. This decline coincided

---

[19] For a full list see Legal Aid Agency (2018).

[20] In 2020 the UK government promised an extra £51 million for criminal legal aid to better remunerate case preparation but the Law Society described this offer as 'woefully inadequate' – see Fouzder (2020).

Table 2.2: England and Wales criminal law firms and offices

	2010/ 11	2011/ 12	2012/ 13	2013/ 14	2014/ 15	2015/ 16	2016/ 17	2017/ 18	2018/ 19
Firms	1,861	1,722	1,656	1,603	1,517	1,512	1,388	1,314	1,271
Offices	2,598	2,415	2,338	2,282	2,172	2,240	1,991	1,998	1,921

Source: Secretary of State for Justice (2019).

Table 2.3: Wales criminal law firms and offices

	Mar 2011	Mar 2012	Mar 2013	Mar 2014	Mar 2015	Mar 2016	Mar 2017	Mar 2018	Mar 2019
Firms	146	140	137	132	122	109	105	94	89
Offices	186	183	181	176	165	150	145	131	126

with the introduction of austerity under the coalition and, thereafter, Conservative governments.

Table 2.2 provides detail for England and Wales as an entire jurisdiction. To understand the situation in Wales we submitted an FOI request to the Ministry of Justice.[21] The data – presented in Table 2.3 – demonstrates that the situation for Welsh criminal legal aid is significantly worse than the overall figures for the England and Wales jurisdiction.

While there has been a 31.7 per cent decrease in criminal legal aid firms across the whole jurisdiction, the figure rises to 39.04 per cent when addressing Wales alone. Further, the decline in the number of offices across England and Wales is 26.06 per cent compared to a 32.26 per cent decline in Wales. As such, Wales has lost a greater proportion of criminal legal aid firms and offices than England and Wales as a whole, with the result that in England and Wales – with a total population of 59.12 million – there are 30.78 criminal offices per person, whereas in Wales – with a population of 3.14 million – this figure drops to 24.9 offices per person. The crisis in access to criminal legal aid lawyers is therefore more pronounced in the Welsh half of the England and Wales jurisdiction. Wales has also experienced greater fee reductions than in

[21] FOI request dated 6 March 2019. Figures accurate as of 18 March 2019. Total figures within Table 2.3 include providers who (i) are physically located in Wales and/or (ii) operate Duty Schemes in Wales (for example, one of the firms included within this table is located within the Stoke on Trent Local Authority Area but provides duty solicitor coverage in Wales).

Table 2.4: South Wales criminal law offices

	2010/11	2018/19
Offices	117	80

the overall England and Wales jurisdiction: although total criminal legal aid expenditure for the whole jurisdiction fell from £1,045 million in 2011–12 (£1,177 million in 2018–19 prices) to £873 million in 2018–19, for Wales it fell from £48.44 million in 2011/12 (£54.65 million in 2018–19 prices) to £36.10 million in 2018/19 (Commission on Justice in Wales, 2019).[22] In real terms, this amounts to a 26 per cent reduction for the whole jurisdiction, but a 34 per cent reduction in Wales. The age of criminal duty solicitors is also rising in Wales – as with rural areas in England: in south Wales, 49 per cent of criminal duty solicitors are over the age of 50; this rises to over 60 per cent in mid and west Wales (Law Society, 2018). This will arguably accelerate the decline in firms and offices offering criminal legal aid work.

In addition to the Wales data, we also outline the south Wales data in Table 2.4, which indicates a 31.62 per cent drop in criminal legal aid offices from 117 in 2010 to 80 in 2019.

The Valleys has been particularly badly hit, as seen from the drop-in offices across local authorities such as Blaenau Gwent (from four to one), Caerphilly (from nine to four) and Rhondda Cynon Taff (from 14 to eight) as shown in Figure 2.3.

Significantly less attention seems to have been paid to the effect of cuts on the criminal Bar. As the Commission on Justice in Wales (2019: 128) highlights, 'Crown Court legal aid defence fees under the Advocates Graduated Fee Scheme reduced by 21% in actual terms in the period 2007 to 2018, implying a total reduction of 45% in real terms' and while the Ministry of Justice reformed this scheme in April 2018, the effect on fees remains to be seen. Additional pressures may be placed on barristers through self-employment (Bar Council, 2020), rendering their position yet more precarious should they fail to obtain work. Barristers have much less direct contact with clients and, as such, the cuts made to the criminal Bar affect the accused – at least directly – much less than the cuts and fee stagnations faced by criminal defence solicitors and legal representatives.

---

[22] As Jones and Wyn Jones (2019) have highlighted, the operation of legal aid has been subject to criticism in Wales, particularly in relation to changes to expert fees and their impact on the NHS's delivery of expert medical work (healthcare is devolved to Wales but justice, and thus legal aid, is not).

Figure 2.3: South Wales criminal law offices

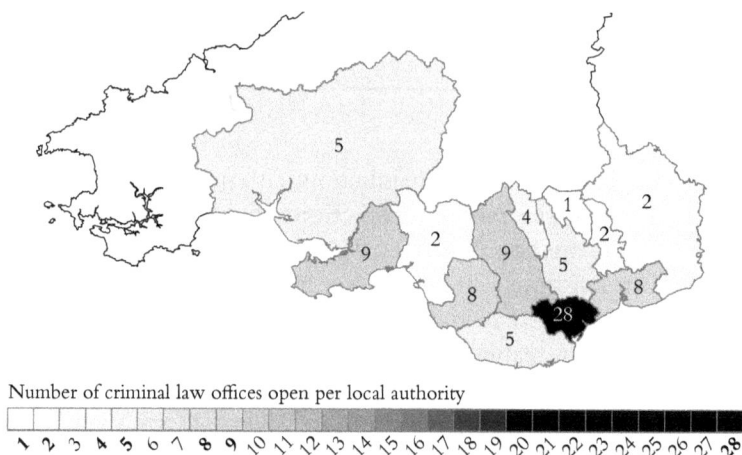

Number of criminal law offices open per local authority

Such cuts – while important to recognize and address – generally affect the Crown Court only and, while it is the Crown Court where sentences are higher,[23] the vast majority – around 95 per cent – of criminal cases are dealt with at the Magistrates' Court.[24] The Magistrates' Court is also where routine miscarriages of justice can occur and, fundamentally, can slip under the radar. Trials in the lower court also attract much less interest from the media and from criminal justice practitioners and are viewed as dealing with the mundane, straightforward and uninteresting (McBarnet 1981; Dehaghani, 2019). For Campbell (2020), austerity has undermined the notion of justice in the Magistrates' Court through an increased focus on speed that may trump any quest for truth.

The demise of the criminal defence professions will further inhibit the ability of those accused of crimes to have their voice heard in court. The accused is largely excluded from processes of justice in the Magistrates' Court; they are typically discouraged from taking an active role in the proceedings (Carlen, 1976; McBarnet, 1981). Yet, defendants are also often compelled to participate in the proceedings against them (Owusu-Bempah, 2017), but are not provided the advice and representation that would allow them to participate in a meaningful way. The accused participants in this study often felt detached, excluded and marginalized from the process (see Chapter 7). While the involvement of a criminal defence

---

[23] The maximum penalty in the Magistrates' Court is six months' imprisonment, or up to 12 months in total for more than one offence.

[24] See Courts and Tribunals Judiciary (undated).

practitioner should encourage meaningful participation of the accused, criminal defence practitioners have neither the time nor the money to facilitate such participation, as we will discuss in Chapters 5 and 6. Indeed, many of the accused are often unrepresented today, signalling an effective return to a time before the mass roll-out of criminal legal aid (see Gibbs, 2016). Issues with suspect and defendant participation are compounded further by curtailments to the right of silence following the introduction of the Criminal Justice and Public Order Act 1994; by virtue of adverse inferences from silence under s 34 of the Act, defendants are compelled to participate in the proceedings against them (Owusu-Bempah, 2017; Quirk, 2017). Such adverse inferences also further devalue legal advice, assistance and representation, placing further strain on the lawyer–client relationship (Quirk, 2017). The result is a less active defence and an increase in potential miscarriages of justice:

> As the police are given more power, and while the police station becomes the location of the trial, or the place where the outcome of the trial is largely determined, the position of the defence lawyer has been weakened. ... Fixed fees for police station work reward lawyers who do the minimum for their clients rather than what is necessary to effectively defend them. (Cape, 2013: 16)

With these issues in mind, we turn to an examination of how vulnerability theory may provide an effective counter-narrative to the neoliberal and austerity agenda.

Vulnerability theory: a radical transformation

It is important to understand how individuals experience the criminal process and achieve access to justice, particularly so when those experiences are affected by austerity and neoliberalism. Vulnerability has been increasingly used within public, political and academic discourse (see Misztal, 2011; K. Brown, 2015); it is a term deployed within the legal and political spheres to restrict – or justify the restriction of – resources to certain groups or individuals such as those deemed not vulnerable (see for example, Ryan, 2015) or those who have not acted responsibly to deal with their own – actual or perceived – misfortune (Munro and Scoular, 2012). It is also a term which is open to interpretation, 'the exact meaning and parameters of [which] remain somewhat elusive' (Munro and Scoular, 2012: 189.) Within academic literature, the term vulnerability can be used to refer to a vast array of characteristics, conditions and circumstances, including, but not limited to, youth and childhood, old age, learning disability, sensory impairment, pregnancy, physical ill-health or mental ill-health, sex work, socio-economic background, and/or geographic position (K. Brown, 2015). Typically, some criminal justice service users – victims, witnesses and (some) suspects and defendants – are recognized as 'vulnerable'. However, their vulnerability status is tied to a particular status or characteristic – victim, disabled, 'mentally disordered' or child. Vulnerability theory views these categorizations as artificial. Underpinned by Fineman's vulnerability theory (2008; 2010; 2013; 2017), our analysis is informed by an understanding that vulnerability is inherent in the human condition and is brought about through our interconnectedness with others, rather than something that is unique to a certain set of groups or individuals. The theory serves as a counterpoint to the classic liberal theoretical position that positions humans as rational, autonomous beings. Rather, vulnerability theory calls upon the state to respond to our shared human vulnerability.

Vulnerability is 'universal and constant' (Fineman, 2013: 21) although one's dependency can vary over the life course (see Gordon-Bouvier, 2020). There are two key aspects of variance: the 'physical: mental, intellectual, and other variations in human embodiment' and the 'social and constructed, resulting from the fact that individuals are situated within overlapping and complex webs of economic and institutional relationships' (Fineman, 2013: 21). It is our flesh-and-blood embodiment – with ontological strengths, weaknesses, and abilities (see Thomson, 2018)[25] – and the manner in which our material bodies interact with the world (Travis, 2017) which render us vulnerable. Thus, it is not simply our embodiment, but also our embeddedness within – and dependency upon – our social relations and institutions that gives rise to our vulnerability. As individuals we may 'attempt to lessen the risk or mitigate the impact of such events [but we] cannot eliminate their possibility' (Fineman, 2008: 8).

Thus, for Fineman (2010: 269), 'the counterpoint to vulnerability is not invulnerability, for that is impossible to achieve, but rather the resilience that comes from having some means with which to address and confront misfortune'. It is not vulnerability that differs – for everyone is vulnerable – but instead resilience that provides this counterpoint. This resilience can be found within individuals, and within social relations and institutions – and it is institutions that hold overwhelming potential in 'lessening, ameliorating, and compensating for vulnerability' (Fineman, 2010: 269). Within this vulnerability approach, the state is compelled towards responsivity and, as

---

[25] At the time of writing (spring to winter 2020), UK nations were variously under lockdown conditions owing to the COVID-19 pandemic. The pandemic drew attention to the fragility of the human condition and to the fragility of institutions such as the police, universities, courts and even the government.

such, may reduce or bolster resilience but not remove or lessen vulnerability (Fineman, 2010). State institutions – contrary to being built around the rational, autonomous liberal legal subject – are centred around the vulnerable suspect and 'constituted for the general and "common benefit", not for a select few' (Fineman, 2010: 274), thus ensuring that everyone has access to resilience building. Resilience can be removed by the mechanisms and procedures utilized within the criminal process: in police custody, for example, the ritualistic risk assessments and the isolation and power imbalance between detainer and detainee may strip an individual of their resilience (Dehaghani, 2021); the often alien and impenetrable legal language or the messy and convoluted criminal process can also deplete resilience (Dehaghani and Newman, 2017) as can the social control and discipline exerted within and by criminal justice institutions and venues.[26] Access to legal aid is also an important resilience mechanism as is access to the means to reach a criminal justice venue. Where an individual does not have access to a court due to (a lack of) means of transport, the state would intervene to address this issue by, for example, improving transport links, providing a means of transport, or by placing courts closer to communities. Relationships – both intimate and professional – can also be a source of resilience but can similarly deplete resilience if strained or of poor quality. Access to a criminal defence lawyer may therefore provide the accused with resilience – notably the ability to mount an effective defence through 'zealous advocacy' – but may also remove or fail to provide this resilience, where, for example, the lawyer is under pressure and cannot spend the time required to successfully defend the case. A vulnerability analysis allows for attention to be paid to the complex web of relationships and alerts us to how decisions are rarely – if ever – made in a vacuum.

More contentious, perhaps, is the proposition that criminal justice practitioners are, themselves, vulnerable and the assertion that resilience should be provided to them as well as by them. The police, for example, may stop, search, arrest and detain individuals, thus restricting their liberty while constructing the case against the individual and withholding key information (see McConville et al, 1991; Hodgson, 1994). With a vast array of powers at their disposal, police officers can use their discretion to discipline and punish. Criminal defence lawyers are also seen as autonomous and sometimes self-serving; they may manipulate their clients and push them towards pleading guilty (McConville et al, 1994). Judges are the gatekeepers of evidence, deciding what is to be admitted, the adjudicators of guilt and innocence, and those that hand down often

---

[26] See Carlen (1976) in relation to the Magistrates' Courts and Choongh (1997) in relation to police custody.

life-altering sentences; the prosecution determine whether a case goes to court and can construct – at least part of – the narrative throughout. Yet, as Fineman would contend, these individuals *are* vulnerable. More difficult perhaps is to argue that they lack resilience. However, within the frame of austerity and neoliberalism, criminal justice practitioners have had their resilience removed or depleted, such as through resource limitations or the introduction of law and policy which forces them to do more with less. Not only does this deplete their resilience, it also, in turn, depletes the resilience of suspects and defendants (see Dehaghani and Newman, 2017). As with suspects and defendants, we can also not treat practitioners as individualized atomized human beings but instead as people with embodied frailties and strengths, recognizing, too, their embeddedness within the complex web of wider relationships.

It is not, however, only individuals who are vulnerable; institutions can also be 'captured and corrupted' by internal and external forces and 'compromised by legacies of practices, patterns of behavior [*sic*] and entrenched interests that were formed during periods of exclusion and discrimination, but are not invisible in a haze of lost history' (Fineman, 2008: 18). Institutions – such as legally aided criminal defence – and the individuals who work within such institutions – that is solicitors and barristers – may therefore also be vulnerable despite being typically perceived as 'powerful' (Dehaghani and Newman, 2017).[27] Some institutions can be less resilient than others, whether because of their complexity, the work that they perform, or the individuals working within them. Further, institutions, such as criminal legal aid, can also lack resilience because of the ways in which they are undermined through political rhetoric and financial constraints (as we explore in Chapters 3, 4 and 5). An institutional vulnerability can alter the response of that institution towards individuals and can, whether intentionally or otherwise, further perpetuate disadvantage (see Fineman, 2008).

We will apply the vulnerability lens to the experiences that emerge at the end of each data chapter (Chapters 3–7). Rather than detract from the voices that we have organized by imposing this theoretical device in the body of each chapter, we will draw out the relevance of vulnerability in the concluding section of each, and then bring these together with a broader and deeper discussion of what vulnerability theory tells us about this experiences in the concluding Chapter 8. While vulnerability theory is an incredibly useful organizing device, it has been criticized for its failure to engage with policy (Kohn, 2014), namely that it provides scholars with a mechanism through which to highlight vulnerability and resilience – therefore useful in setting out broad policy goals – but something that does

---

[27] See also Oakley and Vaughan (2019) in respect of corporate lawyers.

not provide detail on the policies required to achieve these goals.[28] We use it as an organizing device that underlies our understanding of where the criminal justice system sits in society and, mindful of this critique, in Chapter 8 we engage with concrete suggestions as to how resilience can be bolstered or provided by the state.

Conclusion

This chapter has examined the various effects of austerity and neoliberalism on the criminal justice system and, specifically, on certain institutions such as the police, the courts and the prosecution. Much of our discussion has focused on cuts to criminal legal aid and the low fees that are paid for criminal defence work. While cuts to any domain of the criminal justice system can affect those using and those working within it, it is the cuts to criminal defence that cause most suffering to the accused and their families – and perhaps also by extension their communities. An attack on criminal legal aid reflects 'an antipathy not only to state welfare provision but also to procedural justice and fair trial' (Smith and Cape, 2017: 64). The changes to criminal justice during the neoliberal era and the period of austerity are an attack on the welfare state and our collective social safety net, with very real and dire implications for those caught up in the criminal justice system. Difficult questions must be raised in relation to the future of the criminal justice system and, in particular, the future of publicly funded criminal defence. We engage with these questions in more detail throughout Chapters 3–7. Wales has been disproportionately affected and indeed some areas of Wales worse than others. These disproportionate impacts should be known and not ignored.

This chapter has also detailed our theoretical framework, building upon our earlier work in this area (Dehaghani and Newman, 2017; Dehaghani, 2021; Dehaghani and White, 2020). The theoretical framework – a vulnerability analysis – illuminates several pressing problems in the criminal process and, by arguing for a responsive state to ameliorate human vulnerability, provides a strong counter-narrative to the austerity and neoliberal agendas. Although in the data chapters we do not engage heavily with vulnerability theory, they provide the basis for an on-the-ground reality and the foundation for our recommendations in Chapter 8. The following four chapters examine the data, with the first – Chapter 3 – providing a detail on our 69 participants

---

[28] It is, however, worth noting that vulnerability theory provides a framework through which to ask questions and thus interrogate specific institutional arrangements. As it does not dictate the policy and practice outcomes, it can be applied across a range of legal settings and cultures.

by relaying some of the stories of how they came to be involved in the criminal justice system. This provides context to illuminate their views of the criminal justice system and highlight key themes that emerge at various points across the following chapters, namely the underfunding of criminal justice and the level of experience of the accused.

3

The People and Their Experiences

Introduction

In the preceding chapter we set out the impact of neoliberal austerity on criminal justice in England and Wales broadly. The specific focus on the impacts on the police, courts, and criminal legal aid in Wales provided context for the views expressed by participants, who found themselves within a damaged and declining criminal justice system. Such detail grounds this chapter, in which we introduce readers to the participants and draw out how they have experienced criminal justice. Experiences are at the heart of this study; in this chapter we set up the remainder of the book by examining some of the stories of those whose insight and expertise inform our analysis.

To be able to reach an informed view on the experiences explored in the following chapters, it is important to provide the perspectives of the participants in this research. For Newman (2013a: 2) 'debates around criminal justice are necessarily enthused with an array of values, ideologies and interpretive frameworks' meaning that 'any discussion of criminal justice requires that the speaker articulates the choices they have made regarding its purpose'. By this line, the standpoint of those discussing criminal justice is significant and they should never be assumed to approach the subject impartially or neutrally. Such an assumption would be flawed as criminal justice is not merely a theoretical endeavour; criminal justice matters are firmly located within real-life situations, and replete with social contexts and personal implications. Indeed, there are many biases inherent in this study: values inform so much of how we view criminal justice – for Lacey (1994: 34) these are the 'normative implications' of discussing criminal justice – that it is necessary to explore these early on.

The approach in this chapter is informed by legal life writing, which 'offers new ways of advancing legal history and socio-legal scholarship, and of encouraging inter-disciplinary dialogue, both between them, and also with other fields and audiences' (Sugarman, 2015: 32). In order to get a sense of how the participants approached the topics under examination, we believe it necessary that the reader have detail on the backgrounds and histories of participants, and, as such, we do not delve immediately into our data on, for example, the lawyer–client relationship. Our interviews followed a similar approach: we asked individuals about how they came to be involved in the criminal justice system, either as practitioners or accused or family members, before discussing their specific experiences such as whether they can perform their roles or whether they were able to engage in the process. We provide a broad introduction to the participants in this study, their trajectories and backgrounds, and their values, experiences and feelings, thus connecting the personal with the structural. Indeed, as researchers we understand the policy implications of austerity, yet we do not (always) have a sense of how this is experienced on the ground. Within this chapter, we focus on lawyers and the accused although we do provide some detail on police officers.[1] It should be acknowledged that it is the work of practitioners – namely lawyers, and more specifically solicitors – that largely shapes and structures the experience of the accused.

The chapter begins by examining the practitioners, highlighting their routes into criminal justice work. By focusing on their stories, we can gain insight into what kind of practitioners occupy the criminal justice system and how their histories may shape their practice – and their views on practice. We move on to exploring one example of these practitioner views – the opinions they hold on funding of the criminal justice system. That the practitioners were unanimous in believing the criminal justice system to be underfunded means underfunding is an important element of the practitioners' self-identity and of the narrative the practitioners conveyed to us, and forms a key developing theme as we move forward with the analysis in this book. Next we examine how the accused and their families entered the criminal justice system, giving their background due respect. The ways they came into contact with criminal justice frame the perspectives they hold; the detail of their experiences thus underpins the accounts that we draw upon later. Finally, we explore an important element of how the accused view criminal justice, relating to the varying levels of experience different individuals have. Whether or not someone is new to the criminal justice system changes the dynamics of their involvement in a fundamental

---

[1] We focus less on police officers, in part because a great deal is known regarding police occupational cultures (see Worrall and Mawby, 2014) and in part because the police form a small part of our sample. There is also a wealth of popular writing offering accounts of the everyday and common experiences of police officers – see, for example, Satchwell (2016). These accounts were often cited by the officers we interviewed, and one kindly lent us a copy of Inspector Gadget (2008).

manner and represents a second key theme that will be explored further across the course of our analysis in this book.

Across this chapter, we will be setting up the experiences of those we interviewed to illustrate how they fit into the criminal justice system, thus equipping the reader with a deeper understanding of how those experiences have been formed. The reader will be given a glimpse into how and why the experiences of participants have been formed as well as being introduced to these two key themes: the underfunding of criminal justice (for practitioner experiences); and the difference between 'first-timers' and 'regulars' in the criminal justice system (for accused experiences). The underfunding of the criminal justice system – a central theme in this book, which is particularly prominent in Chapters 4 and 5 – is key to understanding the work performed by, the values subscribed to, and the identity of those practitioners. Also crucial to our discussion – and a central theme that will reappear especially in Chapters 6 and 7 – is the varying levels of experience among the accused; the dynamics of the accused's involvement are undoubtedly shaped by their previous experience – or lack of it. These two themes will emerge at various points over the remainder of the book as those we have interviewed have identified them as a central aspect of experiencing criminal justice.

Practitioners and their work

For the practitioners, we can better understand their experiences of the criminal justice system by examining the reasons underpinning their decision to embark on such a career and the circumstances that led or drew them into criminal justice practice. Following Travers (1997a), it is important to use the interview data to give voice to these practitioners as much of the leading work on criminal lawyers (for example, McConville et al, 1994) and police (for example, McConville et al, 1991) has been identified as taking a critical stance that can supposedly speak *over* them. Providing space for these groups to tell their own stories is an important part of drawing out the experiences that we communicate in this book. Relaying how the practitioners came to – or claimed to have come to – the criminal justice system offers the opportunity to outline their experiences in a way that is open to their perspectives and self-understandings.[2] The solicitors in this study were drawn towards criminal work either through a calling or 'social agenda', or out of interest and passion (see Newman, 2013a), or through having 'just fallen into it' (see also Sommerlad and Wall, 1999; Newman,

---

[2]   We use the plural to account for the differences between solicitors but are also aware of Goriely's (1996) insight that legal aid lawyers can hold multiple identities, such as being both 'self-serving' and 'champions of justice'.

2013a). The minority fell into the former category and the majority fell into the latter.[3] Due to the financial realities of practice, legal aid work increasingly 'requires those within it to have a form of moral obligation to move away from self-interest and to want to help others' (Cooke, 2019: 243). DS12 was one such participant who subscribed to the 'social agenda': "You don't do it because you want to be rich. You do it because you, I don't know, it might sound like a cliché, but you do it because you have a calling for it. To be honest, as soon as I got into it, I didn't want to get into anything else." DS12 reflected the attitude of this minority of the solicitors who explicitly held a 'social agenda'; they were in practice to do something worthwhile and the importance of their work motivated them.[4] Remuneration apparently did not factor for this solicitor, who professed such a social agenda. Yet, as will become apparent in the following section, and further in Chapter 5, this was a minority view; most lamented the low wages.

There were also those in our interviews who felt that criminal law was more interesting than other areas of law. There were more of these than ascribed to the 'social agenda'. When asked, "Why crime?" DS3 responded:

'I ask myself that quite a lot, actually, because everybody asks me why. "Why do you want to do crime?" Because a lot of my friends who came through law school, who came through Bar school with me, are doing civil. They get paid four times as much as I would on a case, but this is more interesting ... I find criminal law interesting, and the types of people that you deal with are people. They're not businesses or bank books. They are people. And you have a big involvement in their life, as much as they probably wouldn't admit it, you've got a big involvement in what happens to them going forward, and that's the bit that I like. It's much, much more people-focused, I find, anyway, than civil. I mean, conveyancing is buying a house. Or, you know, trip and slip outside on the street out there. It's much more personally influenced, or personally involved, criminal law. And it's fun. It's really fun.'

For DS3, the work and the people were interesting – and they were both entwined within and the underpinning factor for DS3's choice of career. On a similar theme, for DS7, there was "more to get their teeth" into with criminal work:

'And then, you know, we're not sat behind a desk all day. I think a lot of friends who did other areas of law have left because they just don't

---

[3]   There is, however, some difficulty in separating – and managing – the different types of satisfaction sought through using one label or another (Boon, 2005).

[4]   For a fuller discussion of progressive lawyering in general, see Kinghan (2021).

like it. You know, commercial, property, you know you're sat behind a desk all day. The one good thing about what we do is you make the decisions on a case, you're running it, you run it how you want to run it. Obviously, staff are supervised, but ultimately you have a lot of freedom in what we do, and I think that's why certain people attracted to it. You're out at court every day, you're at the police station, you're moving – you're always somewhere. And it's different every day.' (DS7)[5]

Criminal practice was enjoyable, had variation and freedom, and impacted upon on people's lives. Key to the enjoyment of such work was the opportunity to work with people – this came across in many solicitor accounts. These solicitors worked in this area because of the satisfaction that it gave them, even if they were never going to earn huge sums of money.

Most of the solicitors were, however, lacking a particular motivation to enter criminal practice, and some did not set out to practise it at all. This is akin to Sommerlad's (2012) and Newman's (2013a) insight that legal aid work is not always an active choice.

The romanticized, stereotypical notion of criminal defence work – one presented within TV shows and movies and one that may attract law students – was acknowledged by DS8 as merely mythical:

'I wouldn't say I sort of had the glitz and glamour sort of idea, because while I was, you know, doing the degree, you learn some things, and obviously when I started work experience, it was quite helpful. But I do think it's almost romanticised a little bit doing crime work, you know? And you have all these great happy endings or these big, bad guys and that's just not what it's like in real life!'

Here, as with many of the accounts, this solicitor commenced their legal career with no real goal in mind. They simply found themself practising criminal defence at this point in their career.

We often saw a lack of specific pull towards the law, as in DS7's interview where they expressed studying law as a second-choice option after not being admitted to their preferred degree:

'I went to university to do law as a backup. I wanted to do dentistry, but didn't get the grades in A-level. … Then kind of fell into, again, a training contract at a criminal practice in Cardiff. Training contracts,

---

[5]   What DS7 highlighted here is the importance of personal interactions, examined in more detail in Chapter 6, on the relationships among criminal practitioners and between solicitors and their clients (accused persons).

even back then, weren't common … I didn't really have any experience of crime, but you take the training contract and, and you kind of find it interesting and stay. I never particularly thought of crime as a job. I needed to qualify, so I wanted a training contract, I've paid for the LPC [Legal Practice Course], you know, I need to get a job.'

DS7's career in criminal law commenced out of necessity – requiring a training contract and employment – but continued out of interest. The motivations of those pursuing a career in criminal legal aided practice will be explored in Chapter 5, where we examine the future of the profession.

The prevalence of mixed practices in south Wales – there is only one criminal set of barristers' chambers – and the encouragement, particularly in the early career stage, of practice across legal fields meant that the motivations for barristers were slightly more complicated. Unlike solicitors who were almost exclusively engaged in criminal practice, many of the barristers had or presently also practised in civil, family, immigration or personal injury law. As with the solicitors, however, the barristers pointed towards a similar motivational divide: some had stumbled into criminal practice without a set plan whereas others spoke of a calling. The excitement of the courtroom and, as with DS8 earlier, the glamour of criminal practice, was a draw for BS3. With experience, this was apparently perceived as naïve, but it nevertheless explained why BS3 pursued this career:

'When I was younger, I always wanted to do it. I think I was probably quite attracted to the glamour of things like, you know, the criminal Bar, what it looks like on telly. The idea of standing up for people, arguing in court, all those things were things that I thought was really exciting when I was younger.'

The draw for BS3 could be seen to include a degree of 'social agenda' – the perceived importance of the work they would be doing.

BS13 gave another common 'pull factor', that they found crime more interesting than other areas of law:

'I always wanted to become a barrister and I always wanted to work in criminal law. Very simply that is what I was passionate about when I was studying the various different areas of law. It was always crime that I found most fascinating and that I enjoyed more than any of the other subjects.'

The interest was not enough for some to sustain any sense of passion. In this example, BS5 discussed how they found criminal law interesting in theory but how the reality of practice was quite different:

'So, predominantly in the regions, more and more you tend to have a mixed practice from the beginning. There are obviously some specialist sets. A large consideration for me was I know I find criminal law interesting, prior to going into practice, but I'd never actually done any practice. A lot of people told me, "Don't narrow down your areas too early on," which actually was quite pertinent advice. It's not necessarily the area, having now worked in the system five years, that I've found the most enjoyable day-to-day.'

BS5 seemed to be reassessing their previous enthusiasm for criminal work, having had sustained contact with the criminal justice system and the experience of working within it.

In contrast to those who had been attracted to the criminal Bar, BS7 simply stumbled upon criminal practice without any idea of what it entailed. They appeared to have the choice between practice as a solicitor and practice at the Bar, and between civil and criminal work, choosing the latter in both cases:

'Wanted to be a barrister because I've always fancied the role of an advocate. I didn't come to the Bar intent on necessarily doing criminal work. I came with a view to doing whatever was there. Didn't have any real, you know, idea of what there my future lay because there's no lawyers in my family or anything like that. So I just kind of came to it blind, really. Fancied being a lawyer, and fancied being a barrister rather than a solicitor. … Did a civil and a criminal pupillage, enjoyed both, but it was back in the day when civil and criminal fees, the overall income would have been about the same. And so I was happy to do criminal.'

BS7 seemed to suggest that they were almost surprised to find themselves becoming a criminal barrister, indicating that they were happy to practise criminal law because the income payable for civil and criminal was at similar levels. While BS7 purported to enjoy both criminal and civil, criminal practice may have been preferred because it was viewed as more interesting work, as BS9 explained:

'I just sort of drifted into it and I then quite enjoyed it. It's a damn sight more fun than civil, I tell you, albeit nowhere near as well paid. I mean I basically wanted to be on my feet all the time, and in civil you're on your bum doing papers 90 per cent of the time and then hardly ever getting into court and then it's more, you spend a lot of time negotiating and faffing around rather than just getting stuck in.'

BS9, as with BS7, found themself falling into criminal practice, and was glad to have done so. Their choice was based on interest rather than remuneration and by the excitement and variation of which DS7 spoke. In Chapter 5, where we examine the time pressures barristers face and the impact of legal aid cuts, we are better able to understand the importance of interesting work to sustain barristers in their practice. Within Chapter 5 we also examine motivations to work in criminal practice, given the shaky future of criminal defence during austerity.

With police officers, there was a combination of drift and pull similar to solicitors and barristers (see White et al, 2010), yet their decision to join the force was also influenced by their limited educational performance. For PO6, their grades prevented them from attending college; joining the police felt natural because of their parents' involvement:

> 'I came into it in the late 1980s, virtually straight from school as a nineteen-year-old. I came into it because both my parents had been involved in the police. … And I just, not fell into it, that would be the wrong phrase, but it was seen as a sort of natural thing to do. Toyed with the idea of college, initially, but didn't quite get the grades, so went into it and … took it from there.'

Similar to PO6, PO4 also joined because of their educational attainment – "I left straight from school … I'd always been interested in joining the job but I wasn't brilliant academically-wise in school" – although did so via the cadets. PO4 recounted how a series of attachments – being sent to one part of Cardiff as a cadet, volunteering to work on a high-profile murder case in a different part of Cardiff, and being deployed to the major crime unit in another part of Cardiff – eventually led to "ending up sort of staying on". An important contrast here in terms of career is that the progression routes expressed by police officers in this study were established and clear, markedly different from the accounts of solicitors, in particular. For solicitors in this study, progression mainly involved achieving Higher Rights of Audience in the Crown Court or partnership in a firm, neither of which were statuses that all practitioners would necessarily want.[6]

Across the sample of solicitors and barristers, an important line of reasoning for engaging in this work was that they were good at it – it suited their skills; this rationale also rang true for police officers. This aptitude

---

[6] In Chapter 5, when considering the pressures faced by practitioners, unlike for solicitors and barristers we will not explore the reasons that police officers in this study cited as putting people off policing work. The frustrations largely stemmed from the cultural shift from 'street cop' to 'management cop' (Leo and Reuss-Ianni, 2017). The limited size of our police sample as compared with the lawyer groups means that we do not have sufficient data to explore this in any depth, but would urge for further work on working practices of police officers, particularly with a geographical focus.

was there regardless of their original motivations for entering practice. Yet, by subscribing to this notion of 'drift', legal aid lawyers may often underplay their own skills (see Melville and Laing, 2007). with the money and glamour of commercial practice causing legal aid lawyers to overlook the relational elements of criminal practice; they may have gravitated to such practice because they were actively attracted to work that involved developing relationships with people in need or because they had excellent communication skills and were able to display empathy. This phenomenon was also evident in the lawyers who were driven by a calling. That criminal practice suited their skillset was the reason that BS4 had left personal injury work:

'I liked the advocacy and I liked the jury advocacy more than judicial advocacy, so I prefer to talk to a jury than a judge. I think that I'm better at that. And so, the seeds were sown. An opportunity came to move to here to do entirely criminal work, and I decided that I'd do that. I sort of rebranded myself. ... It was really just being in court and, as I say, addressing sort of lay people – I mean, obviously there's an element of judicial interaction there, but I like the jury advocacy side of things ... completely different skills. If you're dealing with a judge ... you can assume a lot is read, there are shortcuts in everything, there's more formality to the language. I think jury advocacy ... is about working out what makes people tick, what they think about, what bothers them, and I like that aspect. I think there is a psychological and an analytical approach to it which I like, because I like people, and I'm a people person, and I think those skills are better deployed in that area.'

As for a large proportion of solicitors with whom we spoke, BS4 reflected the view of many barristers that they enjoyed the person-centred nature of criminal practice, which is relevant to the discussion of criminal justice relationships in Chapter 6.

We cannot reproduce all the individual stories of how each practitioner came into practice, not even as a potted history or thumbnail biography. What we have done is to provide some common pathways into practice, which serve to emphasize the non-linear nature of the why and how. Some criminal practitioners have a calling but not everyone working in the criminal justice system has made a conscious career choice. Rather, sometimes they have simply 'ended up' in criminal lawyering – or policing – through happenstance. But the common backstories ('social agendas', being interested in the work, finding themselves doing the job without any underlying motivation) all have relevance for underpinning the experiences that come out in later chapters. Having explored how those practitioners interviewed entered criminal-focused practice, we now examine some of the views held of this area of practice.

Funding and its importance to criminal justice practice

As discussed in Chapter 2, this book in part examines the effect of austerity on the experiences of criminal justice. Central to this is the question of funding, a prominent issue raised by the lawyers in this study and an issue that largely frames their own experiences and the experiences of their clients. The concerns about funding – so central as they are to experiences – will emerge as a recurring theme in later chapters (mostly notably through an in-depth discussion about the implications of underfunding across Chapter 5).

Underfunding of criminal justice is a theme that emerges from considering the views of these practitioners; it unites them and to a degree helps define them as it creates a sense of solidarity in the face of a perceived unfairness they all face. The practitioners in our study felt frustrated by the decisions of politicians and the dire situation within which the criminal justice system had been placed. They felt that they were being left to 'pick up the pieces' of the crumbling criminal justice system. Research such as Sherr (2000) and Boon (2002) has shown the inadequacy of much legal education in preparing students and trainees for the realities of legal practice, and the importance of socialization into a relevant legal culture when in practice. The demands of socialization mean that practitioners learn to develop a professional demeanour (see Goffman, 1990). As it applies to those in this study, such a professional demeanour could be understood to include internalization of certain views on the paucity of funding and, especially for lawyers, the view that they are challenged, restricted and punished by a swingeing legal aid regime. This is a defensive worldview that sees them as having to resist external pressures just to do their jobs. This echoes the importance of funding to the criminal legal aid lawyers in Newman's (2013a) study, where it was reported as the most common topic of conversations among lawyers. The discussion here also mirrors more recent work by Thornton (2019; 2020), which demonstrates the fundamental role that underfunding plays in how lawyers understand their work.

For the lawyers with whom we spoke, the criminal justice system was widely seen as a system near breaking point, as discussed in the first two chapters of this book. The practitioners in our study widely felt they were being expected to pick up many of the pieces:

'Chris Grayling's [the former Lord Chancellor] got a lot to answer for. Because the whole sector, from prisons to probation to everybody, has taken an absolute hammering over the last five or six or seven years, and I think is massively creaking. I think rather unfairly now I do think the onus is on the defence to sort out some of the issues. And it shouldn't be.' (DS1)[7]

DS12 echoed similar concerns about how the cuts to the criminal justice system required that lawyers do more with less and deal with the fallout where things went awry. Yet, DS12 also indicated that solicitors were retaining most of the work on Crown Court cases, deciding – because of financial concerns – not to engage the services of a barrister:

'The way we work, we're streamlined. We're cut. ... We do as much as we can ourselves. I do all the Crown Court stuff. At the moment, I'm involved in a like, a three-month trial up in Newport. It's not because – that's not a cost-cutting exercise. Well, it is a cost-cutting exercise, because I can do exactly what the barristers do, so why am I going to give it to them? I didn't come into this business not to make a profit. But you can't come into something like this thinking, "I'm only going to make a profit", you know? There's cuts everywhere, so the criminal defence service, as we might be called, we're bottom-feeders, so we rely on a trickle down of information. If our information doesn't come from the top because they're squeezed in how much they can investigate based on how much manpower they've got based on other things, then we, unfortunately, bear the brunt of it, when things go wrong.'

The cuts to the criminal justice system not only impact upon how much work solicitors perform, but also affect the types of work that they feel willing or able to do and their ability to do that work properly. This also impacts upon their relationships with barristers – discussed further in Chapter 6 – with barristers being passed less work.

All police officers (PO1–6) also highlighted the societal importance of increased criminal justice funding, as in this example:

'Where do you want to spend your money? How do you want to spend your money? Good health, education, and a good system of law and order? It's going to benefit society, isn't it? What's more important? You know, in that order as well. If you're healthy and you're reasonably well-educated, and by that, I mean, you can learn, you may be totally amoral, and you have no hope there, but if you can

---

[7]   Grayling introduced the 8.75 per cent cut to legal aid funding discussed in Chapter 2. Lawyers have called for this cut to be reversed as a starting point to improve the system.

learn the difference between right and wrong and appreciate it. Good health, good education, good law, law and order. Society should be better off.' (PO5)

PO5 indicated, however, that criminal justice is, in their view, less important than health and education. They also premised increased funding on the need to enhance 'law and order' rather than an explicit requirement to improve the access to justice as discussed in Chapter 2. PO2 also acknowledged the politics inherent in criminal justice funding: "It's a political football, the police and the judicial system ... like the National Health Service, they chuck billions and billions of pounds, year in, year out, and they always want more money, you know?" Police officers did not only acknowledge the challenges that they themselves faced as a result of funding cuts, but also recognized the impact of legal aid changes on criminal defence lawyers:

'I know that defence were paid based on activity on the case. Defence are no longer paid on activity on the case; they're paid a one-off fee, which may have additional fees later on, but I mean, it's not like a, "Well if I do this, I can get this, and I can charge this." It's, "There's the case, there's your pot of money to defend that case, and that's it." So I saw, operationally, lots of letters from solicitors, you know, chasing up stuff and throwing their things into the mix, after charge, you know. There's another witness we're going to go and speak to or whatever and managing a case on behalf of a defendant. I'm not sure that happens any more given the new costing structure, and whether they have their one visit in the police-station pre-interview, and they may have a follow-up interview afterwards and that's it, and then it's basically, "I'll see you in court in the morning" ... there's a gap in that regard, that the lawyers may be doing what they need to do.' (PO1)

As PO1 highlighted, the legal aid changes have caused changes to defence practices, particularly the reduction in defence activity and the limits on lawyer–client contact and, thus, the lawyer–client relationship, as we will explore further in Chapter 5.

The steady frequency with which lawyers discussed funding in their practice and everyday lawyer-to-lawyer interactions mirrors that noted by Newman (2013a) – a phenomenon thus not simply unique to England, where Newman conducted his research. This has been echoed in the narratives of lawyers in our study, sometimes as a result of our questions but other times entirely unprompted. Barristers and solicitors were united by their concerns regarding funding; when asked about the most significant issue facing the criminal justice system, participants in our study all noted the issue of funding. It was acknowledged as "the starting point" (BS3); "proper" funding was viewed as something that could make "the biggest difference" (BS4) and it was needed "from the police station" (DS13). Increased funding was viewed as crucial to the future functioning of the criminal justice system:

'If you pay people more, you will have higher skilled people moving into those areas who are able to produce better results than people who aren't that highly skilled. That's a very real concern, is that you are having lots of extremely intelligent, bright barristers going into family law because of the remuneration, and their skills are being used in the family courts, which is great, fine. But ... the criminal justice system is losing out on the brightest and the best because they're going into other areas. There has always been that conflict because civil is always going to pay a hell of a lot more than criminal and family, but, in my experience, there are lots of brilliant, up and coming barristers that ... wanted to go into criminal law, but they are not going into it because of the remuneration. And the system will suffer because of that.' (BS12)

The paucity of remuneration was the most significant concern for criminal practice as it diverted the best practitioners towards other more lucrative areas of practice. This was something that worried many practitioners (see Dehaghani and Newman, 2021a). The quality of practitioners was tied to the issue of funding:

'If you could afford to pay solicitors better rates, that they would be more encouraged to come into that part of the profession. You would perhaps encourage better quality people to come in, because they would know that there would be a future for them; you know, either as practitioners starting off, or when they become senior people and might have their own practices, there would be a profit to be made from it. At the moment, it's barely breaking even. Improvement in the legal aid rates would undoubtedly bring about improvements in the system.' (DS20)

There were also related concerns that the public good inherent within criminal practice was being exploited. Such a view (against the UK government taking advantage of the 'social agenda') was offered by DS5:

'We shouldn't have to have a profession that's reliant upon on some sort of huge social conscience and sacrifice yourself to that to have to come into. ... And the law just seems to be it is changing because the high-street firm is not what a high-street firm was twenty years ago ... you can't have a profession that's just based on just a strong-willed sense of passion and justice is the only thing that's going to get you through. It's got to be a job, for the majority, isn't it?'

The high street firm was seen as one rooted in the community (the importance of local justice will be developed in Chapter 4) and was one that could offer person-centred, holistic advice (the dynamics of the lawyer–client relationship are explored in Chapter 6). The key for DS5 was that the traditional way of practice could be understood as declining and, with it, the likelihood that solicitors would go beyond what they are paid for; "going the extra mile" for the client, purely out of goodwill, will become a thing of the past.

Yet lawyers did not simply recognize the impact of funding cuts on defence practice, they also acknowledged the impact on the prosecution:

'Proper funding of, not just defence, but prosecution as well, because no-one's getting a good service at the moment. You know, we have an adversarial system, so it needs both parties to be adequately funded. And properly funding both sides is the only way to do it. And it's on a cliff edge at the moment. We're – everyone's – just holding on. It's at the point where the system could quite easily fall apart if there were further cuts, because people would walk away from it.' (DS7)

The inadequacy of police and prosecution funding, as discussed in Chapter 2, was highlighted as having an impact on both sides of the adversarial divide. The failure to use highly skilled and knowledgeable prosecution staff was noted as adversely impacting upon the defence, and underfunding was seen to reduce the fairness of criminal proceedings for the accused:

'I think funding of CPS would be a major help. And to an extent funding of the courts. Because I think at the moment the system is of a poor quality, because the police don't have the funding to properly investigate things, or the person-power to do that. Prosecution don't have enough staff who are experienced to be able to properly review things and to chase the police when they haven't done what they need to do. I think the defence are being used as the safety net, to ensure file quality for the CPS, and I think that's quite a dangerous thing. So I think the fairness of trials for defendants would be better served if prosecution, defence and police were properly funded.' (DS1)

Such views on prosecution funding were from solicitors who exclusively performed defence work. Yet the impact of CPS underfunding was also acknowledged by barristers who engaged in defence and prosecution work (and thus had more contact again with the CPS):

'Even more important than [funding] the barristers, is getting CPS properly funded and properly trained and properly staffed. Because the people there are obviously doing the best they can, but they need more money and they need more staff, and that's not happening. So it's, it's on a downward trend. It's going down and down and down. And I don't think the government really want to do anything to help it. And so I think it's those two things. … That's how you would get more justice.' (BS12)

Concerns, again, emerged regarding the decline of the criminal justice system and the reluctance of the UK government to address this, as set out in Chapter 2. The worsening situation was highlighted by DS12, revealing a somewhat Kafkaesque situation for the accused:

'Things are [set] to get much worse, rather than getting better, for several reasons, but going back to what I said from the beginning. One, is the cuts. The continual cuts being made, not just in criminal legal aid and that sort of thing, the continual cuts being made in the depletion of the number of officers to investigate offences. The continual reduction in the use of qualified lawyers within the CPS, who can make decisions on the spot, as opposed to case workers, who are not legally qualified. … Courts are overloaded. You're having a lot more litigants in person who are not qualifying for public funding and don't have the money to pay for their own defence, and so they have to do it themselves.' (DS12)

At the core of each of these issues was the issue of inadequate funding, with cumulative damage to every part of the system. The lack of universality of legal aid provision was highlighted by DS15, who exclaimed that, "Legal aid should be free for all; it was once upon a time." For DS15, "It's rubbish about it being means tested, and it's just a way of preventing people getting legal aid."

The low-income threshold for the legal aid means test, as established in Chapter 2, was considered particularly problematic by many of the interviewees:

'Twelve thousand and something [£12,475] is the cut off. If you go over that you won't meet the means test, you won't get legal aid. I think they should raise that. They should raise that to around about sixteen thousand or seventeen thousand, because anyone who could be on the cusp just won't get legal aid. So, I think they should raise that … I've seen people who have serious allegations against them, just because they work and get, not even a decent wage, they can't get funding. They have to pay for their own barrister. That's not right.' (DS2)

Yet, funding was acknowledged as only the start of any solution (see also Newman, 2013b) because of the extent of the damage. It was, however, recognized as an important step in the right direction:

> 'You know, and that now has gone on for so long that the damage is done, and you can't easily undo it. And I don't want to say you can undo it by throwing money at it because that may not be true, but if they don't throw money at it, they're never going to sort this out, so we get back to at least a semblance of what we should have.' (DS6)

In Chapter 5 we provide a more detailed discussion on funding and the pressure placed on practitioners – and the institutions of criminal justice – although before doing so, we explore, in Chapter 4, the issue of underfunding in the south Wales context in particular.

Thus far we have discussed the practitioner experience, yet equally important – if not more important for the impact that the system has on their lives – are the views and voices of the – often hidden or obscured – accused and family members. Their entry into the criminal justice system – one that is often not born out of choice – is markedly from that of practitioners. Within the following section, we examine the criminal justice experiences of the accused and how these were perceived by practitioners.

The accused in the criminal process

Here we examine the often hidden and marginalized voices of the accused and their families. In doing so, we aim to provide a more holistic understanding of how criminal justice is experienced. Jacobson et al (2016) have highlighted the value of engaging with the stories of those who are drawn into the criminal justice system and the need to redress the dominant focus of criminal justice research that centres on practitioners. Buozis (2017) has detailed how providing access to the counter-narratives of the accused can challenge the dominant status quo of 'law and order' values that underpin much wider discussion of the criminal justice system. Here, we tell the stories of how the accused and their families came into the criminal justice system, ensuring that our subsequent understanding of their experiences follows the perspectives as they define them and builds upon their self-knowledge. We believe that, as with practitioner interviews, there is a need to take these stories at face value while remaining aware of the problems inherent in any social research.[8]

---

[8] Previous criminal justice research, notably that by Baldwin and McConville (1977), has been criticized for engaging with defendants. There, the concern was that the word of defendants – who were purportedly untrustworthy and inherently biased – was given

The accused – like any individual – may have prejudices developed through life experiences and may be influenced by structural and social values and experiences. Although there may be some distinction drawn between those who have, for example, been formally sanctioned for dishonesty and those for whom honesty is central to their career,[9] it is possible that all interviewees are prone to some degree of exaggeration.[10] Embellishments may be driven by self-aggrandizing behaviour, a desire to protect one's reputation, a frustration with the system, an inclination towards telling a compelling story, or a wish to impress. Our focus is not on an objective notion of truth but instead on the reality for the person being interviewed (Miller and Glassner, 2011). We acknowledge that in constructing our sense of self we all may interpret events and create new readings, doing so differently depending on how we want to be presented to others (Goffman, 1990). We therefore do not hold the accused and family accounts we collected to any higher or lesser standard than the practitioner accounts. That said, we acknowledge the interpretation that all research is subject to and thus welcome readers to arrive at their own conclusions.[11]

As with the practitioners, the biographies of the accused and their families provide context for their experiences: the how, why and when they came to be involved in the criminal justice system are important to understanding how their experiences have been shaped and – in some instances – by whom. Participants varied in their experiences of the criminal justice system – some had been involved in the criminal justice system since youth, others became caught up in the system much later in life, and some had experience of criminalization in youth and again later in adulthood. There was, however, an apparent difference between youthful misdemeanours and adult offending. Such was expressed by AC5, who outlined what we

---

primacy over that of lawyers. There is undoubtedly an element of classism at play, which has heightened over recent decades (see McKenzie, 2013). It is worth noting that previous research has shown that the status of, for example, criminal legal aid lawyers is relative to their clientele (see Newman, 2013a). Sommerlad (1996: 298) has suggested that a low status for such lawyers among peers indicates a 'clear reflection of the connection between the status of the client and the lawyer'. The association between lawyers and clients means that the former are tainted along the 'client-type thesis' of professional prestige, with the latter considered somewhat lowly and undesirable (Sandefur, 2001).

9   Ipsos MORI (2017; 2018) show that 54 per cent of people trust lawyers to tell the truth; 76 per cent trust the police.

10   Devereux et al (2009) highlight the limitations of interview-based research with defence lawyers, noting they are likely to give favourable accounts of their practice.

11   It is important to note that some of the accused we interviewed were victims of miscarriages of justice, thus undergoing a markedly different experience from someone who had been accused of a crime they did commit, albeit we heard similar views on the criminal justice system across our interviews with accused persons.

were often told about younger indiscretions being of such small scale as to barely warrant being considered as 'getting into trouble' but that these often escalated as they got older:

> 'I've never been arrested before this day, ever in my whole life, and I've never been in trouble with the police. Like, don't get me wrong: I've had cautions for shoplifting in the street or something as a kid. But that's just general kid stuff, innit? But nothing, never been arrested and put in a police station.'

Here, 'getting into trouble' did not simply mean a caution on the street, but instead something that results in arrest and detention. Other interviewees excluded a night in the cells from this notion of 'getting into trouble', although typically the cautions and detentions were during their younger years and usually involved theft or drugs. The level of offending that constituted trouble was, overall, variable and self-defined. There were participants who had previously been in trouble with the police but were taken aback by the sudden escalation of finding themselves in prison:

> 'Oh, I got caught up in drugs, I did. Because, a whole load of drugs it was, and that's why I got here like. I had a four year, four-month sentence. No. No. I have, fighting, years ago when I was a kid, like, do you know what I mean? But the first time that I've ever been in here in my life.' (AC6)

AC6 was disappointed with the way things had turned out but accepted sole responsibility for the circumstances in which they found themself.[12] As with some of the other participants, their *criminality* was linked with drug use. Similar to AC6, AC2 discussed their involvement in the criminal process as a young person and how involvement with drugs led to further criminality. Yet, they also provided an account of how their life became entwined with the criminal justice system (see also Cloward and Ohlin, 1960; Lea and Young, 1984; Currie, 1985):

> 'Well, I come from Ely [in Cardiff] where there's, drug-riddled, and, you know. I come from a broken family. So, from a young age I was getting into crime, you know, which I was actually doing crime, where, that's all where it started, you know, when we were kids, you know what I mean, like I say, thirteen, fourteen and doing sheds and nicking cars and doing all these kind of things. But ... that's how it

---

[12] Links between drugs use and offending have been explored by Papp et al (2016).

started – but it was normal. That was normal for us, because, you know, we didn't have nothing, so it was, there were, there was nothing for us to do, so it, it just become a part of our life, just going off. And then going to realise that you can make money, then it escalated to, well, you know, you started doing sheds. And we used to screw shops. We, we never used to do houses and stuff. We used to screw shops. You know, we'd steal cars. We'd plough a, a car through a shop, leave it in there and we'd load up the other car and drive off. That's what we used to do. And then – not always like that, you know, we'd use many different ways of getting into shops, you know? So that's, that's, that's what we used to do. But we done that for quite a few years. Then, you know, I started drugs. We hit the drugs, and it was a lot of heroin and crack and stuff like that. So then obviously you're stealing to fund your habit, in't you? Yeah, so in turn … that gets you landed, locked up, you know, for thefts and, you know, violence and things – when you start, you're robbing, you can only rob so much before you're, you're in a spotlight, do you know what I mean? With the police … I ended up in jail quite a few times, probably about nine times all in all.'

While initially involved in the criminal process out of boredom during their youth, they had since spiralled into committing more serious offences as time went on.[13] AC2 relays their involvement in the criminal justice system as an inevitability, and, having had regular contact with the criminal justice system, appears to have internalized the label of 'criminal' (see Becker, 1963). McAra and McVie (2010: 202) have highlighted that 'youngsters involved in serious offending are among the most victimized and vulnerable group of people in our society'. In their analysis, young persons involved in crime have too often been criminalized by the criminal justice system. Following Cohen (1955), criminality, in an example such as that of AC2, also seems to be born out of a lack of opportunities as well as social and economic deprivation. Ely was one of the largest council estates in Europe, regularly ranks among the most deprived in the capital city and is often stigmatized with regard to crime and disorder, with a negative reputation stereotyped through examples such as the Ely riots of 1991. The life experiences of those with whom we spoke, such as AC2, had led them to what might be termed a regular 'life of crime' – an admittedly problematic phrase that, although common parlance, sets people up to

---

[13] Farrington (1995) has conducted influential research on the development of criminal behaviour from youth and across the life course, although such work on 'risk-factors' and young offending has been critiqued by, for example, Haines and Case (2008).

fail and has been shown to be resented by those to whom it is applied (see Gordon, 2018).[14]

For AC4, it was prison that shaped them into what could be termed a 'recidivist offender' (see, for example, Cullen et al, 2011):

> 'I definitely believe that that time when I was in prison, I served twenty-one months out of three years. ... I was a young offender at the time, and I really played up. But I've no doubt in my mind that that conditioned me for further sentences. It did. It was no longer a taboo. It wasn't something that I knew nothing about. I knew it very well, I knew the system, worked it out really quickly, and it set me up for future sentences.'

AC4, like AC2 and AC6, had entered the criminal justice system as a young person and, upon serving a prison sentence, had internalized the label of 'criminal'. Criminality and serving prison time had become normalized and thus provided AC4 with some level of resilience when convicted of further offences. Yet not all the accused who had regular contact with the criminal justice system had internalized their 'criminality' to this degree. Instead, some, such as AC8, had reluctantly accepted their involvement: "I was homeless at sixteen. Been involved with the justice system quite a bit. Yeah, it's, there's always like, to me there seems like they [the police and the prosecution] make the most out of it."

AC8, like AC2, AC3 and AC4, had, however, experienced social deprivation. They had committed offences out of necessity, having been made homeless at 16. There were also, however, participants who were completely new to the criminal justice system and had, by their accounts, led a relatively 'normal' life. Like several other interviewees, AC3 described the trauma, surprise and shock of coming to the attention of the police:

> 'I'm sixty-seven years of age, I'm married, got children, grandchildren. I've always had what I would term a financial background, having had a couple of businesses, successful businesses. ... My experience came as an immense shock to me, immense shock. And by immense shock, I mean a knock on the door at seven o'clock in the morning, right? It was very traumatic.'

In a similar vein, FM4 mentioned the shock that they experienced when their family member was accused, something they framed as a "horrid

---

[14] It is important to consider differences between men and women here as highlighted by Rhoades et al (2016).

journey": "I mean we'd never ever been involved, I mean you know, with the police or anything so it was all really, really alien to us, how it all worked. And it's a shock really when it happens to you because you don't know where to turn." FM4 felt that the process was "alien" to them, evoking the accounts of Carlen (1976) and McBarnet (1981). This lack of knowledge and feeling of bewilderment was evident in many of the other interviews. Accused interviewees and the family members also expressed distrust of the criminal justice system. For AC2, the criminal justice system, and the police in particular, was not taken seriously – especially not on the first contact in youth. AC2 explained:

'I was nervous and excited, you know, generally. But we didn't have really have no respect for the police because the police used to terrorise us. You know, back in like 1997 and that. The police wouldn't give a shit. They'd come by, they'd punch you up, and like – especially when we was, you know, big gangs. Alright, we was cheeky when we was kids, do you know what I mean? And then when they come in, tomping you up with their truncheons – I used to hold them – they have the long bit don't they, the arm, the bell end, they'd give you little jabs in the ribs, and, you know, little chins and that, do you know what I mean? We didn't have no respect for the police, so we didn't do a fuck for the police. The police come, we'd be bricking their cars, do you know what I mean? Smashing their cars up and that's, that's what we would do. So, you know, like I say, it's nothing to be proud of, but that's just exactly how it was. Especially, like, I grew up in Deere Road [in Ely, Cardiff], you know, and it used to be a bit rough, that's how it was, you know?'

Owing to police brutality, AC2 had no respect for the police or, it seemed, any trust in the system (see Hough, 2013). AC9 expressed a similar distrust, but one that was born out of a sense that the police were not there to objectively investigate a crime:[15]

'You cannot trust the police. You cannot rely on the police. You need to gather your own evidence; you need to protect yourself. You need to protect yourself; the police are not going to do it for you! The police are not going to go out looking for evidence, they're not going to go out looking for CCTV, they're not going to go out asking questions, they're not interested if you're innocent or not. They really don't care.

---

[15] This speaks to the problems of police tunnel vision and case construction – see, for example, McConville et al (1991); Findley and Scott (2006); Naughton (2013).

They don't care whose innocent or not, right? They're not interested. You need to be aware that you need to protect yourself.'

Those that once had faith in the police had since lost that faith due to the circumstances within which they found themselves. Worse still, the lack of trust did not end with the police but instead extended to the entire process (see Hough et al, 2010):

'I also worked with the police at quite a senior level in my previous role ... I don't trust them at all now. But it's worse than that, I think. It's not just that I don't trust the police, but I don't trust in the whole legal process. In terms of getting justice for our son, it's not that I don't trust the police officers who were directly involved; I don't trust their managers, the way they handled it. I don't trust the professional standards department, the way they dealt with the complaint. I don't trust the IPCC [Independent Police Complaints Commission, now Independent Office for Police Conduct]. I don't trust the CPS and I don't trust government ministers. It goes all the way to the top that I am completely cynical about the legal process from top to bottom as a result of what happened.' (FM7)

For some, it was felt that prior knowledge of the system would have assisted them in their case:

'I think that they're only interested in making money, and, I think that if you're aware of that, it's okay because you can protect yourself. For instance, if I was aware – if I knew that the police were the way they are, and I knew the prosecution were the way they are, at the beginning. ... If I knew what they were going to do to me, I would have been much better prepared.' (AC9)

While AC9 was surprised at how the police were focused – as AC9 saw it – on only getting a conviction, there were others who spoke more strongly about their views of the system: FM9 saw the system as "corrupt"; SC1 had been "terrified" by the police and thus unable to trust them. FM6 had also been left with a feeling of distrust despite the fact that they had previously experienced the police in a positive light:

'No, I don't trust them at all, anymore, and that's really sad. I mean, it's funny because, like, before that, in my previous profession, I'd worked with police a lot because, you know, I worked in mental health. I had to work with them all the time, and I had a good relationship with them ... I even interviewed them for some project I was working on and they were really friendly ... I don't know if I would say I trusted them then, maybe, because trust is a hard one, isn't it? But I never expected them to – I never expected any of this. I was like, really, shocked and I continue to be shocked.'

Many interviewees expressed anger at having been accused and/or convicted or having a family member in such a position; their experiences and stories were shaped by and through this anger. The anger expressed was often targeted at a system that the interviewees saw as not working to ensure justice. By accurately reflecting this anger, we can allow for a truthful representation of an accused's experience; such is the value of considering the narratives of those who have gone through the criminal justice system in their own terms (Buozis, 2017). For some, such as AC1, these negative experiences started in youth and resulted in loss of employment:

'I've been, shall we say criminalised at sixteen by the police, beating me up. Then to cover their own arses charging me with assaulting them. You know, that was the start of it, simply because I was asleep, you know, against a tree. So, they ripped me up off the ground, threw me against the tree. You know, I was, like, you know, at the time, drunk, and like, groggy. And I said, "Fuck off, you pair of cunts." That was the start of it. So yeah, I was beat up; in the car I was, they were digging my ribs and using all the pressure points and everything else. Anyway, to cut a long story short, that was the start – like I say, it did define me. You can't be too negative about things, but, you know, a whole year later after that I lost my job. At the time I was an apprentice electrician, you know, I was in a good job and everything.'

The disdain for the institutions of the criminal process had become ingrained in their identity. This can be considered a process of 'othering' tantamount to that identified by Weis (2004) and Stahl (2017). Anger at a wider state institution that worked against them was thus internalized. The anger was felt most obviously towards police. AC1's relationship with and anger towards the police spiralled from their initial contact to the point where they were imprisoned for assaulting a police officer:

'Straight away then I always have attitude with the police because I was never treated fairly. I would lash out at them. By twenty-one I was in jail for assault of police. Again, you know, that was just an off-duty copper who thought he would, you know, abuse his power, get involved in something he shouldn't have – it was nothing to do with him. He assaulted me, and yet when I retaliated, I was then charged with assault. Jail. Ever since then my card has been marked.'

This negative relationship was one that AC1 felt endured as the police apparently held a grudge against them. AC1's view of – and relationship with – lawyers was similarly framed as negative: "I did have a solicitor, but they're two sides of the same fence, really, aren't they? Let's face it. They don't actually believe their clients. Yeah, it's all punish them ... punish them on convictions. That's what it's about. It's not about truth or justice; it's just production-line convictions." While AC1 had a solicitor, AC1 did not see any value in having legal representation: "If you want platitudes, you can mention stuff that's going on to your own solicitor, but that's just platitudes. So no, there's no need to talk to a lawyer." They felt themself as not being of any consequence to their solicitor, who was viewed as simply part of the wider system that works against them and, ultimately, criminalizes them. That some accused distrust even their own defence solicitor is indicative of the lack of confidence in a system that is perceived as not producing fair results (Owusu-Bempah, 2017). AC1's disdain also extended to the Magistrates' Court. They considered that the trial was pointless for the accused and simply a chance for the lawyer to play the advocacy game: "It's just a day in the office for him, isn't it? He enjoys his trial. You know, it gives a solicitor a chance to act like a barrister, doesn't it? You know, and they swear by it, but it's not justice. It's not a trial, is it?"

This echoed the views of many lawyers whom we interviewed that, often, accused persons did not take the Magistrates' Court especially seriously (as we discuss in Chapter 7 on lawyers' understandings of the accused). For AC1, issues of trust went wider still – and they also saw trust in the criminal justice system eroding, in part because of austerity:

'Well people of our generation, right, we still have faith in the system, yeah? We believe that there is redress. We can use the law to get by or not. This is where I see things going. In the future, that won't be an option ... he has no redress. He can't use the system to put right a wrong. So he will explode, yeah? It's going to be crisis on crisis. There's going to be a breakdown in societal kinds of support and everything else. People literally will not care. Talk about dog eat dog world? We're going into Judge Dredd territory, yeah? And this is the way it will be. It frightens me that these rights and this austerity tag is just eroding, you know, civil liberties, civil justice ... and now it's going into criminal law and everything. Where does it end? How many more of our rights and freedoms are they going to take away?'

While the views of AC1 may have been tainted by the unfairness that they had experienced, the interview data across these accused persons told us something of the anger of those who had experienced unfairness in the criminal justice system – and are offered to give readers insight into what grounds the accounts of the accused and their families drawn out in this book. In some instances, the anger did not trickle through to lawyers, with some interviewees being neutral or even positive about their interactions with lawyers. The police were the principal target; for example, AC4 showed us their ACAB (All Cops Are Bastards) tattoo on their hand to express their lack of 'faith' in the police to tell the truth. The – perceived or actual – wrongdoing of the police tainted the criminal justice system for many of the accused and their families, often in its entirety. This underscores the importance of ensuring that the police act fairly, as doing otherwise can undermine legitimacy (see Hough, 2013). It is important to note, however, that our sample may not be wholly indicative of the experiences of most accused and family members. The largely self-selecting nature of participation in this element of the research, as discussed in our methods section in Chapter 1, meant that we likely interviewed those who were frustrated and were keen to voice their resentment. AC1 most certainly fell into this category. Another category was those who had suffered a miscarriage of justice; their experiences of justice in error would undoubtedly have some bearing on their feelings towards and views of the criminal justice system.

Thus, although an extreme demonstration of the accuseds' feelings towards the criminal justice system, these experiences are informative when attempting to understand how criminal justice is experienced and will be built on later in Chapter 7 when we examine the broader impact of criminal justice on the accused and their families. There were also differences – purported or actual – between those with very little to no experience of the criminal justice system and those with more experience, as we will explore later. This 'first-timer'/'regular' distinction builds on this section's descriptions of the ways that the accused in our study came into and developed within the criminal justice system.

'First-timers' and 'regulars'

While there are some commonalities between the accused and their stories, there was no singular story and thus no generalizable 'type' of experience. There were, however, notable differences between those who had no previous contact and those who had been through the system multiple times, at least in the way that their stories were told: the 'first-timers' had expressed shock whereas the 'regulars' expressed resignation. This theme emerges strongly from these participants and helps to explain and elucidate the way in which they have experienced criminal justice.

The first time was demarcated – without any prompting – as a unique experience by those who could be considered 'regulars'. This can be seen in the following example:

'Yeah, so like, the first time, we were like, completely clueless to it all, and, like, yeah, like, I didn't know what was happening or what was going to happen next. … And yeah, I found that quite, like, daunting, not knowing where I was or what stage I was in, in the process.' (AC8)

It was, though, practitioners who most frequently made this distinction when discussing their clients' experiences (see also Jacobson et al, 2016; Wooff and Skinns, 2018; Dehaghani, 2019).[16] This helped us turn the more subtle cues as to the difference offered in the accounts of the last section from accused persons into an explicit analytical category – such was the lens through which lawyers already viewed their clients. 'Regulars' purportedly know what to 'expect' (Newman, 2013a; see also Dehaghani, 2017). This distinction between 'first-timers' and 'regulars' may help frame the entire experience of the criminal process for many accused; it may shape their experiences, in addition to shaping the views and actions of practitioners with whom they interact. In Chapter 6 in particular, we reflect further on these distinctions and some of their implications, specifically the impact on the lawyer–client relationship. In the main, however, this was not a distinction expressed as something overt in the accused interviews, but instead something that practitioners identified – often multiple times in the interview – as relevant to the accused's experience:

'It really depends as to whether you've got experience of being arrested or not. If you're a first-time person who's arrested, I imagine it's very overwhelming and intimidating. If you are somebody who has been arrested thirty, forty times previously, it's probably almost routine to the level we wouldn't understand.' (BS7)

The more someone had been through the system, the more they supposedly knew because, as Dehaghani (2017) highlights, experience implies knowledge. The 'old-timers' or 'regulars' were perceived as being accustomed to the experience of being arrested and detained whereas the 'first-timers', with less knowledge, were perceived as experiencing more anxiety as a result of these processes:

'For the old-timers it's no, no sort of great shakes to be arrested, pulled off the street, taken to a cell. It's no, no hardship really. You know.

---

[16] See, also, Kemp and Hodgson (2016) in relation to young suspects.

Some of them, the hard lags are more interested about bail, really, at the police station, if they've been lifted and they've got a bad record, are they going to get bail? For a first-timer, they're always going to get bail unless something is extraordinarily wrong, so the hard, the early suspect, the first-timer is, you know, more worried about the process.' (BS2)

The alien nature of the prison environment was also said to be more difficult for 'first-timers' as they had not yet experienced the culture within prison. Contending with other prisoners and the 'prison culture' was viewed as more challenging for the 'first-timer' than the isolation of imprisonment:

'It must be terrifying is all, you know, I can say about it because if it's the first time you've ever been into custody then it's a totally alien environment. … And that's not because I think it's not even the fact that you perhaps would be in a room on your own. It's the whole experience of being remanded in custody. In prison, you have the prisoners, the culture. Very, very difficult for someone who is not used to it.' (BS1)

Court attendance was provided as another example of how 'first-timers' and 'regulars' may experience the process differently; for the 'first-timers' a court appearance would apparently cause anxiety whereas an 'old hand' would not be particularly bothered by the experience:

'Well, the old hands take it in their stride. The first-timers would be quite worried about it, but again, it's our role to take them through it … I'd imagine for somebody who is really wanting to know what's going to happen to them, it will be horrible; somebody who is used to the system, knows that they're going to get a fine and they can't really be sent to jail, then they'll take it in their stride. So there's a whole range of responses, but basically, the less often you've been in there the worst that you'd probably find it.' (DS11)

The 'old hands' were viewed as less anxious – or not anxious at all – because they had an awareness of the possible outcomes of a court appearance. Going beyond the distinction between the 'old hands' and 'first-timers', DS11 suggested that the less experience someone had the more anxiety inducing they would find the process. Police officers also distinguished experience on this basis, implying that knowledge of the system would not be available to a 'first-timer':

'Yeah, there would be a difference in that, because first-timers don't know the system, and you explain the system to them and it's very worrying for a first-timer to be involved with the law and the system that we have to follow. So, it would be emotionally challenging for first-time offenders.' (PO2)

The emotionality for 'first-timers' was also noted. For 'regulars' – or 'lifetime criminals' – involvement was routine and therefore part of their life, whereas for 'first-timers' emotions may run high, particularly because of the wider social implications of being criminalized (as will be developed in Chapter 7 when addressing the broader impact of criminalization). PO2 reflected this attitude: "I think, if you're a lifetime criminal, it's part and parcel of your life. If it's a one-off, I think it can be very, very emotional. I would imagine very, it would demean yourself within your family and your friends."

For 'first-timers' the worry can be contrasted with the mere inconvenience that 'regulars' – here, 'career criminals' – were said to experience. PO3's account captured this view: "You've got first-timers, who are usually petrified, don't know what the hell's happening. And you've got the career criminals, who it's an occupational hazard."

Part of the distinction here may relate to how seriously different suspects are considered to take the process. The 'regulars' were perceived to be indifferent or treating the process as a 'game' (see Dehaghani, 2017):

'I think that a lot of them see it as a game. I think it's, you know, I think there's a distinction between first-time offenders, or people who first come to, in contact with the police, and those that are habitual offenders or people who have committed several offences or have gone through the system numerous times. I think the people that have gone through the system, whatever the changes have been over the years, they perceive it to be, you know, an opportunity only to the point where they get convicted of which they then take it seriously.' (PO1)

Similarly, PO3 thought that the more experienced accused behaved "as if they haven't got a worry in the world". Instead, they were viewed as "experts" who were more intent on asking for what they knew that they were entitled to rather than worrying about being released. Young 'first-timers' were also, however, deemed to be "arrogant" or at least to have the appearance of being such (see also Dehaghani, 2017):

'Some of them often used to appear very, very arrogant. And know-all-ish. And what it was is bravado. ... An awful lot of the first-timers, or very, very young, these new ones, are, is full of bravado, because they're just trying to bluff it out. And they don't know what the hell's going to happen to them.' (PO3)

The sense of resignation was evident in AC2's interview, where they discussed their lack of respect for the police, as discussed earlier. AC2's contacts with others in prison and police custody made this experience less daunting and, possibly, less isolating and anxiety inducing:

'And I always used to hang around with all the boys, so when I went to jail, I'd always see the boys in the jail. And then in like the police station, you'd go into the police station and you could smoke in there, do you know what I mean? It was different days, like: you could literally smoke in a police station. And you know, you could go in and you'd be looking on the board behind, behind the desk, saying, "Yo, my guy's in, my guy's in, yo, she's in." You know, you'd be shouting through the cell, "Yo, what you in for bro?" Do you know what I mean? That's what it would be like. And, it was just normal, so we didn't, we didn't have no fear of it, and it wasn't like a punishment, it was just something you had to deal with.'

It was recognized, however, by PO3 that the bravado of the 'first-timer' was a mere disguise. It is also possible that 'regulars' put on a brave face and do not know the system as well as practitioners may assume. 'Regulars' may also be at an increased disadvantage because they are assumed to have knowledge of the system and may therefore not receive the attention and information that they may require (see Dehaghani, 2017; Dehaghani, 2019).[17] As noted earlier, the distinction between 'first-timer' and 'regular' was not necessarily one made in those terms by the accused, but instead something that practitioners noted as relevant to the accused's experience. It is therefore possible that the 'regulars' do not always perceive their experience as significantly different from a 'first-timer's' experience. Rather, the categorization may serve as a useful tool for practitioners, within a pressurized system, to determine who requires support and who can – purportedly – 'manage' without. The distinction, although somewhat artificial, is not completely baseless as we, ourselves, found differences between those new to and those with greater involvement in the criminal process. The distinction was not necessarily based on knowledge – or lack thereof – but rather on emotions – shock, fear and anxiety for the 'first-timers' and resignation and boredom for the 'regulars'.

---

[17] We did not explore other factors such as age, neuro-disability or cognitive functioning. What we had was a general finding that everyone is assumed to be more knowledgeable and this blanket supposition merits drilling-down in future study.

Conclusion

Our sample includes a wide cross-section of criminal justice stories, examining how and why practitioners embarked on their criminal justice career path, as well as examining how the accused – and to a limited extent the family members – came to be drawn into the criminal justice system, exploring their frustrations and lack of trust. The overarching distinction between the former and the latter was that practitioners, while often frustrated by or disillusioned with the system, nevertheless retained the view that the system had societal value, whereas the accused expressed cynicism, despair and apathy towards the system of injustice (as they perceived it). Although there will undoubtedly be variation between categories of participants, there are also differences within the categories of participants – most notably with lawyers who did not traverse the same path to arrive at similar destinations.

The aim of this chapter was to provide context to those experiences and to offer insight into the standpoints of those we interviewed, thus providing a rich grounding for the accounts that develop over subsequent chapters. Two key themes emerged from drilling down into the experiences of these participants. First, practitioners detailed the underfunding that so taints their work in and views of the criminal justice system. Second, our focus on the accused can be understood in terms of an important distinction between those accused who were experiencing the process, or aspects thereof, for the first time and those who were more accustomed to the criminal process. The background we have provided for the participants in this study underpins the whole book as it provides insight into participants' experiences. At the same time, two central themes – underfunding and levels of experience – are developed in the chapters that follow. The theme of underfunding will be important in Chapter 4, as we explore how criminal justice works in south Wales, as well as in Chapter 5, where we delve into more detail on the pressures faced by practitioners. The differences between 'first-timer' and 'experienced' accused are important in Chapter 6, where we expand our understanding of criminal justice relationships, and Chapter 7, where we focus on the wider impact for those accused.

Regarding the vulnerability analysis that underpins our work, the exploration of the people who constitute the stories in this book is crucial to providing an insight into how resilience manifests in practice. There will be differing levels of resilience between different groups of interviewees, with variation among solicitors or barristers and those accused or convicted of crimes. Resilience will also vary across the life course and at different stages in professional careers. We cannot make assumptions on resilience and should be open to considering the vulnerability of all. An insight into people's stories helps illustrate the importance of an open mind here as, for example, in considering that there might be lack of resilience among lawyers.

While the lower resilience of the accused faced with the might of the state against them may seem obvious, the lawyers purportedly funded by the state appear as high-status professionals, but they are hindered and made to feel powerless by the underfunding of the criminal justice system. It is evident that austerity impacted upon how those with whom we spoke experienced the criminal justice system (although these are not the only considerations). We have exposed the – often fraught but sometimes congenial – relationships and have considered some of the factors affecting these relationships. These stories also relay to us the importance of the relational: the decisions made, and actions taken, in one arena or by one person or group can affect others, often profoundly. Relationships can be a source of resilience, but they can also deplete our trust or cause us worry, fear and anxiety. Knowledge, too, can provide resilience, but this is not perhaps as simplistic as the distinction between 'first-timers' and 'regulars'. Assumptions regarding one's resilience should be avoided; instead, individuals should be provided the space to relay their lived experience. This also applies to lawyers: while initially assumed to be 'powerful', their story of work may be one of struggle and powerlessness.

This is the first of our chapters to draw on data from the research, offering a glimpse of the personalities and perceptions of our participants. As such, we have buttressed the exploration of the criminal justice system with insight into those who are taking us on this journey. We have done so to assist readers in understanding their standpoints, and give context to their voices – these stories include who they are and what they have done, as well as simply what they say when prompted by us in interview. In so doing, we hope to encourage others conducting research on the criminal justice system and the functioning of justice more broadly to consider insights from legal life writing. This would help centre interview-based research and draw out fuller insight from those who participate in a study. The following chapter will take this process a step further by locating the research in its place, south Wales – another key element of the story, which adds depth and gives nuance to the dissemination of the experiences undertaken in this book. The stories of the participants in this research are inextricably bound with the place in which they experience criminal justice. While the experiences that this book draws upon must be understood in relation to the people who encountered them, the experiences must also be grounded in the south Wales setting, for it is in this setting we met the participants. Drawing upon insight from this chapter, we demonstrate how the experiences play out on the ground in the everyday, regional operation of the criminal justice system.

4

Criminal Justice in Its Place

Introduction

In the preceding chapter we examined the stories of those involved in the research, detailing how they came into the criminal justice system – whether as practitioners or as an accused or family member. This included drawing out key themes such as the impact of underfunding on criminal justice institutions and the role played by the accuseds' level of previous contact with the criminal justice system. We build thereon in this chapter by focusing on the place – south Wales, two decades into the 21st century – adding a further layer of detail that is crucial to understanding the experiences of criminal justice examined in this book. Just as the stories of the participants are important in understanding the experiences that we relay and analyse, so too are the stories that emerge from considering the region in which our research took place.

Criminal justice research has largely neglected the issue of place as a core consideration (Newman, 2016a).[1] This may sometimes be due to ethical requirements such as the assurance of anonymity, but it may also arise out of concerns regarding 'case studies' being discounted through the desire to demonstrate generalizability.[2] Our work is informed by a legal geography approach,[3] investigating the co-constitutive but uneasy relationship between people, place and law (Bennett and Layard, 2015). In

---

[1]   Notable exceptions include work such as Blackstock et al (2014), which highlights the different demographics across research sites, and purposefully selected examples of larger cities and smaller towns to compare.

[2]   If research examines a particular setting and the scholar acknowledges that there is some uniqueness to this setting, then they are sometimes assumed to be unable to highlight applicability to other settings. However, it is possible to have some findings which are unique to one's setting, but which connect with broader trends, or findings within the case study that are not (entirely) unique to that particular setting.

[3]   See also Economides et al (1986).

this chapter – expanding on detail from Chapter 1 (outlining the case for Wales as a site of criminal justice study) and Chapter 2 (describing south Wales and charting some of the impacts of criminal justice cuts) – we focus on the region of south Wales. In doing so, we acknowledge the role of the spatial in shaping the impact of the law on people's lives. While certainly the discussion of experiences of criminal justice can inform broader debates at an England and Wales level, it is nevertheless important for debates to be grounded within the context from which they emerge. We have also attempted to pay attention to both space and time (see Braverman et al, 2014), focusing on criminal justice under austerity while also situating this within a distinct region. By adopting a place – space *and* time – based approach, we ground the research within the communities under investigation (Newman, 2016a). Important to this are the local conditions and circumstances: the impact of austerity does not manifest equally across a jurisdiction. The existence of advice deserts – where there is limited or no local legal aid advice – provides one such example.[4]

We recognize that the question of 'place' is subject to some construction; it is relational and constituted by interactions between those with shared connections (Massey, 2005).[5] As such, although the boundaries of south Wales could be contested – and the notion that there is a shared culture is debatable – the label (south Wales) was understood by those with whom we spoke. This 'south Wales' label is deployed as an organizing device, just as, in the previous chapter, we used labels such as 'practitioner' and 'accused' despite the possibility of broad differences within each category (as demonstrated when considering the varying practitioner motivations behind entering practice). South Wales has utility in helping us frame the research, which can then be taken forward to assess other areas of Wales, or England, for similarities and differences.

This chapter begins by addressing what – according to the interviewees – made Wales distinct from England. This gives an insight into our location, involving those we interviewed, drawing out the 'small-scale' nature of criminal justice in south Wales as compared with (areas of) England. Following on from this, we examine the specific issue of court closures under austerity, detailing the impact of such closures on the experience of attending court and exploring how that experience is becoming more onerous and stressful due to excessive travel demands being made on those who need to attend. We also examine the absence of a women's prison in Wales and the

---

[4]   During our fieldwork, the *End Legal Aid Deserts* campaign was being pursued by the Law Society to highlight the impact of legal aid cuts on local face-to-face provision across England and Wales.

[5]   Place-based methodology has been pioneered by Marsden and Franklin (2013).

necessity for travel caused by this absence. This is an especially idiosyncratic feature of criminal justice in Wales as it means that women who are sent to prison are forced to leave their own country, with provision only across the border in England. Thereafter, we ascertain whether and how similar issues are faced in England as in Wales, underscoring that not all the illuminating experiences we draw out in this book should be framed as distinctly Welsh. There are parallels across Wales and England between, for example, rural areas of both countries.

What we do in this chapter is examine the place of south Wales along the dimensions of both space and time concerns. For example, understanding issues that may (or may not) be specific to Wales, such as around the scale of criminal justice, chiefly reflects space concerns in that they allow us to compare one physical and social locale with another. On the other hand, issues such as court closures, which have occurred under a distinct political programme such as austerity, point to the role that time can play and how emerging ideologies and policies can transform an area (thus incorporating the previous chapter's theme of underfunding as part of our understanding of this place). What emerges in this chapter is a snapshot of how some of those we interviewed detail the criminal justice system in south Wales at the time of their experiences. This provides the reader with insight into the staging within which these experiences play out.

What makes Wales distinct?

According to those we interviewed, Wales, and south Wales, are 'smaller scale' than their English counterparts. As detailed in Chapter 1, Wales has often been neglected in criminal justice and socio-legal scholarship, as well as in policy debates and discussion of practice realities. However, as detailed in Chapters 1 and 2, Wales is distinct from England in numerous ways. While our focus is on south Wales – which is distinct from west, mid and north – the interviewees spoke about 'Wales' as a generality, and told us much about their perceptions of its relatively diminutive scale, compared to England, with regard to criminal justice issues.

Of particular note was the relatively small circuit court in the south Wales area,[6] which was perceived as both positive and negative:

'I think that because we're such a small circuit, small area, there's a good and a bad. The good is that we're friendly and everybody knows

---

[6]   Formally, south Wales falls under the Wales and Chester circuit – one of six geographical areas into which the administration and organization of the court system of England and Wales is divided. Chambers in Cardiff and Swansea cover criminal work in south Wales.

each other in the sense that we, as a circuit, are probably more aware of the judges, how they work, get more trust from the judges. ... It's a bit more local feel, a bit less mercenary feel about it, I suppose and it's easier to deal with the other side because you know who they are. And it's always easier, isn't it, when you know people to do that degree. The bad side to it is that you can a bit complacent, and maybe sometimes you need to be a bit more on your toes. You know, like in, for example, in London, you know, people are not worried about pissing judges off because they don't appear before them day in, day out, so they're perhaps a bit more willing to be, stand up when it's needed rather than rock the boat when you realise that because you're such a small circuit you all have to deal with each other on a daily basis. So, in terms of how that impacts upon clients, that specifically might have an impact in Wales, because we're so small here. A bit too provincial, if you like.' (BS8)

The smaller circuit allows for closer connections and permits relationships to be built, which can help defence lawyers (and by extension their clients) through knowledge of other legal practitioners such as judges. The double-edged sword of the small circuit was, however, also seen to undermine 'zealous advocacy' (see Smith, 2013). The distinction between the closer-knit communities in Wales – or south Wales – was most clearly made in contrast to London – the largest of the UK cities (although not unlike Wales in terms of deprivation, as discussed in Chapter 1). The friendly nature of the circuit – and the sense of community and solidarity – was also addressed by BS3, who discussed the support available in the robing room (where barristers prepare before court):

'I'd say is it's quite a friendly circuit. And when I've been in a real state, I've been able to go, run, into any robing room, pretty much grab anyone, and they've been able to help me. I don't know whether you'd have that same thing in the Midlands circuit, for example. If you were in a chambers in Birmingham and you happened to be in Stafford or in Worcester, and you maybe, you don't have that same sort of like feeling of community, which you definitely have here. Even in Swansea, I could ask people for help.'

While BS3 was based in Cardiff, they would experience the sense of community at the Crown Court in Swansea. This was one of the reasons that BS4 enjoyed practising in Wales:

'It's small. The most distinctive thing about it, I love practicing here. ... The good thing is you don't get away with much down here without people talking about it. So, people with a bad reputation, it gets around. I think it's good to know each other. We have good working relationships. We have opponents where you know you can ring them up and you can, you know, you can sort things out. That's a burden as well, because it means we're working outside the court room an awful lot, but you can get stuff done by being smaller. And when I've been against people from bigger court centres like London, they tend to be much more abrasive and aggressive. It's all about the showing off and the "I'm harder than you are" stuff, and it doesn't get anyone anywhere.'

We will discuss criminal justice relationships, including those between defence and prosecution, further in Chapter 6. What emerges here is that the close-knit nature of the small circuit allowed for discussion between prosecution and defence, which was seen as both a blessing and a burden. It also seemingly reduces – at least the performance of – aggressive advocacy. The aggressive approach, said to be used in cities such as London, was seen as making the process less conducive to 'getting things done'. By contrast, the smaller circuit allowed lawyers in Wales to resolve matters easily. However as suggested, the small scale of the local circuit was not viewed by all as a positive:

'I think with the small circuit thing, it does create difficulties because if you do get into a personality clash with a judge, you're going to be in front of them a lot and it can impact on how you can deal with clients. Whereas if you're on a much larger circuit, or if you're a London-based circuiteer, chances of you even appearing before that judge repeatedly are very small, so you can perhaps be more robust, more curt in your encounters with them.' (BS9)

The possibility of developing 'a bad reputation' with others, particularly the judge, could therefore impact upon how others interacted with the lawyer and, perhaps most notably, upon the experience for the client. As alluded to by BS8 earlier, there was an awareness among lawyers that the close-knit nature of the circuit meant that falling out with a judge could be disastrous for a client. It also meant, however, that lawyers were often able to gauge how a case would develop and, as the lawyers saw it, thereby give the client more accurate advice regarding, for example, whether to run the trial or whether to plead guilty. Again, contrasts were made with London, where lawyers were seemingly better able to perform 'zealous advocacy' (see Smith, 2013).

According to those we interviewed, south Wales also differed in relation to the types of offences that the system processed, with a further element of scale. Comparisons were frequently made between south Wales and London, and often other large UK cities. Lawyers in south Wales were said to deal with fewer drug-related crimes, fewer gun-related crimes, and fewer serious crimes than their English counterparts:

'We've got certain types of crime here that you don't have the same kind of levels of gun crime and sort of proper gang-related drug crime like in Liverpool. I did a case in Liverpool for three and a half months and they've got massive drugs cases all the time, because that's where the drugs come in. We haven't got that level of serious crime.' (BS5)

In particular, the English capital city of London was identified as a comparator for Cardiff by some such as DS16: "I don't think it's anywhere like London. And we don't get gun crime in Cardiff really at all do we? Sure, there is the odd gun around, but we don't have, we don't have gun crime on a regular basis, whereas we do in London."

We were often told by practitioners that the nature of the criminal justice issues they encountered among their clients was less extreme than what they saw in English cities based on the experiences of taking cases outside of Wales, through the stories of their colleagues in other locations, or through their knowledge of current affairs.

It was not simply lawyers who remarked on this difference. AC2 had experienced the distinction between Welsh and English cities and the different crimes within these cities:

'It is much more violent in, in like London for instance or Manchester. You're much more likely to get shot or killed by just getting stabbed, rather than here, you'll get slashed up or – you will get stabbed. You'll get stabbed in the leg or the arse, or, you know, you'll get stabbed in a place where the people know, and if they argue or something, they know they're just going to hurt you. So, they're not going to kill you. Whereas the difference with like them ends, they will kill you; that's the difference ... Cardiff and Wales in general is a lot more laid-back than – you go England, no-one wants to kind of look each other in the face, do you know what I mean? Here people do. That it's much more sociable still, even with the environment we got, it's still more sociable and people are still linked in many ways.'

It was claimed that while serious offences – such as knife crime – were committed in Wales, the motivation behind these offences differed between English and Welsh cities: in the former, gun crime was common and stabbings were carried out to kill, whereas in the latter people were stabbed *only* with the intention of harm, but ostensibly not very serious harm. The reason was that Wales is purportedly much more "laid-back" than England, with the people in Wales being friendlier than those in England. However, for PO5 the rationale for the difference in the type of crime was not due to friendliness, but instead that Wales does not have cities or towns commensurate in size to the urban areas in England, and that Wales does not experience the same type – or levels – of deprivation as England:[7]

'We don't have the conurbations with London, Liverpool, Manchester, Leeds, Bradford. Anywhere you like, you know, we don't have this massive stretch. Yeah sure we still have areas that are slightly underprivileged perhaps in housing, maybe even in education, but massive strides are made all the time to try and put that right. You know, you look at the regeneration of the waterfront in Barry, the regeneration in Swansea, the regeneration in Cardiff in particular with the Bay and how even the schools have improved down there. You look at how they try and regenerate things in the Valleys.' (PO5)[8]

The differences in the types of crimes had an impact, it was alleged, on UK government spending on criminal justice and legal aid in Wales. BS10 claimed that priorities reflected the reality within English cities, as opposed to Welsh cities:

'For criminal legal aid spend on advocacy so, and not including police station work and the like, but in terms of what is spent on providing representation in courts in criminal cases, only 75 per cent of what is spent in England on a per capita basis ... there's a whole political aspect of trying to work out where [the Ministry of Justice] will devote the money to in terms of criminal defence, and I suspect that that is done very much reflecting the priorities of the big metropolitan areas in England. So, what are the criminal defence needs of London, Manchester, Birmingham? Rather than what perhaps are the priorities here in Wales. ... And they consume an awfully large, disproportionately large amount of the overall budget of criminal legal aid spend, for example, on terrorism cases ... organised crime, criminal gangs, that sort of thing.'

---

[7] Although, as we note in Chapter 1, Wales has much higher levels of relative deprivation than England, often more so than London.

[8] The regeneration in the Bay area of Cardiff has served chiefly to gentrify the area, to the disadvantage of those living within Butetown (mentioned as the site for the public meeting of the Commission in Chapter 1) (Phelps, 2019). In particular, the regeneration of the Bay has been criticized as a vanity project that failed to address the needs of the local community (Crockett, 2017).

The priorities for the UK government were ostensibly issues of national security – such as terrorism – rather than issues of local concern or, as BS10 framed it, "the community-based crime that we have here" – such as house burglaries. The issue was raised by other barristers; the resource allocation decisions were also said to have an impact upon the sustainability of practice in Wales:

'It's not as sustainable to practise in crime here than it is elsewhere. The reason why is there's not the quality of work in Cardiff than there is in Bristol, Manchester, Birmingham. So, forget about London; I'm talking about the regional centres, okay? So, cuts for legal aid disproportionately affect us because we just don't have the volume and quality of work of elsewhere.' (BS1)

For BS1, the "quality" of work referred to well-paying, substantial cases. There were also distinctions made with the English Midlands and other large cities like Manchester, specifically how the differences in offences committed there, as compared with Wales, changed the nature of a barristers' workload:

'In the Midlands there's more mortgage fraud, big drug work. Here you don't get the really big – you don't often get the really big conspiracies, the really big drug cases, and you don't really get the big gang violence. I mean, if you're in London, it's just routine: gangs, stabbings, shootings. Thank God we don't really have that in Cardiff or the surrounding areas. … But when you think Liverpool is one of the big centres for drugs, London is one of the big centres for drugs, and Manchester is one of the big centres for drugs, you do get much more of the massive cases in those areas than you do down here.' (BS9)

On the larger circuits, there were larger cases. This was identified as especially significant for the barristers in our study. For BS2, larger cases resulted in differences with workload:

'I think there's more career progression in London. When I was in London, the people over fifteen years' call didn't do rubbish. They didn't do ABHs [actual bodily harm], they didn't do Section 20s, they didn't do affrays, they just left that all to the junior people. They were more interested in cultivating a big case practice. Here, there just – you get people over fifteen, twenty years' call doing burglaries, affrays, rubbish trials, just because they've got to be in work that week. They've got to, they've got to earn some money. Do you see what I mean? So … you're more likely to find someone of twenty years' call doing an ABH trial or an affray trial in Cardiff than you are in London or

Birmingham or Manchester. ... You know, you have to fill the working week with whatever you can get. So, I think there's that aspect I know from having been in London and having been in Cardiff; it shocked me when I came down here that you get people of twenty years' call doing an ABH trial. It was bizarre, to my eye, but it's what happens.'

The type of work meant that more senior barristers were unable to get stuck into 'big cases' – the sort that may be career defining – and were having to instead engage with the "rubbish", low-level offence work that is typically seen as uninteresting and unimportant, mirroring Dehaghani's (2019) findings in respect of police work. It also affected career progression and earnings, something that could further exacerbate the precarity of defence practitioners, as discussed in Chapter 2. Given that the fees payable in cases concerning 'more serious' offences are higher than those fees available for work on 'less serious' offences, the effect of fewer serious cases being tried in Wales thus has an impact on the remuneration available to defence practitioners and can further exacerbate their precarity yet again. There were also concerns that the viability of practice hinged on the 'numbers game' as explained by Newman (2013a), wherein lawyers become pushed to focus on working through as many cases as possible (and risk reducing clients to numbers on a list). The 'volume work' was arguably necessitated by the smaller fees payable for "rubbish" offences; it impinged upon the standard of the work lawyers could do. Concerns were also raised about the sustainability of small practices within the broader frame of engaging in 'volume work' to remain viable as a practice (see also Dehaghani and Newman, 2021a):

'I mean it is different from bigger cities. I mean, I do tend to do work around [England and Wales], and yeah, I can see how in bigger cities there is a dearth of client care. That's possible. But the reality of that is that those firms who have got a larger number of clients coming through and a greater pool from the legal aid fund will be able to survive, whereas south Wales has been historically been a lot of smaller companies, a lot of one-man bands. It's just going to be impossible for them to survive with legal aid cuts, with legal aid regulation, with all the requirements that are placed on you to just have a firm with SRA [Solicitors Regulation Authority] compliance. We're in a different position of, there is quality being provided but how long can it last?' (DS5)

While larger practices – uncommon in Wales – are not inherently lacking in client care, it is possible that the larger firms lose the close contact with their clients, particularly through large-scale discontinuous representation (McConville et al, 1994). Thus, not only have legal aid regulation and cuts had an impact upon the viability of defence practice in Wales, such developments may also force the move towards larger practices, a model that DS9 thought would be unworkable in Wales (see Dehaghani and Newman, 2021a):

> 'There is no Tuckers [English criminal defence firm] in this area. You know, the biggest firm in the UK, frankly, they haven't – and it's not by coincidence. You know, I know some of the partners of Tuckers. They don't see a future in terms of their business model here … there's not enough volume for them. There's not enough work to keep them going, effectively. … Because we don't have the volume that you'd certainly get in London, Manchester, Liverpool, those types of criminal hubs, so they haven't bothered … and we always have been a nation of high street practices, and lots of practices … crime is our, our largest income. And there's only one firm in Gwent that is crime-only; the rest are all high-street practices. And even in Cardiff, there's only … one firm that's crime-only. Everybody else does other things as well. So, we are still a high street practice country, nation. And it's that issue. That affects your bottom line in terms of your profit margins and … if you're not making money then you're going to lose the firms, and if you lose the high-street firms, where do you get access to any justice, not just criminal justice? If your high-street practitioner in Tredegar closes? You know, in fact, I think you, I could probably bet you ten pounds that if you walk down Tredegar high street, you're not going to find a solicitors' practice, because they can't afford to dabble in bits. You either have to go all in or not at all. So as a nation of high street practices it's a very Welsh issue, that if you lose one aspect of it you can't afford to run the rest, so you close the firm down, and then the rural areas especially, if they, you know, they want a defence solicitor, they've got to come to Newport or Cardiff.'

DS9 expressed particular concern for remote, 'left-behind' areas in the Valleys such as their Tredegar example. The amount and type of work available in Wales, it seemed, necessitated the existence of small firms practising in criminal-only and high street practices offering advice and representation in an array of areas; there were very few firms in Wales offering criminal defence alone. The Commission on Justice in Wales (2019: 397) notes that 'high street firms are found throughout Wales' but 'they are the category of law firm most generally found in rural and post-industrial areas of Wales'. The Commission also suggested that solicitors are more likely to operate in high street firms than in England, and caution that Wales is seeing a significant decline in high street practice, which challenges the provision of access to justice across the country. Closures of banks and businesses, and the wider decline in the high street, are having an impact. Fee reductions and changes in legal aid regulation have also promoted the death of the high street practice across many small towns of Wales, the effect of which is taking justice further away from communities. Such insight will be developed in Chapter 5, looking in more depth at legal aid cuts, and, thereafter, in Chapter 6, considering the impact of cuts on the lawyer–client relationship.

Criminal justice in south Wales (and Wales more broadly) has been distinguished partly on the basis of scale. Indeed, scale was the dominant characteristic discussed by those we interviewed when comparing Wales with England. This notion of scale refers to the size of the practitioner community and the type of work that is available to practitioners. Having addressed one of the distinguishing features of criminal justice in south Wales – the space – we now turn to consider the issue of time in relation to court closures, which have occurred over the past decade and have continued during our research.

Court closures in south Wales

The court closure programme (discussed in Chapters 1 and 2), featured heavily in our interviews as something that, since 2010, has adversely impacted Wales. The impact of court closures – one of the most visible, yet neglected, aspects of the austerity programme – was something that was seen to affect south Wales particularly badly and was removing the possibilities for local justice (see Newman, 2016a): "We [Barry] no longer have local Magistrates' Courts. … And we're taking away the local aspect of justice. You know, go back to tribal times if you like: the local chieftain administered justice. That's how we get common law" (PO5). As such, justice was being removed from communities. The closure of courts can exacerbate the problems of trust. This was identified by DS13:

> 'I think it's a stressful experience in itself, having to go to court, but having to go out of your area, I think people do feel that they're not, especially in the Crown Court, they don't feel, if they've got a jury trial, they don't feel that they're being tried by their peers, essentially, because it's a whole new area that sometimes they've never been to, they're only going there to be listed in court. So, it does build into the lack of trust.'

Of particular concern was that the accused may feel that they were not being tried by a jury of their peers. As we saw in Chapter 3, and will explore further in Chapter 7, many accused and family members lack trust in the 'fairness' of the criminal justice system. The decline of local justice may be a notable aspect of this distrust. Within an adversarial system, such as in

England and Wales, jury trials ensure – or allow for – representativeness and thus engender the public's and the accused's trust in the system. The issue of local justice was also discussed by DS6:

'Wales doesn't really have the same large conurbations as other areas, and I think that Wales tends to be, I was almost going to say "tribal," but small communities. Proper communities … I think you get, around Wales, these communities that know their area and understand what's needed in their area so that where we used to talk about local justice, in England, to a great extent, you can actually concentrate the local justice in one or two courts, covering a wide area and they will understand, the benches there, what's going on in this very wide area because there is this sort of continuity of behaviour, or whatever, or the issues will tend to be the same. But I'm not sure that in Wales it's right to be closing the courts and assume that, for instance, Cardiff can understand what's happening all the way up in Rhondda Cynon Taff and places … assuming some sort of homogenous population is so much more wrong for the Welsh population, and I think that they really ought to be looking to stop this closing of courts because local justice can be seen by people as fairer, as more just.'

The quote indicates the existence and operation of local legal cultures (see Church, 1982). DS6 discussed the importance of local justice and knowledge of local issues as something specific to (or at least, worse in) Wales. As compared with England, where cultures and what DS6 termed "continuity of behaviour" were said not to vary significantly within a wide area, Wales was said to have a much less homogeneous population across its different towns and regions, with variation even within south Wales, such as between the Rhondda Valley and Cardiff city (only 15 to 20 miles by car). The impact of court closures was such that cases from the Valleys were not being properly understood where they were now tried, that is in Cardiff. The notion of community is generally considered to be strong in south Wales (as discussed in Chapter 1) and may be a reason for the perceived "friendliness" that AC2 noted earlier.

Justice research has shown that for rural communities in particular, there is often an emphasis on the importance of personal relations, with day-to-day life characterized by intimacy and high visibility (Eisentein, 1982). Within small areas in particular, people and their family histories are known to others in the area, active social networks allow the community to be attuned to local events, and there is a relative homogeneity within rural – as compared with urban – communities, all of which creates a significant social cohesion (Edmondson, 1996). So, while DS6 critiqued the assumption of homogeneity for south Wales as a whole, what we can understand is that the towns and communities across the region may each be individually homogeneous, hence accounting for their difference from one another. In such scenarios, the expectation is that personal relationships and shared histories keep the local community functioning, with any system of justice that is too alien for the local community being rejected (Fahnestock, 1993). The importance of such considerations in many parts of Wales has impacted upon lawyers' service (Franklin and Lee, 2007), with lawyers perhaps adapting their practice to suit local conditions in the manner suggested by Boyum (1979). Thus, in such areas, the functioning of local institutions of justice may be notably different in smaller and more remote, rural or post-industrial areas.[9] The demographic differences between these areas and larger, urban areas, such as disparities in income levels, may also have a particular – or peculiar – impact upon a case, as BS2 noted when comparing Cardiff and the Valleys:

> 'So last week I did a fraud which was a Cardiff case which, on the Friday, got switched to Merthyr. Now, the jury comes from a different demographic. A Merthyr jury – this was a fraud; the guy was spending hundreds of thousands of pounds. Now in Cardiff that would have been alright because the level of spending and the level of money that we were dealing with in that case isn't massive to people with a house in Cardiff. But here, to have a jury in Merthyr, having inherited a house that was worth a quarter of a million pounds which in Merthyr is a massive house, down here it's a tiny house? That made quite a difference to that case and the whole way we had to run the case, yeah, became a lot harder.'

Thus, the different income levels between Merthyr and Cardiff altered the jury's perception of seriousness. There were also different types of work between Merthyr and Cardiff: "Merthyr is a lot more violence [cases] and, you know, just drunken behaviour, whereas Cardiff is slightly more sophisticated the work, if that's the right way of putting it" (BS2). The people of Merthyr were also viewed as "more anti-police", which could have the result of "hardly [obtaining] a conviction in Merthyr Crown Court for anything" (PO3).

While the Valleys are still served by Merthyr Crown Court, it appeared that more work was being sent to the other south Wales Crown Courts, all located in cities (Cardiff, but also Newport and Swansea), with the effect

---

[9]   The value of understanding criminal justice in rural Wales has been recognized by Koffman (1999). Moody (1999: 9) has identified a broader 'rural neglect' within criminal justice research, with Donnermeyer et al (2013: 80) considering the rural 'marginalised and even invisible' from such scholarship.

that, with a decrease in footfall, Merthyr Crown Court could be at risk of closure. The often long and complicated journey to court – an important, but often neglected, aspect of the criminal process – necessitated by court closures was claimed by DS13 to be "a punishment in itself" for the accused. We can thus consider the issue of the journey to court as a punitive aspect of the criminal process, with the process itself often being the punishment (see Feeley, 1979). There were frequent difficulties in getting clients to travel to courts, and at times it was near impossible: "Public transport isn't always available, especially not to get to court for nine, ten o'clock in the morning. And if you don't drive or have access to a vehicle, it can be nigh-on impossible to get to the nearest court" (DS13).

We were told, by practitioners, how travel had an impact in every area that we studied; this was not a local issue, court closures created travel problems across the region. These issues were evident in the western section of our south Wales sample:

'Well if you're, if you worked along north Carmarthenshire, so Llandovery up, your court is Llanelli, or even if you stray into Breconshire your court is Brecon. So, you know, you have to get to Llanelli Magistrates' Court, they tell you to be there at nine. Of course, that's ten, and basically you should be there by half past nine ... lots of them arrange lifts, and the difficulty quite often is that the lift doesn't transpire, or these cars aren't particularly reliable. You know, it's more likely to have a breakdown or whatever because that's the quality of the car that their friend has got. So, travelling for clients has increased hugely.' (DS11)

They were also evident in the eastern section:

'East Gwent encompasses quite a large area, it goes up to Abergavenny, the nearest court for them, Cwmbran. Cwmbran and Newport, I think, are the only two, yeah. So, it can be a fair journey, especially being arrested up in Abergavenny and you live up there, and they have to pay for it themselves, so I think they can be out of pocket. Plus having a day off work ... and parking at Newport is hard, because you have to park in the Asda car park and you've only got three hours, so a lot of them end up with tickets if they end up sitting there and they arrive at half nine and the matter doesn't get on until after half twelve and they get a ticket, or they'll spend money on taxis or buses and have to leave super early. So, I think there needs to be more courts really. There used to be more, but they're centralising everything now, so it makes things harder for defendants to get to court ... I would say most of the clients I represent don't drive or have a motorbike licence and they're usually on benefits, nine times out of ten, so they can't really afford public transport unless they jump on the bus and then get another bus in order to make their court date.' (DS2)

With this problem thus felt across south Wales, it cannot be assumed that all accused persons have adequate – or any – access to their own mode of transport. To add to the problem is access to public transport either in terms of public transport provision (as noted in Chapter 2, some areas of Wales are poorly connected) or in terms of financial provision to use public transport. Even where the individual does have access to their own means of transport, there may be limited or no parking facilities near the court, as highlighted earlier. Limited access to transport – or parking – can make it difficult for the accused to attend court on time and may discourage the accused from attending court at all. Court closures, compounding other issues of disadvantage, may increase the stress associated with attending court and may limit an individual's ability to access justice. The issues posed by centralization of courts and, more generally, the court closure programme, tend not to be acknowledged by local communities until they need to access a court (Newman, 2016a). The court was not part of most people's experience of their towns and cities growing up and they would become aware of the location of the court only when required to go there. Court centralization especially impacted defendants who lived further away from the main population areas such as Cardiff:

'I think all of this predominately is down to funding, but you know, you've closed Bridgend Court, Barry Court, Pontypridd Court … those three courts have all gone into Cardiff Court. If people are travelling from – what's the furthest distance? Probably Bridgend, I would say. It's quite a distance to come all the way to Cardiff, especially if you don't drive. If they're getting public transport from Bridgend or Barry all the way to Cardiff, and they've got to be in court for ten o'clock, it's putting a lot of pressure on people. A lot of these people are struggling financially, as well, and you're asking them to potentially take two bus trips, or public transport, whatever it might be, to get to court because we've closed their local court in Bridgend, you know? And we're asking them to come all the way to Cardiff. It's quite a lot of pressure on them. … If it was the other way around and we were having to go to Bridgend I wouldn't have a clue where to start when it came to – what's the best bus to get? And what's the time? They're probably meant to leave two hours before, I would imagine, at that time in the morning to get to Cardiff – nine-thirty? So, there's too much pressure on them because if they're late for court they're having more warrants, and they're being arrested.' (DS17)

Again, the difficulty of travelling to courts from less well-connected areas – albeit, as the crow flies, nearby – places the accused under significant strain.

Compounding these difficulties and frustrations was the issue of case adjournments. DS16 outlined how cases being halted and postponed has an impact on travel:

> 'I remember having a client coming from Porthcawl, and he was worried about the money because he'd only get the money back, you know, if he's found not guilty, and then he can make an application, but he's also got to pay his own train fare stuff, and, you know? Of course, the judges, well what can they do? They can't do anything about it, but it's, you know, five quid there, five quid back, he's on like fifty-three quid a week, whatever it is, that's a lot of money, isn't it? And also, frustratingly, sometimes it doesn't sort of happen. You go to court and nothing happens, and it gets adjourned and you have to come back again.'

The difference for this client would have been exacerbated by court closures; previously, they would have travelled around six miles from Porthcawl to Bridgend but after Bridgend Magistrates' Court closed in 2016, this left them with a journey of closer to 30 miles to Cardiff. The effect on case adjournments allied to court closures is made clear in the following example:

> 'I mean it's become worse over the years. Yesterday I had a chap who had to get the bus from Abergavenny down to Newport and because of the timetabling had to leave at seven o'clock in the morning to get to court in time. Court wanted to adjourn it to the following day and objected to that just because money-wise I think it cost him ten pounds, and he didn't have that. You know money-wise, spending that twice in a week probably is going to be really difficult for him. But I mean lots of clients have to travel. And the courts, with their listing policy, certainly at one stage in Gwent we had Caerphilly Court and Newport, and Cwmbran and Abergavenny, and the court would list things at their own convenience. So, the cases that related to the Caerphilly side of the valley, which could be quite a fair distance off, were being listed in Newport. Which meant that clients were having to come down, either with their lawyers, or get a sort of two-hour public transport journey down. Now Caerphilly's shut so now it's only Newport and Cwmbran that are running, so everybody on that side of the valley, which is Rumney and Bargoed and all of those, has to come down to Newport. Which is a long way.' (DS1)

DS1 highlighted how financial impacts were a significant consequence of adjournments. Travelling to court, while difficult for many accused, presents particular problems for those already facing financial hardship, such as those on means-tested benefits:

> 'Where it's a real issue is where you have, if somebody is on benefits. They've got a family. They can't afford it. It's not cheap. Whether they're going by car, train, bus, whatever, it's not cheap. So, there is that, and it's, it will be difficult for them. And somewhere along the line, you know, there's a fear that, well, they've got to get to court; if they don't get to court, they're going to prison because it's breach of bail. And I wonder whether the kids have to do without some food the day or two before in order that the money is there to get to court and back. You just don't know with these things. But where they're going to court because they're having a trial, and perhaps a trial is going to take a week or sometimes longer – even for a simple one, it can take longer – how do they manage? They couldn't possibly have the money to travel. If they're working, they're not going to have income for that period, you can be fairly sure. They're not going to get benefits for that period because they're not available for work, as well, because they're in court. And I must admit, I do wonder how those people cope ... a lot of people are hand to mouth nowadays.' (DS6)

The financial impact of court closures on the accused highlights that travel problems could be experienced anywhere across the region. As such it is important to recognize that difficulties with travel were also noted even within Cardiff: "Cardiff's a big place. When I say 'big', it's a funny city Cardiff. It's narrow and wide. You know, I've got clients in Ely who can't get here on time for court" (DS15). This highlights that travel problems are not only experienced in rural and remote areas; although travel may be a greater encumbrance outside the city, travel problems – encompassing geographical as well as social and economic factors – can also be experienced in the Welsh capital city.

The stress of attending court, while compounded by the aforementioned issues, is also further exacerbated by the concern that failure to reach court on time may result in imprisonment through breach of bail. It may also not only put individuals in financial difficulty by virtue of having to pay for travel to court, but can also further increase financial difficulty through, for example, necessary unpaid absences from work as noted by DS6. DS18 raised similar concerns, but also discussed the lack of UK government concern for those experiencing such problems:

'If you've got to come from Bridgend to Cardiff, God I've no idea what it's cost. I mean it's fairly expensive from Barry but God knows how many buses you've got to change, or train'd be simpler but more expensive to get there. But of course those people who make these decisions couldn't care less about things like that. If someone's got to eke out the bus fare from their Universal Credit, and you're not going to get any unfavourable headlines in the Daily Mail for that.'

As noted earlier, failure to attend court can amount to a breach of bail and thus result in the issuing of a warrant for the accused's arrest. DS9 explained that some clients would await the warrant because they could not afford to go to court:

'I've had clients say, "I can't afford to get to court. I'll, I'll take the government wagon when they come and pick me up." That's the reality of it. You know, they haven't had their benefits or they're drug addicts, so of course they haven't got the money for the bus because they've spent their last ten pounds on a ten bag from the dealer on the corner. Yeah, so they're not going to get to court and then they'll just wait for the warrant to be issued and for the police to come and pick them up.'

Yet not all accused are similarly pragmatic about the warrant being issued. For some it can result in significant anxiety and distress, to the point where an accused may threaten suicide. An example was provided by DS7:

'Well, the individual I spoke to today was threatening to kill himself. He's rang the court and said the same thing. Because he's not without his problems, and he just can't afford to get to court, and doesn't want to be in a custodial setting. And that's a risk, as soon as they issue a warrant. So, his options are, don't come, if he can't get here, they may very – we were trying to avoid the issue of a warrant today, this afternoon, but if they do issue a warrant then he can come to Newport and surrender to that at the court, but he may face another Bail Act, what's called a Bail Act charge. Or he waits until he can afford it, perhaps, and then there's more chance of a Bail Act offence, because he hasn't surrendered to the warrant as quickly as he should have, perhaps. Or he gets picked up by the police. And if he gets picked up by the police it's a night in the cells.'

Challenges also emerge through police station closures (as detailed in Chapter 2), particularly the effect of these closures in interaction with court closures. Many solicitors in our research (who themselves attend both police stations and courts) identified this connection, as highlighted here by DS11:

'So, you know, you're down to one court for the county and one police station for the county and they're not in the same town! So, whereas years ago, you know, if you had somebody held in, they'd be walked up the steps to the court which was there, so Ammanford police station, back steps from the court straight into the court room, now they're being taken to Llanelli. Carmarthen Court has closed, Ammanford Court has closed, so for Carmarthenshire it all comes down to Llanelli. Quite often on a Saturday duty in Llanelli we'll find out that people are brought out for minor stuff, because … they're talking about drunk and disorderly, that sort of stuff, or because they're homeless and they haven't got a flat, so the police will keep them in for court on the Saturday and quite often you'll see people coming down and you think, "Why on earth has this person been dragged here?" but they're still dragged halfway around the country.'

Police station closures have thus also taken key sites of justice away from local communities (Newman, 2016a). The detention – often miles from home – appears disproportionate to their alleged – often 'minor', that is, inconsequential public order – offending. Yet not only are individuals being detained in distant police cells, they are also having to make the – often uncomfortable – journey between the police station and the court, most likely in a police car or court transit van. The disproportionality of their arrest and detention seems even more marked when the offence for which they are arrested was non-imprisonable:

'The worst, talking from experience, that I've ever been involved with [was] a fifteen-year-old on a Section 5 public order. So not an imprisonable offence, okay? He gets arrested in Burry Port, gets taken in the car, en route to Llanelli, gets told Llanelli is full, go to Ammanford. En route to Ammanford he is told Ammanford is full, go to Haverfordwest. En route to Haverfordwest, he gets told Haverford West is full, go to Brecon. And that's how the custody suites are run. You've got overflows. So, if Haverfordwest is full then they're going up to Brecon at the moment, or down to Haverford West … and vice versa … there can be significant travelling involved.' (DS11)

The accused was taken five miles to Llanelli, another 26 miles to Ammanford, a further 50 miles to Haverfordwest, and finally 82 miles to Brecon, a total in excess of 150 miles (and three hours by car).[10] This could have been

---

[10] One could most certainly also argue that this 15-year-old should not have been detained for a public order offence (see, generally, Dehaghani, 2017).

avoided by a call through to the station in advance and is most likely a rare occurrence. However, the distance between the accused's final destination – Brecon – and their place of origin – Burry Port – is a substantial 58 miles by car. Such journeys in Wales are often more complicated because of geography, as discussed in Chapter 1.

The experience may be one that is somewhat – although likely not entirely – unique to Wales. We conducted our research at a time of austerity, which has impacted both England and Wales. As such, many of these findings may translate broadly into the English context, as well as to other areas in Wales. There is, however, one feature of the criminal justice landscape that is unique to Wales: the constitution of the prison estate.

Prisons in south Wales

A significant difference relayed to us was the lack of a women's prison in Wales. As discussed in Chapter 1, Wales has five prisons in total, including the UK's first 'super-prison' (HMP Berwyn). However, absent from the Welsh prison estate is any provision for women (see Jones, 2018). This, along with the absence of a Category A prison and problems with local authority accommodation for those leaving prison, was criticized by BS10: "Well the one obvious [problem] is the lack of a proper prison estate which we should build here. We've got no local authority accommodation, and no female prison, no Category A prison. Appalling. And unjustifiable."

Many of the families in our research spoke of the stress and expense caused by having to travel to prisons (see also Dixey and Woodall, 2012). Often these prisons were remote and frequently there were several locations to travel to over the course of a sentence as family members were moved within the Welsh – and/or English – prison estate. The absence of a women's prison in Wales created particular difficulties for women prisoners:

'Any particular problems in Wales, yes there's no women's prison in Wales. That's a big one. And we've got, hang on, one, two, three, four, five other prisons, male prisons? What on Earth is going on there? So, you know the nearest one is just over the bridge there.' (AC4)

The length of time that it takes to get to and from the women's prison near Bristol was said to create stress for those women appearing in court. BS1 discussed these effects:

'It is an absolute disgrace that there's not a woman's prison in Wales because if a female prisoner is remanded in custody in a trial in Swansea, she has to travel every day from Eastwood Park in Bristol, which is a two to two-and-a-half hour journey. So, to get [to] court for half past ten or ten o'clock, she's up at about half past five and on a bus at about half past six. ... And then of course they've got to get back. So, they're leaving at half past five, they're probably getting home, back home, going back to prison, in England, at half past eight, something like that. It's disgraceful.'

The length of the journey from prison to court necessitated an extremely early start for the female prisoner; this raises concerns, which BS1 alluded to, regarding an accused's ability to participate effectively in the case against them. Attendance at court could also adversely impact upon the stability of placement within the prison estate because even travel to court *within* Wales can result in significant periods of time away from the prison. This was explained by BS2:

'If they get brought from Swansea to Cardiff, they'll sometimes lose their cell, in the eight hours that they're away. So, you get a lot of defendants saying, 'I don't want to come to court. I'd rather do it over the link. If I get brought up from Swansea to Cardiff, by the time the end of the day happens in Cardiff, and I'm being shunted back to Swansea, they'll ring up and say, "Well his cell has gone. You're now being shifted to a different prison somewhere else." And so, from their perspective, the stability and the solidity of staying in the same place is helped. If they don't come to court, there's no risk of them losing their spot, as it were ... that's a factor which they tell me is important to them.'

Thus, for BS2, there has been a perceived increase in live-link due to the inadequate prison estate. The court closure programme, by moving courts further away from communities, has necessitated long periods of travel, thus also enticing or forcing the accused to 'attend' their trial via live-link. The problem with live-link in all such cases, however, is that it can lead the vulnerable innocent accused to plead guilty (Gibbs, 2017; Dugan, 2019).

This raises important questions regarding defendant participation in the criminal process, which is limited not simply by legislative policies (see Owusu-Bempah, 2017), but also by the on-the-ground realities of policy decisions. The problem posed by travelling long distances between prison and court can also impact upon a lawyer's willingness and/or ability to meet the accused before the hearing,[11] which may lead the lawyer to encourage live-link consultation with their client instead of meeting in person. BS2 discussed this:

---

[11] It is also potentially limited through the implementation of legislative policy.

'For practitioners, I mean in Wales, the prisons can be quite a long way away, especially for female defendants. Eastwood Park is the nearest one to south Wales. So, you'll have someone in Swansea arrested and sent to Eastwood Park, you know, a good two hours away from Swansea. It's near Slimbridge, you know, in Gloucestershire. … If you're a practitioner and you want to have a conference with your client, you can save yourselves a day if you just have a conference over the link, which is what I've done in the past. I don't want to be driving down to Reading Jail, or Dartmoor. It's a disaster for me. You know, I can get the work done on an hour's slot for a pre-trial conference.'

The lawyer thus also has an incentive to use live-link. The use of live-link becomes more onerous for the lawyer and awkward for the accused when discussing the options surrounding a guilty plea. We explore, in Chapter 6, the problems the accused faces regarding guilty pleas, and how this complicates the lawyer–client relationship. Here, BS2 highlighted the role of live-link vis-à-vis pleas:

'It really causes more hassle on the plea hearings, when they're deciding whether to plead guilty or not guilty, there may be some debate in their mind going on and then you've only got ten minutes to talk to them, and sometimes, their decision on plea is not straightforward. You're trying to explain to them the law, you're trying to explain to them the shape of the case against them. That's their last chance to get 25 per cent credit at plea, plea and trial preparation hearing. After that it's going to diminish down to a lesser credit. So I've sometimes found that it's quite difficult at that stage. If someone is definitely pleading not guilty, it's not a problem. It's really in those shaded grey areas where you're trying to say someone, "Listen, you're up against it here. What do you want to do?" They often feel pressured in that ten-minute slot to reach a decision, and there's plenty of times I've said to them, "Look, if you're in two minds, just say not guilty, and then we'll see" because you can always go from not guilty to guilty but coming back the other way is a whole load of grief.'

Daw (2020) has identified the pervasive creep of remote appearances into criminal justice over recent years and Gibbs (2017) highlights how little we know about its impact on justice. To judge from the lawyers in this study, live-link may not be the most useful medium for discussing complex legal matters or the strength of the prosecution – or weakness of the defence – case. The difference between sentence length depending on the timing of the guilty plea can be significant; the importance of the timing of the plea considering the various discounts seems to be difficult to communicate during live-link.

It is not necessarily – or solely – the live-link that creates this urgency, rather it is also the limited time that the lawyer has with their client that can create anxiety in decision making (an issue to which we return in Chapter 5 when examining the time pressures faced by barristers). The communication barrier which manifests through live-link was explored by BS5:

'If you've got a girl in Eastwood Park, most of the early hearings short of the trial, will be over the video link. And if she pleads guilty, the sentence will be over the video link, so you'll never actually be in the same room with her at the same time. Yeah, not being in the same room as a client has a massive bearing on the case. If I'm to ever crack a client, if they're to ever actually listen to the advice I'm giving them if they're guilty, if they're in the same room as me, I 100 per cent get what I want; over a video link it's probably 50 per cent. It's, you know, the impact, the immediacy of it. You can get what you want.'

BS5 also raised the issue of cracked cases – where the trial date is set but the case does not go ahead because the defendant pleads guilty or the prosecution has no evidence to offer – and the importance of the lawyer obtaining what *they* want. This raises concerns regarding the power dynamic within the lawyer–client relationship (Mulcahy, 1994). The use of video link seemingly creates a disconnect between the lawyer and the client and thus makes even more challenging the lawyer's task of explaining law and procedure and, arguably, the client's task of understanding the information provided. Therefore, not only are there imbalanced power dynamics at play between the accused and the lawyer, the ability to build rapport and discuss the detail of the case is further hampered by live-link, potentially placing yet further pressure on the accused and shifting power thus further away from them. Added to the communicative difficulties presented by live-link is the vulnerability of the client, such as where the client has limited educational attainment (see Dehaghani and Newman, 2017), which makes providing advice – and, crucially, ensuring such advice is understood – an even more demanding task:

'But when you're talking to clients who are not, you know, as educated, not from the same background as us, they're not as engaged in the process, they're not listening? I mean, there is a place in the system for the video link, so, the way it facilitates the process, but really, it can never be used as a substitute for face-to-face contact with a client I would say.' (BS5)

The background noise in the prison restricts the ability of the prisoner to understand what is occurring and being said on the other side of the live-link. Live-link may thus restrict prisoners' opportunities for engagement with, and effective and expressive participation within, the criminal process through 'sensory bias' (McKay, 2015; 2017).

The absence of a women's prison in Wales – and thus the necessary travel involved – may not only adversely impact on the female accused's ability to make decisions regarding her case, but it may also interfere with her ability to receive visits from children and other family members (see Rees et al, 2017). BS4 explained:

> 'In south Wales, Eastwood Park in Gloucestershire's the closest prison. It hasn't got a mother and baby unit now, so a pregnant woman being sentenced to prison would then have to go to Surrey, you know, further away from the family. It is a massive concern. They're even further detached then from their family and communities. And I think there's a very high percentage of prisoners in Eastwood Park who don't receive visits from family members, because you can understand that if … they tend to come from, unfortunately, from a certain demographic. The costs of travelling from west Wales, from Swansea, from somewhere in the south Wales Valleys to Eastwood Park is very, very expensive. Not easy to reach there by public transport, really, you'd have to have a car. Or money to pay for a taxi from the railway station. But it's not easy – you'd have to get to Gloucester somehow, and then. So, it is difficult, and it is a real problem for women offenders.'

As BS4 notes, women who are pregnant – or who have recently given birth – are placed at yet a further disadvantage by being taken even further away from home to the nearest mother and baby unit. The issue of travel – a recurring thread throughout this chapter – has been raised yet again, particularly the financial ability to travel to these sites of criminal justice. For prisoners, their imprisonment takes them further away from their communities, and for female – and some male – prisoners, this means across the border to England, often very far away from home (see Jones et al, 2019). The universal issues posed by, for example, live-link meetings are exacerbated in Wales compared to England, with the former's higher levels of court closures and, especially, the absence of a women's prison. However, there are aspects where there might be fewer distinctions between England and Wales. In the next section we will explore some of these similarities as relayed to us in our interviews.

Similarities with England

Thus far we have presented Wales as distinct from England, and it is in many respects; however, there were also points where those we interviewed made little differentiation between the two countries. In this section, we will explore some of the ways in which the most prominent features of criminal justice that seem to define Welsh experiences may not be distinct to Wales. Rather, these represented regional differences within and between areas of Wales and England. We see common trends in this south Wales sample and their experiences in various locations in England. A tongue-in-cheek, facetious answer as to whether there was a difference between England and Wales was given by BS14: "Not necessarily. The only reason I'm smiling is just like the Valleys culture of fights, but that's, erm, bouncer stuff."

When asked about their perception of the differences in more detail (and with greater seriousness), BS13 drew on their experience working across English courts:

> 'Other people might disagree with me. But I'm not Welsh, I'm English and I worked in England, and I work across the border. I'm in London quite a lot, so I've been in court centres in the Crown Court, in the Magistrates' Court in England and in Wales … I've not noticed a difference between the two. I think it's similar, the issues are the same. You have some court centres that seem to be run in a much more efficient manner, but I don't think that's to do with being in England or in Wales, I think that's just to do with the court centre and the staff and how many cases they have going through it, going through the court. So, there isn't anything that I would say that I've picked up on in the short time I've been in practice that would differ between the two countries.'

Issues around court management were mentioned by both BS13 earlier and DS15 in the following quote, but these, in both instances, were not viewed as something that could distinguish Wales from England. Rather they were seen as something that was unique to the court itself:

> 'I think it's the same whatever. Whenever I've spoken to colleagues from away, you know, certain courts have different quirks, certain courts are hanging courts [courts that are tough on defendants], but they – we all have the same problems, the same difficulties. I can't think of anything that's happening here that's not happening in a court in England. … But it's no different. It's exactly the same. You know, the police are escaping their need to do things diligently by releasing people under investigation. So, you have a tranche of cases where just nothing happening on them for years and years and years.' (DS15)

The problems DS15 found with police were apparently the same problems encountered across England. DS4 also agreed on the common problems with police across England and Wales:

'I tend to look at police station reports from all over the UK ... and I think it's pretty similar, to be honest. I think nation-wide there are problems with access to the client in the first instance, getting proper information from the police in the first instance, trying to get the cases dealt with expeditiously in the police station in the first instance. Then there are issues post-interview with having any influence over charging decisions and what happens, next steps. And then again there are issues once the client has been released under investigation or on bail, there are issues communicating with the police as the investigation is ongoing. I think that's nationwide. There may be some local variances between particularly difficult forces, or whatever, but I think it's the same issues all over.'

DS4, like BS13 and DS15, noted local variances, this time in relation to the police. DS10 noted how South Wales Police were "awful" on the whole, with some "amazing" people working for the force, but South Wales Police could not necessarily be distinguished from any of the other 42 territorial police forces in England and Wales:

'There are obviously issues when it comes to regions and different circuits compared to London, but I don't think, in my experience anyway, there's anything from the Welsh system that says, "This is really bad." Apart from obviously the fact that South Wales Police are terrible and underfunded like the CPS and everything else like I've already said. You know, I speak with every force in the country, pretty much, because I've got clients all over the place, and when I say South Wales Police are awful, it's like anywhere. You get some really bad people, and you get some really amazing people. I think that South Wales Police especially do suffer from issues of resource. I don't know about leadership. It's only probably, I don't know who it was, but they have a historical issue and we are, as I am, entirely biased because we had a client who was part of the Lynette White stuff. ... And the Lynette White and everything you can read about that from in the public domain, the BBC stuff for example, is very useful for opening their eyes to how badly things can go. So, when you've got South Wales Police at the heart of that, that doesn't help. That being said, when I've dealt with individual officers, they've always been great.'[12]

---

[12] The policing budget provided to Wales does not take account of the increased need when policing a capital city – see Chapter 1.

With notable miscarriages of justice cases occurring in south Wales in the 1980s and 1990s such as the Cardiff Three – as alluded to earlier with the mention of Lynette White (see Chapter 1) – and the Cardiff Newsagent Three, some of these lawyers did suggest that the local force had a negative reputation. However, on an individual level, as with DS10's quote, most officers were "great" or at least reasonable, as we will discuss in Chapter 6 when examining relationships.

As noted earlier in the chapter, there were differences highlighted by participants regarding the greater rurality in Wales and the absence of large cities. The rural–urban divide emerged as a key insight that could link areas of Wales and England together in terms of criminal justice experience (see also Newman, 2016a). This was expressed by DS7, noting that, "Wales is more of a rural area, so it's probably more comparable to the sort of areas north of London than a big city." Concerns were raised that rural areas – in both Wales and England – were struggling for criminal defence provision:

'I think, maybe not necessarily Wales in particular, but definitely rural areas, they're going to have less people going forward for criminal [defence work]. You know, they keep cutting our fees, they keep cutting legal aid, reducing the number of firms that have got legal aid contracts.' (DS17)

Previous research has pointed towards the common criminal justice issues experienced in rural areas (Hester, 1999 on Traveller communities; Barton et al, 2011 on raves; Donnermeyer et al, 2011 on agricultural crime; Fyfe and Reeves, 2011 on wildlife crime). In rural areas, domestic violence may also be more pronounced (Squire and Gill, 2011). Rurality was noted by DS11 as a similarity between Wales and England; rather than distinguishing Wales from England, DS11 suggested that differences between urban and rural exist in both countries:

'Well, there are areas in England which are similar in terms of being rural and remote and not having many courts and police stations; there's lots of overlap with areas of England. The only difference that you can absolutely say that's a definite is the Welsh language. ... So, I would say that ... most of it is from the geography, but there's areas in England where there's similar geography: I'm thinking of Cumbria, South-West, you know. The difference between Swansea and rural Carmarthenshire is the same as the difference between Birmingham and Cumbria, probably, isn't it?'

DS11, a first-language Welsh speaker, identified the prevalence of Welsh language in more rural areas of south Wales. For DS11, the ability to speak

Welsh in such areas is "important" because "they will have a lot of trust in you if you are speaking Welsh to them, because if they want to speak Welsh and you're speaking Welsh to them – and I'm thinking now about north Carmarthenshire, so rural areas." Thus, in such communities with many first-language Welsh speakers, DS11 points out how using the language will give an extra level of connection between lawyers and clients, which may be relevant for the lawyer–client relationship discussed in Chapter 6. Yet, it is noteworthy that DS11 also commented on the shared obstacles of criminal justice provision in rural English areas. Welsh language aside, perhaps there are many shared rural experiences across Wales and England.

In addition to the shared rural similarities outlined earlier, some interviewees remarked on the shared cultures of post-industrial areas:

'Valleys attitude is totally different than Cardiff and Newport attitude, and Swansea attitude. I honestly don't think it matters which of the Valleys you're from, the attitude tends to be more or less the same … I would say in England, because I spent a year or so up in Cleveland and the Yorkshire have got a similar attitude to the Welsh … I think it comes down to whatever the industry is. You know, heavy industries, steel, mining, that type of industry, because it goes back, it's work hard, play hard, isn't it? And I think that's got a lot to do with it. So, like, when you come to the south east [of England] … I think the attitudes are different than say, for argument's sake … the middle of the Black Country, we're talking Yorkshire. You know, and they're very similar to Welsh, because the people's attitudes are very similar. But, so other than that, the justice system is what it is, isn't it?' (PO3)

As discussed earlier, there were suggestions from interviewees that Welsh people supposedly differed attitudinally to the English and that there were variations between the Valleys and the Welsh cities. As PO3 suggested earlier, the attitudinal differences between England and Wales are perhaps a sweeping generalization and there may be shared cultures, attitudes and values among post-industrial areas regardless of whether they are in England or Wales.

Another contention discussed earlier was that Wales lacked the serious crimes that were committed in England. However, BS15 was quick to point out that the difference was not necessarily about severity, but the volume of very serious offences:

'The one thing that we don't have as much of is gun crime, but I was talking to various officers during the course of a trial we've just finished, and they're saying it is becoming more of an issue. I mean I did a murder last year which was two brothers who … shot and killed somebody. It was a drugs execution, which was unusual for south Wales, but it's there ... there is a lot of knife crime in south Wales. I mean virtually every murder I've done in the last two years has been a stabbing, with people ... what I find extraordinary is maybe in the past, people would, if they had a problem, they'd go to sort it out with their fists. What they tend to do now is they get a knife, and they kill them! Which is an extraordinary response. Which is why you get so many youngsters being convicted of knife murders, and as I said, in the last two years I have done, every case, realistically has been ... a knife murder. And deliberately arming yourself with a knife and going out of your way to find somebody to kill them ... is certainly a worrying trend and it's something that is happening more and more. ... It's the volume: that's the only thing.'

Such discussion returns us to the question of scale explored earlier in this chapter but offers an alternative slant that suggests Wales is not that different from England here in relation to the volume of serious crime. BS15 remarked that murder trials are not unusual in south Wales:

'There's always a murder running in one of the south Wales courts ... it's very unusual for there not to be. Yeah, I think that's a reasonable observation to make ... there was, there was one yesterday, which pleaded, in Swansea, that was a murder which went as a manslaughter. There's one in Swansea starting next week. I start one in Swansea in May; I've got a Cardiff one in June ... one that was running in Cardiff which we finished two weeks ago, there was another one running in Newport ... to some extent, you will often find two separate murder trials running, one in Newport, one in Cardiff, or one in Newport, one in Swansea.'

The issue of volume is potentially closely related to population size: Wales simply has less volume of serious cases, not because people in Wales are less likely to engage in serious crime, but because Wales does not have the large urban areas – such as London, Birmingham and Manchester – that are found in England. The differences between Wales and England for BS15, as for many of the other solicitors and barristers in this section, may thus be demographic and/or economic. What emerges is that the south Wales experience is worthy of note, but any assumptions of some inherent Welsh exceptionalism need to be probed and caveated with comparison across the country as with regions between Wales and England.

Our aim in this section is to acknowledge the similarities between Wales and England and in so doing provide both transparency and accuracy. The nuance of the narratives and variety of personal experience has made any form of accurate quantification difficult to impossible. But there were a number of common refrains throughout the interviews about criminal justice in its south Wales setting: the notion of a distinct Welsh (legal) culture; the Welsh language; the challenges faced within rural areas; the smaller, closer-knit feel of Wales and the impact that this may have on practice; and the difficulties of travel around Wales, exacerbated by absence of transport provision.

Conclusion

In this chapter we have examined issues of national and local specificity as determined by the interviewees and, having positioned this research within the south Wales region, we have provided context for the specific findings that follow in later chapters. In addition to offering detail on the issues impacting upon, inter alia, criminal defence, we have also discussed in considerable detail the issues of court closures following austerity and provision within the prison estate. Transport obstacles and limitations, particularly to these sites of criminal justice, should be acknowledged and addressed. While much of this book, and indeed this chapter, sets out the differences between Wales and England, it would be remiss of us to neglect the similarities identified by some of those we interviewed. The law and the operation of justice must be set in context to be properly understood (Holder and Harrison, 2003). This means the acknowledgement of 'place' and its relationship with economic, political, social and other such systems. We recognize that a number of the subjects addressed in this chapter and throughout the book may be found across the England and Wales jurisdiction: issues identified in Cardiff, Pontypridd and Swansea could be replicated in Carlisle, Pontefract and Sheffield. It is important to also consider culture and the presence of the Welsh language as a difference between Wales and England. Indeed, practitioners identified Welsh as a difference – "a unique thing that we have" (BS3). Yet, as identified by DS7 – "that's not as much of an issue as some people would like to make it" – the language was not at the forefront of many experiences, particularly as most participants did not practise in Welsh and had limited experience of dealing with cases where an accused used Welsh. If we conducted this research in the north or west of the country, language would likely have taken on more prominence and represented a stronger element within our place-based approach.

The meaning and applicability of 'place' is always a site of potential conflict (Massey, 2005) and, as such, there is scope for debate about whether our depiction of south Wales holds as an organizing device in how other people would understand the area. Whether readers are of the view that Nottingham could replace Newport, that Wales and England are similar should not be assumed. What we have done is highlight issues of space and time that we have been told play out in south Wales, analysing how they might be relevant to criminal justice, thus contextualizing the experiences in this study. These distinctions and synergies merit consideration. Drawing attention to some of the similarities and differences between England and Wales provides both a contribution to understanding aspects of the criminal process – and the wider justice system – across the entire jurisdiction yet *also* fills – at least some of – the void that exists in socio-legal criminal justice research on Wales. The court closure programme – while taking into account distances as the crow flies – does not consider the distances in actuality where towns, by virtue of geography, are awkwardly set apart, such as in the Valleys. The disproportionate impact of the court closure programme would not be known were it not for a study that acknowledges the importance of place. Recognition of the local may spark discussion on how, for example, court closures affect English local authorities with large rural components such as Cornwall or Suffolk. With a move away from physical hearings, the relationship between law and space/place is fundamentally altered (see Hynes et al, 2020).

Location is also important to understanding the issue of resilience and vulnerability. Resilience is influenced by the connections that shape a place; networks and institutions may frame an experience, in relation to both the interpersonal and the physical. By locating people within the place that they live and work, we acquire an insight into how their vulnerability plays out. A close-knit legal community might, for example, bolster the resilience of some solicitors and barristers, bound up with the communitarian political ethos in Wales as discussed in Chapter 1. This raises important questions about whether and how this experience might be distinct to south Wales. At the same time, inadequate court and prison facilities may reduce the resilience of those 'processed' through the criminal justice system, with the accused and their families potentially having a different (worse) experience of criminal justice than some in other locations. Place impacts on resilience and is key to understanding vulnerability. Unless we raise and explore how the space of south Wales at this current time plays into the vulnerability profile of those in and around the criminal justice system, we cannot begin to understand their varying levels of resilience.

Building on Chapter 3, with its focus on the people of this research, we have given detail on the place central to our research, thus providing context for the three chapters that follow. Rather than integrating such information into a general research methods chapter, this book has provided full-length chapter treatment relating to local detail, something that could be considered a deviation from the 'norm'. Some studies have provided but the barest of detail of where and when; we believe that including this detail, where possible, provides for a richer account. Local conditions and divergences between and within regions are important to the questions of how justice is delivered and experienced. Alternative lines of inquiry regarding the impact of, for example, law and policy on the ground can thus be pursued. By widening the scope beyond generic conceptions of austerity and actively fixing our study of criminal justice under austerity in south Wales, we provide another level to our work, and invite others to engage in a dialogue about what aspects of our findings may be seen elsewhere, or may be specific to the region or country. Further, by engaging with questions of locality informed by the data, we have situated the people and, now, the place at the forefront of discussion, thus stimulating consideration of, for example, legal aid cuts on legal practice (discussed in Chapter 5), in both general – across the jurisdiction – and specific – impact on impoverished areas such as the south Wales Valleys – terms. For too long Wales – and the regions, cities, towns and villages within it – have been overlooked and simply assumed to be the same as England. We have shown that this assumption is unfounded. The next chapter will see us begin to drill down into the insight provided by the experiences of these people in this place, as we consider some of the main pressures that practitioners identify from working in the criminal justice system under austerity.

5

Pressures of Practice

Introduction

In the previous chapter we assessed how criminal justice issues played out in south Wales as the location of our study, thus outlining the context of the experiences at the heart of this book. The chapter detailed defining features of the space and the time of this location, such as the relatively small scale of the criminal cases and the impact of austerity on an issue such as court closures. In this chapter we flesh out the specific criminal justice experiences that occurred in south Wales, considering the pressures that practitioners faced in their practice. These pressures frame the experience of practitioners and, in turn, shape the experience of the accused.

Criminal legal aid is subject to lower remuneration levels than other areas of legal practice; criminal legal aid lawyers have typically been viewed as 'low status' compared with other lawyers (Sommerlad, 1995; 1996; 2001).[1] Those practising in legally aided criminal defence work are becoming increasingly deprofessionalized in relation to the tasks that they must undertake and their role in relation to the court. They are required to engage with increasingly formulaic processes; restrictions are placed on the initiative that they may seek to take. Their remuneration has stagnated and been reduced; the financial value placed on their work is limited. Within these circumstances, legally aided criminal defence lawyers have been labelled 'alienated workers' (Newman, 2016b; Newman and Welsh, 2019); their diminishing profession attracts little wider respect and internalizes negative messages. Alienated workers may feel powerless and time deprived, making their work inherently more stressful (Boni-Le Goff et al, 2020). Within this chapter we consider, in more depth, the issues deemed to be central to understanding the experiences of criminal justice. We address specifically the challenges that practitioners face within their practice. These challenges – presented

---

[1] See also Moorhead (2004).

through the frames of 'time' and 'money' – are inextricably linked. Owing to the pressures of practice caused by years of neoliberal and austerity-driven policies (as discussed in Chapter 2), the lawyers in this study had little of either. They were paid insufficiently for essential work, they felt pressure to work quickly to compensate for the insufficient fees payable, and they were bothered by what they perceived as undue encumbrances on their time. The nature of legal aid work required practitioners to work faster or, in the euphemistic language of the government and the courts, as *efficiently* as possible.

Access to criminal justice is premised on the role of the criminal legal aid lawyer, who, in addition to advising and representing the accused, also liaises between the accused person – and possibly their family – and the courts, police and prosecution (Newman, 2013a). Thus, the challenges experienced by lawyers are of great significance to the wider criminal process (see Dehaghani and Newman, 2017) and to the experiences of criminal justice for the accused and, by extension, the family of the accused. The pressures upon lawyers may have impeded access to justice for the accused. After examining the pressures on lawyers, we examine the ripple effect upon the accused and family members.

Yet, we begin by delving deeper into legal aid funding – an issue identified as of great importance to the lawyers in this study. Financial restrictions have reshaped practice, generally in a manner that will negatively impact upon the service they provide. We then move on to explore specific time pressures practitioners identified as impacting their work, providing a discrete example of pressures in detail by focusing on the experiences of barristers. This highlights how the financial restrictions both play out and are worsened in the practice of preparing for cases. Following on from this, we examine the precarious future of criminal defence in the light of the pressures identified. Finally, we consider the apparent lack of public understanding on the problems facing the criminal justice system.

This chapter carries on the theme of underfunding that was first articulated by practitioners in Chapter 3 and as was developed in Chapter 4 in the specific south Wales context. Whereas the discussion in Chapter 3 was more about the impact of underfunding on their identity, and our application of underfunding in Chapter 4 spoke to the impact of underfunding on the local criminal justice system, in this chapter the focus is on the impact of underfunding on practice. By considering how legal aid cuts have caused solicitors to reduce the service provided to clients and exploring concerns over the sustainability of the criminal Bar in a climate of such cuts, this chapter illustrates the pressure exerted upon practitioners, the institutions and the clients that they should serve. The pressures of practice that directly or indirectly stem from underfunding are key to understanding how the criminal justice system functions.

The problems with legal aid funding

As discussed in Chapter 3, there are notable problems with the underfunding of criminal legal aid. Solicitors and barristers alike outlined the negative impact of legal aid funding on their practice and, by extension, on access to justice within criminal proceedings and the broader functioning of the criminal justice system. Criminal defence lawyers consider that they have been set up for failure because of the financial conditions under which they operate. These financial conditions work against good defence practice and lead to uncertainty regarding the role; the fiscal context is central to questions of profitability, viability, and level of service provided (Welsh, 2017; Thornton, 2020).[2] A prominent feature of the interviews was the changes to the legal aid landscape and their impact upon the work of criminal lawyers. For BS15, "The reality was, I always used to think we got paid too much and now we don't get paid enough." The profitability of criminal defence work was absent for those interviewed:

> 'They get paid buttons, really. What we do as a firm, I don't know what we would get for it. I think we get paid as a firm a hundred and sixty-five pounds to go for a callout at Llandrindod Wells [police station]. And we would pay our solicitors, you know, sixty, seventy pounds to attend. So, the profit element, when you have to, you know, look at the back-office staff, rent, rates, and all the rest of it to pay out of that relatively small amount of money.' (DS20)

DS20 suggested that the rates paid have rendered incredibly difficult the possibility of firm survival. The sense was that these poor rates reflected a lack of appreciation for the work of the criminal defence lawyer, criminal legal aid was an "easy target" and had been dismantled and degraded because the public cared little about "criminals", as we discussed in Chapter 2. BS1, for example, considered the general sense that politicians have worked against criminal legal aid, indicating that the political undermining of legal aid emanated from Conservative and Labour alike (Hynes and Robins, 2009):

---

[2]   The quality of legal aid work more generally has been degraded – see Hunter et al (2018) for a discussion of judges' perceptions of legal aid work, and Cooke (2019) for an exploration of legal aid in the round.

'This is not a party-political point because it started with Labour, actually. It became seen, initially, as a way of bashing criminals. So, by talking about slashing legal aid, it made it sound like they were being tough on criminals … there's no votes in funding defendants. Like I said, no voter thinks it's going to happen to them. But I'm afraid it does. It happens to their sons. … They can't believe it when it does.'

The importance of highlighting the way antipathy to legal aid has extended over the political spectrum has been highlighted by Robins and Newman (2021). As discussed in Chapter 2, the problems of underfunding have been amplified under austerity but are deeper rooted.

Some lawyer participants shared examples of how little they were getting paid for work, which helps to put detail onto the broader point. DS1 told us about a trial they had shortly before our interview:

'I had a five-day trial in the Crown Court that had been going on for eighteen months. It had been listed for trial before, we had a load of conferences, and it went for a five-day trial and the defendant was acquitted, and we got paid nine hundred quid. And that includes the Magistrates' Court. And my satisfaction level about that was very low. … We had a dangerous driving trial, a listed trial. We were able to prove that the client was innocent because his car had been in a garage on the day of the incident – his neighbour was crackers, who was the complainant. Listed for a trial, prosecution pulled it on the day of the trial before a jury was sworn, we'd had maybe eight hearings, loads of conferences. You know, a chap with no previous convictions who was very worried, and we got paid two hundred and sixty quid.'

This example illustrates the amount of work that can go into a trial and the frustrations regarding the payment arrangements where the trial does not go ahead. In this case, the lawyers had conducted a significant amount of work only to be paid a relative pittance later. There were also concerns about the amount of time that a lawyer has available to spend with a client, particularly when it is the client's first time in the criminal justice system, as indicated by DS1 and as explored in Chapter 3. DS1 discussed the disparity of payment between criminal defence and other areas of legal practice: "All other lawyers are able to charge at somewhere between a hundred and fifty and two hundred quid an hour. With legal aid, you pretty much, you're lucky if you're getting forty an hour. You know, it's forty-four seventy-five for preparation in Magistrates' Court."

Solicitors talked about how the funding situation impacted upon their work, particularly the research and preparation for cases. DS2 provided an account of a difference in how they conducted their practice as a result of underfunding (see also Dehaghani and Newman, 2021a):

> 'It's a problem because back ten years ago, if there was a road traffic collision, I'd go out and go to the road and have a look at it and take pictures. I'd go around and speak to various people about the incident. If it went to Crown Court, I'd go to Crown Court and seek out Counsel and make sure Counsel have everything ready for the case. Now with the legal aid cuts and the way things are, you don't get paid for any of that, and there's less incentive to do a good job other than pride and responsibility and they can only carry you so far, especially with a firm that wants to make money, like every firm does, otherwise we couldn't stay open. I can't go out and do the best job that I can do and justify it. I just can't. I mean, on the more serious ones you can, but on the less serious ones, which are still serious for them, you can't justify it. There's no incentive to go out and do anything above and beyond what you're expected to do and that's really, really sad.'

DS2 discussed the "goodwill" that lawyers were being forced to operate on – and it was something that could only carry them so far. There were concerns that "less serious" cases were not receiving the required attention and that some of the best-practice preparatory activities that lawyers may engage in were being neglected or ignored. The impact of financial pressures on case preparation discussed by DS2 – and raised by many solicitors in this research – mirror previous literature such as the findings of Stephen and Tata (2006). For them, the need to take on an increasing volume of cases to make the finances work meant avoiding client support or interviewing witnesses. A lack of finances thus results in a lack of thorough preparation, which can have serious negative consequences for accused persons. Other solicitors discussed the impact of legal aid on how cases were approached in court (see Newman, 2013a):

> 'There's still a financial pressure as well. If you're getting paid, for argument's sake, three hundred pounds to do a legal aid case, like a shoplift, and your client wants to bring in a thousand witnesses ... I don't have the hours to sit there. You're not being paid per hour; you're being paid per case. So, I can be in court for five minutes, and get paid the same as if I was there all day. Do you see what I mean?' (DS12)

Solicitors also spoke of the impact of legal aid on the quality of advice that they were able to provide to clients in police custody (see also Kemp, 2018). DS4 provided one such example:

'The main problem is we get paid fixed fee for police stations, which is a hundred and seventy-seven pounds, odd, plus VAT. And being able to deliver a really good service to a client who's in a police station on that fixed fee is a real challenge. Because, you know, you could spend hours and hours and hours at a police station with a client, and sometimes you need to. But you've always got in mind that you're on that fixed fee. And it is a challenge, definitely. So I think the poor legal aid rates are the biggest factor in not being able to, sometimes, provide the client with the best possible service.'

The rates payable thus affected the level of service provided to a client. Lawyers had to make a decision regarding the amount of time and resource that they were prepared to – or able to – spend on a case. Welsh (2022) highlights the risk that taking on criminal legal aid work can place on solicitors' firms. Barristers also recognized the financial pressures on solicitors:

'Getting investigations done, statements taken. When you've got labour, time-intensive trawl of potential witnesses, solicitors are getting paid so little under the current rates they don't have the staff, they don't have the time, they don't have the resources any more to really get stuck into a case, so you're doing it on a, it tends to be the bare minimum to make a competent job as opposed to a Rolls Royce service. Whether people can expect a Rolls Royce service on legal aid, I don't know. But it, the solicitors are cracking at the seams even more than barristers at the moment. Their rates are horrendous. Most of them make a loss on general crime and rely on a few really big cases to put them back into the black for the year.' (BS9)[3]

When faced with the same dilemma, BS9 had different views on how far barristers would compromise quality of service as compared with solicitors:

'It's a difference between the bar and perhaps solicitors – and I may be doing them a disservice – but I still don't know any barrister who would advise not to plead guilty in a hopeless case just because he wanted to earn more money, but ... I have seen that happen from solicitors.'[4]

---

[3] A "Rolls Royce service" indicates the best standard of service and reflects language used by a custody officer in Dehaghani's (2019) research in police custody to refer to the level of service provided to detainees.

[4] Having not observed practice for this research we are, of course, unable to verify whether and how such differences played out.

One of the impacts of legal aid noted by DS18 was that levels of practitioner benevolence would be reduced. This reduction has a negative effect on the nature of the lawyer–client relationship (as we explore in Chapter 6), as it does on the way the accused and their families feel about the criminal justice system (as we consider in Chapter 7). This was alluded by DS2 earlier and clearly expressed by DS18:

> 'In common with all publicly funded services I suppose it … diminishes the amount of goodwill there is in any system, whether it's teaching, nursing, local government, whatever it may be. Because if people … find themselves under pressure, expected to deliver more work for stagnating or less remuneration, then it will create a degree of ill-will, and … whereas there would be slack in the system so you might help people out, when you're not getting paid to do it, there will be less of that goodwill around, in any environment that's treated in that way.'

With a system under strain, there is a need – perhaps, a built-in expectation – that lawyers will 'go the extra mile' and help hold it together by engaging in tasks over and above what they are paid to do. However, if these lawyers are frustrated and fed up, it may be less likely that they will act out of kindness. This was reflected by DS12:

> 'If somebody doesn't qualify for legal aid, we will have to instruct them on a private basis … we've got to be paid so that we can go up to, you know, you've got to send a solicitor to court, you've got to read the papers. Most of the time we'll work out a fee, and it's not a silly fee. … But you know, if you've got some single mother being done for stealing, and for whatever reason, she's not going to qualify we're not going to – you know, we'll probably, to be honest with you, most of the time we'll take the hit on something like that and we'll just do the case because we're there anyway.'

Helping clients for free would no longer be feasible; lawyers now had to do more (paid) work to get by. More experienced lawyers noted how they were having to take on a greater workload to turn a profit:

> 'I can tell you that every one of us – well I've been there for twenty years – you have to do three times the amount of work if not more to earn the same as you did fifteen years ago. Well fifteen years I was a junior-ish barrister, a junior barrister – I do much more serious cases, many, many more, to earn almost same, more or less, as I was, well, certainly a decade ago if not fifteen years ago. From that point of view that's insane, and it's unsustainable, really, in the long run.' (BS1)

One result, and coping mechanism, was the push for 'volume work' as discussed in Chapter 4 – a larger number of cases that could be dealt with more quickly. DS4 explained (see also Dehaghani and Newman, 2021a):

> 'You probably work out how much work you need to do on a case and know that the fixed fee comes nowhere near it … in order to try to make a living out of this, the only way round the fixed fees is to have a lot of work. So that the volume increases, so that you're still getting lots of work in. And sometimes when that happens, because you're so busy, you can't give a certain client enough time that they really should deserve on their case. We try our best, but sometimes it doesn't happen.'

The volume – or 'sausage factory' (Goriely, 1996; Newman, 2013a) – approach necessitated by the decrease in funding also meant that lawyers were unable to spend enough time with their clients. DS13 reflected on this effect (see also Dehaghani and Newman, 2021a):

> 'Well, the fees are extremely low so I think – and I think it's probably different when you're more experienced doing it, but I think a lot of solicitors they can't spend the time with them because they don't have the funding to do that … it's just a matter of going through the motions in terms of funding.'

While practitioners were often unhappy with this situation, they viewed it as the pragmatic reality with which they had to contend. The 'volume work' was also seen to create or exacerbate workload problems, as BS8 indicated: "'You have back-to-back cases that are very stressful, you'd probably find, I'll be honest, that you wouldn't have put as much preparation into their case as you would or would have liked to." The pressure and intensity of work was difficult for practitioners. Clients – who want their lawyer to possess detailed knowledge of their case and who value time with their lawyer – may feel at a disadvantage and thus in an especially unequal position vis-à-vis the state (see Newman, 2013a).

Financial incentives for criminal lawyers lead to better quality work, while financial disincentives result in distracted and less motivated lawyers (Gray et al, 1996; Fenn et al, 2007). The lawyers in our study felt that the legal aid system did not properly reward them. One potential impact will be on changing the nature of what lawyers feel they can do. Emotional support is a crucial part of the lawyer's duties (Cooke, 2019), particularly at the police station (Pivaty, 2020). While not strictly necessary to the lawyer's role on paper, this emotional work is important to the lawyer's role in practice; it is possible that the problems arising through legal aid funding, as discussed in this section, may undermine the provision of emotional support as lawyers feel less willing to put additional time and energy into their work (see, for example, Dehaghani and Newman, 2017). There are many reasons why, in Chapter 3, the issue of legal aid funding was central to the lawyers' discussions of their work. As discussed in Chapter 2, there are numerous other problems with the criminal justice system, and we will explore these later, with the implications of inadequate legal aid funding, particularly the impact on the lawyer–client relationship, being explored in Chapter 6. Next, we draw out how the problems of legal aid funding led to time pressures for many of the lawyers interviewed.

Too little time

The reductions in legal aid funding placed lawyers under considerable workload pressures and thus left them with little time to conduct their work. In this section, we examine how lawyers were often expected to pick up cases at short notice and increase their working hours during periods in which they had done less previously. To provide concrete examples of what this meant in practice, we focus on the workload of barristers. Barristers have long worked under pressure (Morrison and Leith, 1992) and, as a result, have been limited in the work that they can perform, often resulting in poorly prepared cases.[5] The functioning of the courts further exacerbated any pressures, particularly 'micro-management' of cases driven by a desire for efficiency (see Chapter 2):

> 'There's a lot of time pressure which never used to be there. ... It's not that long ago that a case would be listed in the Crown Court, and the first listed would be the trial listing. ... They try to micromanage cases now, so you have hearing upon hearing upon hearing and cases where you think, 'Well, why are we here? Who needs to know this, we can sort this out.' And I mean most cases resolve themselves that way, so do you really need these hearings? "Which witnesses do you want? How long are you going to be with this witness?" I don't bloody know, because I don't know what he's going to say! "Well if he agrees with everything I say, he'll be two minutes; if he doesn't, I'll be twenty minutes." A lot of it is based on this attempt at cost-cutting. It's not to do with efficiency, it's an attempt to cut the costs of running the courts.' (BS8)

As BS8 highlighted, the desire to cut costs has resulted in unnecessary hearings. The claims of 'efficiency drives' from the Ministry of Justice are thus

---

[5] For Morrison and Leith (1992: 91), 'time is short, and pressures are constant'.

bogus as the actual reasoning is to just reduce the amount of money spent on criminal justice, hence facilitating such inefficiency. These comments reflect a common frustration among participants that, in the name of efficiency, too much time was being allocated to the minutiae of cases. Trust in lawyers to resolve matters between themselves has waned, the court appears to exert more control over the proceedings, and lawyers are expected to predict the time taken on tasks. This has undoubtedly been driven by practices of new public management (as discussed in Chapter 2 in relation to neoliberalism). The effect was counterproductive, with more work on cases instead of less.[6] The stress and frustrations produced through court procedures were often exacerbated by the last-minute nature of some of the work:

'As well as the remuneration and the chaos, you get the five PM list that comes in, where it comes in at five, six o'clock. If you're lucky it'll come in at three, four o'clock. You'll have five trials, three sentences, three guilty pleas. You're supposed to prep them all from five o'clock then that evening, get up in the morning, prep that, do that list which will go until about three, four o'clock, you come out of court, you look at your email, there's the list for the next day ... when you saw a Magistrates' Court list in your diary you would think, "Alright." You've just got to suck it up for twelve, for twenty-four hours, where hopefully you're free about four, five o'clock when the list comes in, prep the list as much as you can, make a note of everything that isn't there, and call the CPS in the morning and say, "I haven't got this on that, I haven't got this on that, I haven't got this." Try and deal with it all before court starts then deal with talking to witnesses, seeing which witnesses have turned up and getting confirmation on guilty pleas. Prosecuting the list. And you do it all again at four, five o'clock then the next day.' (BS12)

It was a relentless churn for many. The work of barristers in England and Wales can be typified by the short notice with which they pick up work and the cases they need to balance (Tague, 2007). Having such little time to prepare impacted on the service these barristers felt able to provide, as discussed by BS6:

'Obviously in that situation you've been up 'til whenever reading the papers, you've got so many things to think about, and really ... what

---

[6] Hoggett (1996) has outlined how new public management reforms in the public sector more broadly ignore the individual in favour of a fictive universalism, which acts to provide a justification for an increased intensification of labour practices.

you need from the client is to give you as much information as you can so you can get on with it. And usually you don't have very much time to get that information out, and so I think in that situation often their needs are not always at the top of the list of priorities at that moment ... I think in terms of offering reassurance and giving them time, and answering all their questions, you just can't always do that in that situation.'

As noted earlier, lawyers may often perform 'emotional work'; however, as BS6 indicated, the time limits on consultations, exacerbated by the 'last-minute' nature of barristers' work, may deplete the ability of the lawyer to provide such emotional support. There were effectively restrictions placed on their practice caused by taking cases on at such short notice. Barristers discussed their awareness of such problems, and the need to accept such problems and adapt accordingly:

'Oh, it is difficult. Especially when you get in last minute. Say now if there's disclosure issues, you can have a very good idea of what the case is ... but a piece of evidence might support you and help you with cross-examination or whatever. But you have an idea what the case is about ... quite often, especially the more junior you are, you will receive trials, Crown Court trials, sometimes complicated ones, fraud cases, cases involving representing somebody who if they're found guilty will go to prison for a long time. You will get it last minute.' (BS11)

Relatedly, at Crown Court especially, listings were said to have exerted significant time pressure on most of the barristers in this study. They felt that the process through which cases were listed to appear at court created additional burdens that worsened the problems caused by underfunding (as discussed in Chapter 3). BS13 relayed how these listings impacted on the time that barristers could spend on case preparation and client contact:

'So, in the Crown Court if you've got several cases that you're dealing with in the morning, but, for example, a client is late or a solicitor is late, or one case is heard before the other ... you're then under pressure to conclude a conference as quickly as you can basically. But those periods, can be difficult, because you're having to say – and again this is about being honest with the client – "This case is going to be called on in ten minutes time. We need to get through X Y, Z." If you need to ask for more time, you have to ask for more time to do that, but it can feel quite pressurised sometimes to make sure you're in court on time ... but the reality is you can't do justice to that client without having the necessary time to advise them on everything that you need to at that stage in the proceedings.'

The listings, crucially, affected the amount of work required by the barrister, often – as barristers suggested – needlessly. As BS13 indicated earlier and according to BS9, cases can overrun. This may, in turn, make the scheduling of work more difficult. Barristers may often be required to flit frantically between cases. While the court may aim to make the process more "efficient" (as suggested by BS6 earlier), the unpredictability of the process can sit in tension with this aim. Further, owing to difficulties presented by court listings, barristers may be required to 'juggle' their work and, at times, drop cases often at the last moment. This has an adverse impact upon the client and the lawyer–client relationship, as discussed further in Chapter 6. BS9 highlighted this here:

'If things overrun it's quite hard getting cases put back for a few days so you can retain continuity, so that causes late returns. Cases are taken out of the list because they understandably over-list, so when things crack, they can pull something in. But if that case then doesn't crack, they then have to push the one that doesn't get on off, and half of the time that's then relisted when you can't do it and you've done all the prep, you've had the conference, you've built up a rapport. So, it really annoys clients, and it causes double-prepping and a lot of wasted prep you simply do not get paid for.'

Given the problems created by these listings, barristers would generally prioritize the highest-paying work, with the caseload being organized around murder and rape cases rather than affray, ABH or smaller-value thefts. Thornton (2019) has identified how barristers adapt to the financial situation within which they operate; they make decisions about what work to take on at any moment to ensure that they are selecting the most remunerative option and can thereby maximize potential profit. As highlighted by BS5, it may also mean that barristers decline to work for the CPS "because their fees haven't changed since 2006":

'And what happens at the moment is that defence cases you generally prioritise over prosecution cases. So, you might have a week where you've got a defence Section 18, and a prosecution rape, but you'll return the prosecution rape ... but keep the defence so that the defendant doesn't have to have a change of barrister at the last minute. It means that the prosecution often don't necessarily get the barrister of their choice as well, but their fees are even worse.'

While listings were a common problem for barristers in south Wales, there was some suggestion that other areas were worse:

'Now here, the listing here, although I whinge about it, it's not as bad as other places. For instance, in Hereford and Worcester etc, they have what's call the "warned list" system, so they will say that your trial will come into the list in any time within a two-week slot, and you're expected to keep yourself available for that. ... If it doesn't get in, you've wasted two weeks and you can't take other work to cover it. It's ludicrous. ... You lost continuity, because no one in their right mind is going to keep themselves free on the off chance it comes in then, so you get late returns, the counsel having never met the client before, people having to re-prep and doubling, trebling of work. Clients unhappy because you turn [up], "Who the fuck are you? I've never seen you before. What do you know about my case?"' (BS9)

Again, the workload pressures in combination with way in which cases were listed meant that cases were being passed to others, thus undermining the rapport between the barrister and the client, and thus further undermining the lawyer–client relationship.[7]

Among the barristers interviewed, there were concerns that judges were not particularly forgiving of the pressures that barristers faced, although it was acknowledged that some judges were more empathetic than others. For BS9, "It has always been an issue but it kind of goes through periods depending on the judges." BS9 explained judges' attitudes with specific reference to the practice of cross-courting (whereby lawyers take on cases in different courtrooms on the same day):

'When I first started up in [the Midlands] one of the judges there, he would be apoplectic if you crossed court and kept him waiting for thirty seconds, and when he went there was a more relaxed attitude. And certain judges here now are not so relaxed about it. So it depends on which judge is sitting and how fragile is he, if he's having to sit there for ten minutes being kept waiting. ... We had one recently who was a very busy barrister. I used to be in Chambers with him. He's still a mate of mine. And we'd be, typically, in the good old days in Merthyr with ten cases, thirteen cases each on a Friday. And we'd both be cross-courting like mad, but the judges

---

[7] This has a similar effect to the situation with overloaded solicitors passing around cases as and when practitioners had the time to deal with them identified by Newman (2013a).

knew that we'd get the work done. And they allowed it to a certain extent. Then he got made a judge and he banned cross-courting. ... There needs to be more recognition by the judiciary and flexibility built into the listing day so that counsel can do his own cases to avoid double prep, to avoid wasted expenditure, to allow clients to have continuity of representation, and all the hassle that goes with [changing representation].'

As BS9 highlighted, even those judges who engaged in cross-courting practices when at the Bar could be unsympathetic to the plight of barristers. It was felt that judges needed to be more cognizant of the pressures that barristers faced and that listings had to be more flexible to take account of the unpredictable nature of cases. Time pressures were not only faced by barristers, however. Both solicitors and the police also struggled to manage their workloads, although for solicitors the issue was the amount of work required to make their business viable; for the police the pressures centred on paperwork and administration.

Time pressures, in various ways, were a common motif among the practitioners, as was the concern regarding increased workloads – pursued in the name of bureaucracy and management – and mounting form filling and box ticking. Added to these pressures were budget cuts that made the mounting work even less manageable. We unpick these in the following section, focusing in particular on the implications of the aforementioned problems on the future of the criminal defence profession.

The future of criminal defence

The legally aided criminal defence professions are inherently – at least following austerity – precarious; it has been remarked that 'the prospects for criminal legal aid in England and Wales are bleak' (Smith and Cape, 2017: 63). As noted in Chapter 2, there are serious concerns about the future of the criminal defence profession. Of particular concern is the dearth of individuals entering the profession and the ageing population of criminal legal aid lawyers, particularly criminal duty solicitors. These issues are caused, either directly or indirectly, by the dire funding situation.

In Chapter 3 we learnt that most of the lawyers we interviewed did not enter criminal defence due to any great conviction (such as for what we called the 'social agenda'). It may have been interesting enough to steal their focus while, as for most, they just drifted into criminal practice without any obvious pull. If financial remuneration was so unattractive as to actively deter lawyers, then the chances of appealing to all but the most socially committed minority would be limited. The lawyers in our study thus spoke in stark terms about the future of the criminal defence profession (see also Dehaghani and Newman, 2021a):

'The real cuts have affected everybody … the number of providers in, you know, Cardiff and Gwent have dropped significantly. I was a partner in a firm, and we stopped doing crime because it didn't make money. And I think lots of firms are in that position at the moment where they are considering their future in terms of crime, certainly legal aid crime. And that's one of the problems that you've got with crime, is being able to offer a young lawyer a worthwhile salary. And, because you've got to work your way up the system, so you're going to spend the first few years doing police-station call-outs and Magistrates' cases. You know, pardon the expression, the shitty end of the stick. But you're going to be on a salary of what, fifteen or sixteen grand? You know, you can earn that at sort of middle-management in Tesco if you wanted to, but you've got to deal with the pressure of the job, the issues of the job, the judicial bullying from the district judges and the magistrates, three AM callouts to the police station and that's the salary you're being paid. Why would you do it? Unless it's your calling, which I think is unfortunately this position we're in with crime these days, unless it's something you really want to do, they're not doing it. Which is why we've got this crisis of criminal legal aid lawyers, that there's no youngsters coming through.' (DS9)

The pessimism evident within this quote stemmed from the funding cuts and the impact that this has had upon recruitment into the criminal defence profession. DS9 went on to recount how "my last trainee did crime for, probably three years qualified" but has since taken a job in London for Price Waterhouse Coopers where "they've offered him sort of seventy-thousand pounds and a fast-track promotion". The practical reality of funding cuts – and the related ability of firms to take on trainees, as addressed earlier – meant that firms were unable to recruit young lawyers. These young lawyers were also – understandably – deterred from joining or remaining within the profession. As DS9 highlighted, the gruelling work for criminal defence practitioners (as also discussed in Chapter 3) such as the calls at anti-social hours, the abuse from the judiciary, and the general pressures, make the job, in light of the remuneration available, an unpalatable option (see also Newman and Welsh, 2019). For those who choose to enter the legal profession, criminal defence work proves an unpopular choice as suggested by DS17:

'There's no – hardly any new people coming through. And that shouldn't be the case, there should be more funding and more incentive for younger people to come into crime because we need a criminal justice system; we're always going to need legal aid. But starting out again, I probably wouldn't go into it and that's because of the work and the money.'

Such an account echoes Harris et al (2021) in their highlighting of how difficult it is for a legal academics teaching criminal law at a university to recommend criminal defence as a viable career choice to their students. In this vein, the rising cost of tuition fees was another deterring factor for junior lawyers that we were often told about:

'We do a lot of work experience. It's an interesting area, isn't it, especially if you're sixteen, seventeen. You know, "I want to be a criminal lawyer." But at some stage after you've incurred your fifty thousand pound plus university tuition fees and your LPC fees are even more, how are you going to pay back seventy thousand pounds on what you earn as a criminal legal aid lawyer? I was lucky enough, my debt was very low for my generation. But they've got huge debts to shoulder, haven't they, and you've got to start earning money … I mean it's difficult to persuade somebody to do a profession if you're not going to be properly numerated for it.' (DS5)

Young Legal Aid Lawyers (2018) have illustrated that the resultant debt that new lawyers shoulder, in combination with the (relatively) low remuneration within criminal legal aid work, can inhibit entry into legal aid work. For DS5, the cost of qualifying as a solicitor was thus compared with how much the criminal solicitor would earn from criminal legal aid work, and it was acknowledged that young lawyers could not be expected to be driven by goodwill alone. Indeed, one of the lawyers in our sample noted that they were only able to practise because of their partner's income:

'Police station reps particularly and duty solicitors, they're not getting any younger and at some point, they're going to need to retire and what's going to happen then is that there's going to be a huge gap. What I would say is the friends that I've gone to university with, whether they're training or whether they're still paralegals, I probably couldn't work in crime long-term if it was – I've got a good partner and my partner helps out a lot – but if it wasn't for the fact that my income's more of a side-income, I don't think it would be enough to support a family and a household, especially not as a younger person when you've got to pay off all your LPC loans.' (DS8)

Sommerlad (2012) has highlighted the marginality of such legal aid work – more privileged social groups have options and will focus on areas of law with higher status. Those who lack privilege – Sommerlad talks along class, gender and ethnicity lines – will find their only choice for a legal career is in a 'degraded' area such as criminal legal aid. Criminal defence with its low remuneration and high workloads – as DS17, DS5 and DS8 indicated – will appeal to only the most passionate or desperate (see also Newman, 2018). The profession and those working within it could be considered precarious. Not only is legally aided criminal defence as a profession in sharp decline, lawyers engaging in such work may be unable to sustain a living from their own work alone, thus exacerbating their precarity. The precarity of the legal profession was viewed as particularly marked in Wales:

> 'The younger son is considering doing law … work placements in London firms. Regrettably, that's where I think young talent is going to end up from south Wales and Wales generally which is a shame. But when you're talking about being paid seventy-five grand in the London firms to do your training contract there's no comparison is there?' (DS5)

Even the Welsh capital city could not compete with the pay on offer in the English capital city. DS5's response reflected data reported in Chapter 2 showing a paucity of criminal solicitors in some parts of Wales:

> 'Well it depends where you are, doesn't it, in mid Wales, north Wales? At the moment it's very difficult to find anybody. I've got a friend who's got a practice in mid Wales, and they can't get anybody, and I think that's going to come, there are still youngsters who want to come into the profession in south Wales, but I think that's going to become the same. … Why would you go into a profession when you could be earning twice as much doing a job, and another type of law or working in another city? Despite how much you might enjoy the job, it's an impossible conundrum to be faced with.'

Issues of recruitment were thus marked in more rural areas of Wales; however, it was also acknowledged that the trend would eventually make its way to south Wales. Others pointed towards the impact on more remote (often, post-industrial) areas within south Wales, such as in parts of the Valleys (see also Dehaghani and Newman, 2021a):

> 'I mean, even in Abergavenny there were probably about ten firms of solicitors when I first started; there's now three. And in Ebbw Vale, two or three, out of, maybe – there were ten or fifteen. So, it's just declined and declined and declined … and I think if you waited another

five years … the, the figures would go down dramatically, there's just nothing in it for them, why would you do it?' (DS19)

This was not only a regional or national problem, of course; similar trends will stretch across the jurisdiction. Barristers also experienced problems with recruitment, reporting the decline of the criminal Bar, both locally, and across England and Wales:

'Generally, criminal law, or the criminal Bar, is dying from the ground up. I would be amazed if there's a criminal Bar in fifty years' time. … You look at all Chambers around the country, and you look at the criminal teams in each of those Chambers? They're just getting smaller and smaller, and older and older. And it's because legal aid is obviously killing it.' (BS12)

That the criminal Bar might be declining in this manner was a major anxiety among the barristers with whom we spoke, articulated in more or less bleak terms in every barrister interview (BS1–16) that we conducted. BS2 reflected on this and how they now spoke to others about their work:

'I think it's a troubling time ahead for the criminal Bar … I used to have students come with me, and I'd be evangelical about the job and say, "This is a terrific job, it's a good career, if you're passionate and you're interested, go for it, because you'll really enjoy it." Seven or eight years ago, things started to change. Now, if people come with me for work experience, I'm putting amber lights in their way, and red lights, when I used to be wholly green. It's a much different landscape now to juniors coming through, which is a great shame.'

While a career at the criminal Bar was once viewed by BS2 as a "terrific job", the "landscape" was now viewed as very different; the decline has been quite recent and somewhat coincides with the advent of austerity. It is therefore not simply solicitors who are discouraging students from engaging in criminal defence practice; barristers also feel reluctant to encourage students to engage in criminal defence at the Bar, yet such problems went beyond recruitment. This was suggested by BS11:

'Retention is the main problem. Retaining people. They'll come in, they'll start off the mixed practice, and then they'll go off. I think retention is an issue, in any event, with kind of young people at the Bar – at the legal profession, actually. You'll see a lot leaving and then not coming back.'

From a financial perspective, sustaining criminal work proved difficult for barristers, some of whom, as a result, decided to focus on more lucrative areas of legal practice. As BS15 noted, "I'm not going to do crime and my principal reason for that is money." BS12 also highlighted poor pay as a crucial factor that would discourage lawyers from engaging in criminal practice:

'And the misleading thing is you get paid two hundred pound a day for it, which you may think is, "oh that's amazing, that's a thousand pound a week". That is an unbelievable amount of money for a lot of people. It's a huge salary. But you, you'd have to pay me double to do that, just the sheer amount of work and stress and quite frankly you're putting your practice on the line a lot of the time because there are things that happen that you just think, how has that been allowed to happen. ... It's really tough ... go family law or civil law and it's a dream.'

Although remuneration is not necessarily poor at the Bar, it was not seen to reflect the pressures of criminal practice. It was also acknowledged that more senior barristers were still well remunerated, thus giving the false impression that work at the criminal Bar pays:

'And I think that, the worst part about it is that criminal law, probably for QCs and Silks, still pays really well and they're having an absolute ball of a time, some of them. And even the very senior, junior practitioners that are doing these huge fraud cases, especially maybe in London.' (BS12)

It was also recognized that some senior barristers, particularly those working in London, were well remunerated and were able to engage in "big" cases. Yet, this reflected only the "top ten per cent of the profession" (BS12); the remainder were suffering immensely and were either resigned to accept their lot, particularly for those who were "ten, fifteen, twenty years in [and] looking for other jobs" (BS12). Therefore, the minority were doing well, but the majority were struggling. Many of the barristers with whom we spoke discussed the significance of the recruitment gap, yet some also noted, as earlier, the issues with retention:

'We do have some junior members of Chambers, but we've also got a huge gap ... between people of my call or just below, so sort of 2002 through to, I think, 2012, so about a ten-year gap ... it reflects the fact that [this is] the stage where people are starting young families, isn't it? So, people coming into it at that stage, people start off and then have just had to walk away from it. Now I hope that the people who have joined us and are below that gap ... are going to be able to make it all the way through, but we'll have to see. ... When they get towards the end of their twenties, when they start thinking about families, then that's going to be the point when we'll see whether they'll make it through or whether they will step away from it ... the worst case scenario would be, if in twenty years, we haven't got any criminal Bar ... and this is not unique to the Bar: it's also happening in the criminal solicitors.' (BS10)

BS10 reiterated the effect of criminal legal aid cuts on both solicitors and barristers and how this may later adversely impact recruitment. Reduced funding was creating both a crisis in retention and recruitment and was reducing morale, which BS6 noted was "really low". Part of the effect was that, while barristers were still earning good money, they were unable to have a life outside of work:

'It just the workload is getting heavier and heavier and heavier, the pressures are getting heavier, what's expected of everybody is getting greater, and the money is getting less. And when I first started at the Bar ... there was kind of a feeling as though it was almost like a lifestyle, you know? So, there was a lot of socializing outside of work ... you kind of felt like you were part of something. ... Because people did sort of see a lot of each other, not just within work but outside as well ... people just haven't got time and are so stressed at trying to do the things that they have to do for work, and nobody's got time to go for a drink after work or go for lunch or whatever ... obviously you can still earn a good living at the criminal Bar. Nobody is going, "Oh, boo hoo, again, I earn five pound fifty an hour," but it's actually, for the level of stress and the number of hours that you do put in, people are starting to wonder whether it was worth it.' (BS6)

The pressures of work, in addition to reducing the ability of barristers to have a healthy work–life balance, also created significant challenges for women. Some of the most talented and popular members of the local Bar had recently moved on to careers outside practice (see also Bar Standards Board, 2016).[8] Of particular note was the exhausting nature of the work and how this was incompatible with having a family. Cooke (2019) has noted

---

[8] The impact upon women was noted as a serious concern among the barristers we spoke to. However, owing to our concerns regarding anonymity, we have not identified the gender of the participants in this study. Issues of anonymity have also restricted the material we felt able to use to speak to this subject as much of the detail on gendered experiences would have led to interviewees being identifiable.

that women in legal aid work often find themselves with a dilemma between furthering their legal career and/or continuing with a cause they believe in or pursuing their desire to have children, and that these were not typically seen as complementary. This is a continuation of the problems of recruitment but introduced a further context – gender. The gendered problems were identified by several barristers in this study, such as BS4:

'Since September, we have lost from the criminal bar in Cardiff, three senior criminal female practitioners. We've got an issue with retention after maternity leave, as well. But this isn't only limited to women, this issue. The problem is this … it's mentally exhausting and it's just really hard work … working forty hours a week would just be lovely … when I'm in a case I work sixty to eighty hours a week. And we're constantly bombarded with emails. By the time you leave, that will be full of emails and most will be totally irrelevant: they're just asking for boxes to be ticked and, you know, buck being passed and stuff like that. It's exhausting. And then we've lost two recently. They're both fantastic, and they're both really skilled barristers, lovely people, everything you'd want in your criminal barrister. … But they just said, you know, "Enough … I want a job where, a different working environment where it's less abrasive, where it's more regulated, and I just want out." The hourly rate sometimes is just ridiculous. It would be below minimum wage.'

Unlike solicitors, barristers are often self-employed and remuneration for their work can thus be unpredictable. The amount of work involved also, as noted earlier, is not reflected in remuneration. The antisocial working hours and unbearable workloads (see Bar Council, 2017) made caring responsibilities difficult. To further worsen the problem, the hyper-macho culture – described by some such as BS11 as "bullying" – meant that barristers, particularly female barristers, were leaving the Bar. There were concerns that they would not be the last ones to leave – and that there was a particularly worrying (and evident) gendered element to the problem (see Bar Standards Board, 2016). The balance between work and life, particularly caring responsibilities, was noted by BS6:

'Doing criminal law, there's no way that you can only work so many days a week, it just doesn't work like that. If you want to do trials and practise properly then you have to work Monday to Friday. But the way I got around that was by trying to take more weeks off a year, so taking say school holidays off or whatever, and that made quite a big difference. And just, the attitude has changed massively between, certainly the clerks I think were historically very difficult about it. …

There's a lot of women who are quite senior in Chambers and perhaps have felt as if they've had to do it, to get through it, and why should things be different for younger people? There's quite a lot of resentment towards people ... but just the job itself, the fact that you often have to work until late into the night, you have to work at weekends. It's very difficult when you've got children, and I think even though ... there's no obvious reason why that should be different for women than for men, it just is a lot of the time and women take on a lot more of the caring responsibilities.'

The care work that women perform far outweighs that performed by men and was a major problem cited by women barristers by the Bar Standards Board (2016). As such, the gruelling work required of criminal barristers weighed heavily on women. Added to these pressures were the unsympathetic attitudes of some within the Bar, but also from clerks and the judiciary. The wider culture of the Bar was also said to be unpleasant:

'But there are lots of other issues, and one of them is definitely that women I think find the, I was going to say the confrontational nature of it. Nobody goes into it unless you're happy to be to some extent confrontational ... there's nobody at the criminal bar who isn't able to fight their corner; you wouldn't be there otherwise. But I think the way that judges speak to people, I think that often women find that more difficult. I say that, but actually I wonder if it's just that women are either happier to admit it and happier to do something about it.' (BS6)

The unhealthy work–life balance combined with toxic working conditions may increase the incidence of mental health problems in the profession (Collier, 2020), particularly among junior lawyers (Junior Lawyers Division, 2019).[9] There was also widespread pessimism across the solicitors and barristers that we spoke to about the future. This was reflected by DS12 giving the specific example of barristers facing increased competition from solicitors with Higher Rights:

'The junior Bar are already struggling because people like me ... I have the Higher Rights, I practise in the Crown Court. I do my own Crown Court work. I have done for a number of years. ... When I first started doing it the Bar were all up in arms, you know, "What's this solicitor doing up here?" and I'd just say, "Look mate. I'm an advocate. I read

---

[9]   For a fuller discussion of the structural and cultural components underlining high levels of mental health problems in the legal profession see Jones et al (2020).

the same book as you. I argue the same points of law as you. It's just my qualification's different, and my robe looks a bit different. But there's nothing you can do that I can't."'

That solicitors have rights of audience in the Crown Court is not necessarily a problem in and of itself but may compound some of the already existing problems within the Bar – both would be competing for the same work and, as criminal legal aid cuts continue to bite for solicitors and as they search for profit, there is likely to be an increased presence of this branch of the profession in the Crown Courts. These issues were created not necessarily by solicitors who have rights of audience, but by the funding situation for criminal legal aid generally. DS12 went on to explain:

'I don't think you're going to find a lot of young people looking to the criminal justice system as a career choice. That's what I think's going to happen. And there will be more cuts. There will be more cuts; the cuts will be deeper. But they will cut and cut, and there'll be nothing left there to cut, and that's when there'll be a problem because there will not be people there to represent people who need representing and can't afford to be represented.'

The decline of the criminal defence profession not only raises issues of recruitment and retention, but also signals a diminishing of access to justice for the accused. The feeling among some lawyers was that the government was making a concerted effort to degrade the criminal legal aid system and undermine criminal defence:

'When it became a bit more obvious what was happening, I tended to assume that it was the government's long-term approach to dumb down the defence service so as to make life easier for the police and the CPS, because if life is easier for the police and the CPS, it's cheaper. And I'm still convinced that is the model they're working on.' (DS6)[10]

This section has captured the fear and doubt among these practitioners for the future of legally aided criminal defence, and for the criminal justice system in this part of south Wales. This is a major implication of the underfunding we explored in Chapters 2 and 3. There was, though, an awareness from the sample that, given their understanding of the negative public perception, few

---

[10] As we have argued elsewhere, the reduction in lawyer resilience has undoubtedly increased the resilience of the police and prosecution (Dehaghani and Newman, 2021b).

would care about the decline of legal aid-funded criminal defence lawyers. We will now turn to exploring those public perceptions.

Wider understanding of criminal justice problems

The negativity of public perceptions of criminal legal aid lawyers was widely discussed by the lawyers interviewed, with such opinion being said to stem from unhelpful media and political portrayals of legal aid (see Hynes and Robins, 2009). Lawyers acknowledged the reputational problems with criminal defence, particularly the apparent misconceptions regarding financial remuneration:

> 'Clients get the impression that you're a money swindler, get in get out, I'm onto the golf course this afternoon. That's the impression that the general public probably hold about the legal profession when you get to court. Dispelling that is massive, and actually the main part of dispelling that is making them know that you care about them and what happens to them, because if you don't, if it comes across like, "Yeah, he may know his stuff, he may know the case, but I don't feel like he actually cares what happens to me," that is probably a huge barrier and their walls go up then and the defendant ... doesn't get out of the justice system what he deserves. ... There are good practitioners and there are bad practitioners, but it's getting over that stigma amongst the public that lawyers are probably untrustworthy.' (BS12)

BS12 acknowledged that this myth had an impact upon the lawyer–client relationship; dispelling the myth was essential to ensure that the accused person trusted the lawyer. It was not simply clients who held an inaccurate view of criminal legal aid lawyers; the average layperson was also said to have no idea of the realities of legally aided criminal defence work:

> 'Joe Bloggs has no understanding whatsoever. The misconceptions are huge. Firstly, the amount of, everyone thinks we're millionaires, no-one really understands the amount of work that goes into it, the unsocial nature of it, the arguments that it causes with family because I can't be where I'm needed. I can't pick up the kids tonight because I'm down the police station. I can't just walk out of a trial for instance ... you'll be in a trial, witnesses can't come back the next day, we're running late and it's seven pm when you're leaving court. Or how does that work when you've got to pick up the kids from school? It doesn't. ... That causes stress within the family. And you're never not working. The only way this works is if clients have your phone numbers because if

they're arrested, they need to know that they can speak to someone. And you just get calls all the time.' (DS7)

Again, as with BS6 earlier, the nature of criminal defence work has a negative impact upon work–life balance and, in particular, upon the families of criminal defence lawyers.[11] Yet, the ability to be 'on-call' is essential to a workable lawyer–client relationship. As noted earlier, the gruelling nature of criminal defence work is not reflected in the remuneration for such work, and while the public may perceive criminal defence lawyers as having lucrative careers, the reality could not be further from the myth; it was not the "land of milk and honey" (DS7) that the public may claim it to be. The concern was that the public tended to derive their views of criminal justice from the media (see also Daw, 2020), which The Secret Barrister (2020) casts as the notion of 'fake law': a false understanding of how the justice system works based on media disinformation. DS13 expressed some of the similar sentiments we found among the lawyers in our study:

'That builds into what I said earlier about the media's portrayal of the system, and there's a lot of distrust in criminal defence solicitors I think, in terms of the general public. But that's because they don't understand the system and don't understand the role ... I think people have more faith in the police than they do in defence solicitors, but that's mainly because of the articles that are written about lenient sentences and things.'

Unprompted, numerous lawyers – in double figures – stated that reports in tabloid newspapers, such as the *Daily Mail*, were a problem for criminal defence lawyers. One such example was DS11:

'But the PR for criminal solicitors is rubbish ... you see a report a quote in the Daily Mail saying that this toe-rag has had a hundred and fifty thousand pounds worth of legal aid to fight his case, or these are the five top-earning criminal barristers who are earning X, or X amount of million a year off of legal aid. And it's very, very cynical, but it works.'

Some lawyers claimed that the legal profession generally presented itself poorly, with particular concerns raised regarding the photos that accompanied

---

[11] Forstenlechner and Lettice (2008) remind us that, even when working in a well-paid area of law, junior lawyers will often be disheartened by the time pressures they face and worn down by the demands made of them.

reports of the industrial action protesting against legal aid cuts taken in 2018. Such a sentiment was expressed by BS11:

'I don't think lawyers help themselves. Many still drive round in flashy cars even though, you know, they can't afford it. I remember ... when the strike happened a couple of years ago, and one of the barristers, you know, young female barrister outside the court on strike had a very expensive handbag in her hand, and the Daily Mail picked up on that ... I think some people still feel the need to live a certain lifestyle which is expected of lawyers, which just isn't true. You can make a good living as a lawyer in south Wales, but it won't be these kind of huge figures which people used to be able to earn back in the golden days of legal aid.'

The public perception is of privilege, wealth and the good life – the 'fat cat' image reported by Hynes and Robins (2009) may have become ingrained in public consciousness.[12] Viewing the photos of barristers on the picket line in wigs and gowns alone is enough to produce some manner of cognitive dissonance in laypeople and is unlikely to generate much sympathy as such symbols of professional high status are obvious class signifiers. The dominant image disseminated from the legal profession is typically that of a successful commercial firm (Collier, 2005); to be a legal professional is fundamentally linked with the achievement of high pay. The perception that barristers are elite professionals who drive expensive cars or carry designer handbags may undermine the message that the criminal Bar – and the criminal defence professions more generally – face serious financial constraints. The image detracts from the precarious reality of criminal defence. BS11 also indicated that, beyond remuneration, there was a need for the legal profession to more clearly emphasize the risks of undermining criminal defence:

'But there's more issues than just salaries. I think we're not good at communicating that, and that needs to be communicated much more. People need to know ... that there is a greater chance of miscarriage of justice. That there is more of a chance that they won't be able to find somebody who'll represent them. That there is a chance that if they are accused of a crime, that they will be in huge debt afterwards

---

[12] Francis and Sommerlad (2009) have shown how the legal profession has long been engaged in a project aimed at maintaining social closure for those hailing from backgrounds rich in social and cultural capital. As such, it is little wonder that this elite image has become ingrained despite the reality of precariousness (see Sommerlad, 2012).

even if they are found not guilty. I think these messages need to be sent more powerfully.'

Gibbs and Ratcliffe (2019: 7) suggest that public legal education is lacking and it is 'difficult to find high quality independent information about how the criminal justice system works'. They report that most accused persons do not know enough about the system to understand what criminal lawyers do, which is part of a wider lack of knowledge about the criminal justice system in general. Sommerlad (1999) has documented the increasingly antagonistic stance of the public towards criminal legal aid lawyers, with Newman (2013a) reporting that they felt unappreciated and undervalued. In these interviews, DS6 stated that the public only acknowledged the importance of criminal defence if they had been through the criminal process themselves:

'I don't think the public do have an idea of us. Those who rely on us and have a good experience of a defence lawyer have one view; those who have been cross-examined as witnesses for the Crown may have a totally different view of course; those who have never been in the system but read the Daily Mail will have another view ... it's difficult to know what the public think of us because there are polarizing views, and so many of them are just untrue ... those who are able to think about it and understand it will realise that, like it or not, we are an essential part of the criminal justice system. You can't operate without us. And if we lose our skills the criminal justice system is a complete nonsense. But I don't think there are many people out there who actually understand that.'

For DS6, people only recognized the value of criminal defence lawyers when they had relied on them. If this contention is true, it is obvious why the lawyers felt so unappreciated as it is only a very small proportion of the public that find themselves in these circumstances. Further, as highlighted when discussing accuseds' experiences earlier in Chapter 3 and later in Chapter 7, our interviews would cast doubt on whether all those who do rely on criminal defence lawyers would come to appreciate them. Whether the accused understand the pressure or not, those interviewed were largely antagonistic towards their lawyers.

Solicitors and barristers in this study frequently raised issues of their being disliked by the wider public. Some, such as BS4, thought they were so disdained that lawyers were not considered worthy of public funding:

'I know the general public don't care about what lawyers are paid, they just don't think we should be paid anything at all, do they? I mean if you went out and asked your average Daily Mail reader, "What should a criminal defence barrister be paid?" The answer would be, "Nothing." You know, "They shouldn't have defence," but, that's not the case. ... It's really important and it should be properly remunerated. Just, all people want is to be paid fairly for what they do.'

DS9 thought it understandable that clients did not consider the pressures exerted upon legally aided criminal defence lawyers. Specifically, DS9 questioned why their clients should know or care about these pressures; the clients were – understandably – only interested in matters pertaining to their own case:

'I don't think they care. I don't think I would, if I was a defendant. Why is that my concern? I don't go to the GP thinking ... "What are you being paid?" All I want to know is how you're going to treat me. You know, what's going to happen to me in terms of my lump or whatever it is, whatever my condition is? How you're funding your practice or what you're being paid is no concern of mine.'

One of the consequences of misunderstandings of criminal defence work is the ease with which cuts are made (as discussed in Chapter 2):

'No there's no votes in crime, is there? You know, we're the whipping boys whenever it comes to anything like that people always, friends, even friends say, "Well, how can you represent guilty people?" And you're like, "Well do you realise, do you know, the percentage of people that are arrested that are actually charged? Because it's very low. Or the amount, the percentage of people that are vulnerable?" No, I don't think the public really understands it. I think they think ... we're there just representing guilty people and trying to get them off on technicalities. Which isn't the way it works. Technicalities tend to be the facts. So ... they don't get it. ... The only sort of exposure that a lot of people have to it is reading press reports about horrible people doing horrible things ... they assume that everyone going through the criminal justice system must be a horrible person doing a horrible thing. Because they don't see that that is the tip of the iceberg and then the bottom of the iceberg is a load of people who haven't.' (DS1)

Again, DS1 raised concerns that media reporting of criminal cases contributed to this misunderstanding of criminal defence work. Rather than acknowledging that those who are not guilty may nevertheless be suspected of an offence, it is assumed that those accused of crimes are, in fact, guilty. The public does not understand the complexities of the law and the media do not always report in a manner that reflects such complexities (see The

Secret Barrister, 2020). The idea that criminal legal aid was not a "vote-winner" was a refrain we heard repeatedly from the lawyers in this study. It means people do not think about or take seriously the problems of criminal justice. For BS16, "People would be amazed, honestly, at their public justice system and how it's creaking." There may be a lack of understanding of the problems facing the criminal justice system. This lack of understanding may allow the criminal justice system to be further decimated. Political will to improve the system is absent because being perceived to be lenient on 'criminals' is simply not a popular cause.

Conclusion

This chapter has highlighted some of the pressures faced by the criminal justice system, and, in particular, the pressures faced by practitioners. Following the more contextual Chapter 3 (on the participants) and Chapter 4 (on the place), this was the first of three chapters to consider the issues raised at interview in greater detail. As such, it was important to begin by considering the working conditions of the practitioners as, to a large degree, this sets the context for the accused's interactions with and in the criminal process. The state of legal aid is placing criminal defence practitioners under significant strain (Newman, 2013a; Smith and Cape, 2017). Their practice is undervalued and underpaid, particularly given the amount and level of work required on a case. The pressure is further exacerbated by 'efficiency' and 'cost-saving' measures that require practitioners – both lawyers and police officers – to engage in bureaucratic accounting exercises. For barristers, the pressures are yet further compounded by cultural factors such as bullying and a lack of sympathy from others. This makes it difficult for women to enter and remain in the profession, but also creates more general – non-gendered – issues with recruitment and retention. Young lawyers are discouraged – whether of their own volition or by others – from entering the criminal defence professions. The issues with recruitment and retention are perhaps more pronounced in Wales than in England. The result is a pessimism regarding the profession generally and the sustainability of the profession specifically. This is further compounded by a lack of public understanding regarding the pressures faced by criminal defence, particularly that which is legally aided. The unsympathetic attitudes of the public towards criminal defence practitioners emerge, in part, through unhelpful – and often misguided – media and political discourse. There are thus numerous and various challenges facing criminal defence and, by extension, access to justice for the accused.

We have accepted the accounts of the solicitors and barristers in this study, not as we are in thrall to them and see them as arbiters of truth, but because these are their stories. Some points may be embellished, and others contested or challenged, but, as with the accused in Chapter 3, they are the lived experiences of these practitioners. We appreciate that their accounts of their financial struggles may not attract automatic sympathy from the wider public, not simply because they are misleadingly labelled 'fat cats' by the media, but also because they work in a profession which, despite its problems, could be perceived as relatively privileged. For some ordinary working class people, the profession is one that many may only dream of succeeding in – or, indeed, entering. Yet, it is important to remember that to ensure access to the profession, those entering it must be adequately remunerated. Social mobility may be impossible to achieve if one is languishing on barely more than minimum wage after spending upwards of £50,000 on a university education (see Young Legal Aid Lawyers, 2018). The precarity and relatively low professional standing of the criminal defence professions (see Sommerlad, 2012; Thornton, 2020), in addition to rising concerns regarding access to justice, is also problematic if considered within the frame of access to the profession. However, this also has an impact on the incidences of poor mental health and stress experienced within the profession (Junior Lawyers Division, 2019; Collier, 2020).[13] The lived experiences of criminal defence practitioners and their dissatisfaction with the profession are important when attempting to understand their interactions with others within the criminal process. For Cooke (2019), the reduced well-being of – what she considers – a precarious legal aid workforce will limit their ability to provide client care; the damaging impact of austerity must be understood as a problem that impacts on lawyers and clients alike.

The pressures of criminal practice highlight the lack of resilience experienced by – and provided to – solicitors and barristers reliant on income through legal aid. The precarity of this work should be understood within the vulnerability frame – criminal legal aid lawyers and the institution of criminal legal aid itself should be considered vulnerable. With this recognized, we can understand the ability of austerity to strip their resilience. There is a resultant lack of resilience provided to these lawyers through, for example, the absence of support and sympathy for those engaging in criminal practice from public and government alike. The lawyers in this study did not feel appreciated or supported. The ability of these practitioners to do their jobs is thus impacted, which reflects a reduction in their resilience. There will also be downstream effects, chiefly to the strength of the lawyer–client relationship, as we will explore in Chapter 6. The reduced resilience of these lawyers also presents an effective curb on the resilience of the clients who rely upon them: if lawyers feel unable to investigate or prepare a case

---

[13]   Francis and Fleck (2021) have shown how legal aid lawyers can also develop vicarious trauma through working on emotionally potent caseloads.

as they should and/or if they cannot spend the time with clients that they would like, then the accused is receiving a lower standard of care. It is in these circumstances that we begin to question whether inadequate funding has undermined access to justice; the institution that should equip the accused with resilience is being challenged. Although this is fundamentally an argument about the quality of justice, the precarity of these lawyers is also illustrated by essential doubts regarding the quantity of justice, and whether there will be enough lawyers in the system to provide any kind of service to the accused in future. The profession is thus also precarious; applying a vulnerability lens helps us understand the significance of this precarity for profession, lawyer and client.

This chapter has commenced the process of expanding on the detail from Chapter 3 – on the backgrounds of practitioners – and enriches the exploration of criminal justice experiences in south Wales from Chapter 4, offering greater discussion on the pressures facing criminal legal aid and the undermining of access to criminal justice. This issue is felt across south Wales and, following Thornton (2019) and Welsh (2017), indeed across the England and Wales jurisdiction. Yet, the challenges facing criminal defence are not entirely unique – the police, the CPS and the judiciary are all working within a crumbling criminal process (see Nicklas-Carter, 2019). Harris et al (2021) have called for greater recognition of the interconnectedness faced by those within and those encountering the criminal process. Giving voice to those often marginalized necessitates a prioritization for the accused and family members to get their narratives across, to the detriment, perhaps, of more general discussion on the pressures facing lawyers. In the next chapter we shift our focus to key relationships in the criminal process, examining the interconnectedness and interwovenness of these experiences, and explicating how underfunding and time pressures have undermined these relationships. The next chapter thus takes our exploration of practitioner pressures a stage further to explore the impact on casework and clients.

6

Criminal Justice Relationships

Introduction

In the previous chapter, we considered some of the pressures that criminal justice practitioners faced and the resultant negative impact on the criminal process. The chapter examined problems stemming from inadequate legal aid and the way that this undermined criminal legal practice. In this chapter, we consider how those pressures impact upon relationships – operating within the parameters imposed by underfunding – between different parties in the criminal process.

Within this chapter we examine the experiences of 'others' in the criminal process, specifically those accused of committing criminal offences, interrogating how various parties within the criminal process understood their own experiences and those of others. The roles of actors within the criminal justice system may have a bearing on the values within the system (McConville and Marsh, 2014). In particular, the shift between 'due process' to 'criminal control' has signalled an anti-accused ideology with increasing police corruption, decreasing evidential standards, lawyers' antagonism towards clients, harsher sentences, and inducements for guilty pleas (McConville and Marsh, 2014). Indeed, previous research has pointed towards the need to investigate interactions between key actors in a holistic manner (Newman and Ugwudike, 2013).[1] Through examining interactions and relationships, we can understand how the process is experienced and, crucially, how it operates.

A prominent subject emerging from our research is how important it is for good relations to be built between various actors. While individuals and parties to the process may hold different worldviews and possess varying responsibilities, it was evident that essential to the functioning of the

---

[1]   Newman and Ugwudike (2013) compared the experiences of defence lawyers and probation workers in their interactions with defendants.

criminal justice system was the establishment of some common ground. Yet, some differences – such as the perspective of the arresting police officer and the suspect protesting their innocence – may be irreconcilable and, in some instances, we may prefer there to be greater distinctions between, for example, the views of prosecution and defence, particularly on matters such as negotiated settlement. Of particular concern is the danger of the courtroom culture and how it may cause a shift in the defence lawyer's mindset away from the needs of the accused person (their client) and towards the needs of the prosecution and the state they represent (Heumann, 1978), thus working against 'zealous advocacy' (Smith, 2013).

We begin this chapter by examining practitioner relationships within the criminal justice system. Our focus is on how solicitors and barristers forge relationships with others working in the criminal process. We then consider the place of the accused by exploring how practitioners view them. What emerges are the judgements and assumptions that are made by practitioners about the accused. Thereafter we consider the interactions that constitute the lawyer–client relationship. The lawyer interviews are used to highlight how practitioners think relationships are best developed and the challenges that they face in fostering good relations. We end by examining one particular challenge to the relationship through the example of the sentence discount for an early guilty plea. This is shown to impact the lawyer–client relationship and shape the involvement of the accused in the criminal justice system.

This chapter builds on the theme of underfunding that was highlighted by practitioners in Chapter 3 and developed in Chapters 4 and 5, by drawing out also the theme of the accused's previous experience of the criminal justice system. It also picks up the importance of the other theme we identified in Chapter 3; the impact that the prior experience of the accused person has on their place in the criminal justice system. Relationships, in terms of what lawyers expect of clients and how they think that clients digest the information provided by lawyers, fall within the 'first-timer' versus 'regular' dichotomy. As such, this chapter should be read through that lens, and the practitioners' views of their relationships grounded in the different assumptions they make about clients as set out earlier.

Practitioner relationships

Relationships are at the heart of the criminal justice system. Flower (2018) characterizes criminal justice as being made up of 'team-work'; she identifies the criminal defence lawyer as part of this team – alongside police, prosecutors and the judiciary. In this section, we consider that team approach and, in particular, the approach taken to the development of those relationships by the lawyers in this study. Blaustone (1990) has set out the often underappreciated importance of interpersonal skills in legal work, noting that working with others is a key part of the lawyer's role. The solicitor–barrister relationship was discussed at greatest length, although we also examine the relationships between defence lawyers and the police, prosecution and judiciary.

The relationships between barristers and solicitors were said to be crucial, particularly, as BS9 explained, for the benefit of the client:

'It's much easier to work with a firm that you can trust, and they can trust you. ... They know when you say you need X, Y and Z done at a particular time, it does need to be done. There are solicitors that I routinely work for ... we don't just communicate nine to five. We'll be emailing and calling each other up to sort of eleven o'clock at night, twelve o'clock at night if things need doing. The lines are always open. And a very good working relationship with a good solicitor is hugely important. It increases your ability to do your job for the client, significantly.'

With transparency and communication, the relationship between these parties improves; this can have a positive effect on case progression through the system. Important to the relationship for BS9 was "in person" contact; those interactions "at the other end of the phone", such as with those based in London, were inherently more strained.

Generally, the relationships between solicitors and barristers in south Wales were said to be positive. This, in part, came about through the small size of the circuit (as discussed in Chapter 4) – a "small pool" for (BS7) – which meant that barristers "tend to get to know the defence solicitors" (BS7). Solicitors were viewed as particularly valuable for engendering positive relations between the barrister and the accused: as BS3 expressed, "When I gave advice, the solicitor would back it up." While, in this instance, BS3 was supported by their solicitor and appreciated the help, there were broader concerns that the solicitor–barrister relationship was changing:

'The solicitor doesn't get paid to come to the court hearings that you do now, so they only turn up if its, as a PR exercise really, for the client, on the first day of the trial, to make sure they're alright, or if you've got lots of defence witnesses that they have to help with and take statements from and marshal, and so that's only really when you'd see a solicitor during the trial. I know people think they didn't do anything apart from sit behind you and take a note, but they did that much more, you know? They looked after the client, dealt with their concerns when you were busy dealing with other barristers and the things you had to do, they would be the front of house dealing with all that, while you were busy in the background doing what needed to be done for the trial. And they had a good relationship – normally the solicitor would have a relationship with the client, much more long-standing than you had.' (BS8)

The dynamics of the relationship between the barrister and solicitor were changing, and this, as BS8 highlighted, has emerged from changes to the criminal legal aid landscape and, specifically, the inability or unwillingness of the solicitor to attend court. Indeed, due to "constraints of the money", it was more common for "a paralegal trainee [to] sit behind counsel, where [it] used to be that the lawyer would do a lot more of that" (DS1). This may also have an adverse impact on the barrister–accused relationship, the level of service offered to the accused, the experience of the accused, and, potentially, the outcomes of the criminal process.

The relationships that the defence had with the police and prosecution were also commented upon.[2] DS6 expressed the dominant view of our lawyer sample, that relationships were founded upon professionalism:

'One word: professional. Four words: professional on my part. It can be difficult if you form friendships, especially if you form friendships say with police officers. You may have to cross-examine that police officer, you know, and it can be an issue. And the same with, you know, judges, CPS … you've got to keep it professional.'

This professional relationship between the police and defence was said to be beneficial for the accused: "We get far more done down the police station by being nice to officers rather than just going down there like a bull in a china shop" (DS7). Indeed, Blackstock et al (2014: 341) suggest lawyers in their study 'considered it important to cultivate good working relationships with the police in order to gain maximum information about the case and to open up possibilities for negotiation'.[3] Such value to this relationship was identified by lawyers in Newman (2013a), who reported that a 'them and us' approach would not help the lawyers' clients. The need for amicable relationships between the defence and police was seen as more pressing for solicitors than for barristers:

---

[2] McConville et al (1994) previously questioned relationships between defence lawyers and the police, and whether they adversely impacted the accused. For example, they were suspicious of how legal executives that represent suspects at the police station were often former police officers.

[3] See also Pivaty (2020: 166–7).

'Most solicitors have a very close relationship with the police, unlike barristers. It's in our interest to keep things sweet with the police, whereas a barrister, it's not in their interest. They can go in guns blazing because they don't have that much interaction. The police are usually pretty good. ... They don't want to cause any problems. Unless there's a specific problem which has to be addressed, I'm not going to be a pain in the police's behind, just for the sake of it. Some solicitors put on a show for their clients and push their police around for no reason really.' (DS2)

DS2 here accused some solicitors of what Mungham and Thomas (1979: 179) label pyrotechnics: 'the demonstration of sustained aggression and a fancy piece of theatrics ... deliberate manufacture of emotion and display'. As Newman (2013a) identified, aggressive displays towards police offers are an easy way to win clients over (and a means to ensure client satisfaction even when a solicitor might not actually have put much work into the case). Yet, as Newman (2013a) also notes, such anti-police displays were generally fruitless; solicitors realized that an antagonistic attitude towards the police was unlikely to allow for much progress on a case. It may be in this context that solicitors in our study largely recognized the need to be courteous towards police officers as doing otherwise could be counterproductive. As was also noted, barristers were purportedly better able to distance themselves from police officers and therefore take a more adversarial approach. The dynamics between solicitors and the police in south Wales was also noted as more positive than elsewhere: "Solicitors generally have a great relationship with the police in this area. When I was working in [south of England], it was a bit, it was a little bit different: they were more stand-offish, the police" (DS2).

Following Blackstock et al (2014), it appears that smaller towns and more rural areas are the types of locations that can lead to closer relationships between police and lawyers as the two sets of practitioners come to develop a shared history. There may have been an element of this in our south Wales sample, as befits the nature of the place (discussed in Chapter 4). However, not all solicitors in our research celebrated such amity. Indeed, this friendliness was highlighted as something that could be problematic by DS16 (see Welsh, 2022):

'I found coming to Wales very strange because it's very friendly. I'm not keen on that! So, when I practised in London, there's a hundred police stations in London, if I'm a duty solicitor for central London, that covers eight police stations, so I'll be buzzing backwards and forwards. I never come across the same copper twice, I just didn't ... at Cardiff, I do see the same police officers over and over and over and over again, and I don't think it's good that the lawyers and the police officers are so friendly ... they know a lot about each other, they know a lot about each other's personal lives, "Hey Dave, see the rugby?" It's like this in the solicitor's room, and then we go in, and I think it must be very difficult to maintain an adversarial stance, or to make robust representations.'

But DS16's was very much a minority view that was not repeated by the other solicitors; DS2's stance, by contrast, was widely held. That a hostile dynamic was not generally presented might problematize the adversarial contest – and this concern underpinned DS16's worries about solicitors and police being too friendly. Some of the accused and their families showed concern regarding the implications of this personal amity on professional practice. The closeness of the relationship between solicitors, and the police and prosecution signalled corruption for FM9:

'I've done a little bit of homework, and I've found out that [lawyers] are known for working with the police and working with the CPS ... you can see that they're all in it together, and they can go get a conviction, and it's a lot easier. This judicial system I think absolutely stinks.'

These relations formed an important part of FM9's anxiety over whether their lawyers were acting in their best interests: they saw their solicitor as too friendly with the police and considered this to be the reason for their family member's conviction. Yet not all solicitors spoke positively of the police. DS9, for example, stated, "My impression of policemen is not very high, I'm afraid ... their culture is pretty appalling." Overall, though, there was a less adversarial stance taken by lawyers than an outsider might expect (see also McConville et al, 1994).

While lawyers tended to have a less critical view of their relationship with the police, police officers provided a negative impression of defence solicitors:

'It wasn't a case of getting to the truth, you know, it was just a case of manipulating the witnesses and the magistrates. The defence solicitors aren't there to serve justice; they're there to serve their client and try and get them off no matter what. Whether they're guilty or not ... How many solicitors know that their defendants are guilty? They had their consultation in the cell, but I'm not sure they tell them, "Yeah, I did it." "Okay." Counsel is supposed to represent them. You know, it's a big game.' (PO4)

The view was that solicitors had little interest in the pursuit of justice and were instead concerned with "getting their client off". This also represents the public's rather cynical view of defence lawyers as discussed in

Chapter 5 – and especially in the account we provided of AC1's lack of faith in the justice system in Chapter 3. Although there were differing opinions on the degree of friendliness, authenticity of relationships, or potential deeper antagonisms, the consensus among the lawyers at least was that relationships worked well between prosecution (and police) and defence. Indeed, solicitors emphasized the importance of working together with the prosecution: "I'm of the attitude that it's cooperation; it's not conflict. Cooperation gets you so much further than just automatically going in and being, 'Right, I'm against you. You're prosecuting. You're my enemy'" (DS3). Such views represent some level of pragmatism within the adversarial system. DS1 thus raised the notion that criminal practitioners work together, echoing what has been called the 'court workgroup' (Heumann, 1978; Young, 2013):

'CPS, the majority of them, yeah, they're great. I've got colleagues who have gone to CPS in the past, I've got friends in the CPS. You know, court is a bit like school … you've known people for a very long time, so you know the clerks, you know the prosecutors, you know the ushers and everything, you all go on court-users' dos and socials and stuff … work is left at the door … everybody seems to rub along quite nicely.'

Yet, these good relationships were becoming harder to nurture because, as explained by DS7, it was "only in court" they get to meet so "you've seen them socially now and again, but, listen, they're not people you generally have much to do with to be honest". The difficulty of achieving contact with the CPS was cited by several solicitors. Many identified the issue as one of resource, affecting police and CPS alike (speaking to the general impact of austerity we outlined in Chapter 2):

'The biggest problem I find is getting hold of the CPS and the police. That I find extremely difficult, just not being able to get through. I think that's a problem in that there's a lot of unmanned police stations, and when an officer's based at an unmanned police station it's nigh-on impossible to get through, and the thing with CPS is you just get no response to phone calls or emails. I don't know if that's because they're understaffed, though, but that's the biggest frustration.' (DS13)

The small-scale nature of the south Wales circuit did, however, allow for a positive working relationship between defence and prosecution:

'I think the relationship between prosecution and defence barristers is good in south Wales because it's very rare to be just a defence barrister. There's not many people who start just solely defence and have never done a prosecution brief or vice versa. There is a general understanding as to the pressures the other person's under, and then that can develop more discussion between the two of you.' (BS7)

The combination of defence and prosecution work necessitated by the size of the circuit made for a mutual appreciation and understanding of the pressures facing both prosecution and defence. However, the police were perplexed and frustrated by the closeness of relationships within the small south Wales circuit: "I've known where the judge and both barristers were in the same chambers. And then, I've been in one case where they were also all changed places the defence becomes the prosecution. So, again that's something us people don't understand" (PO3). The phrasing of "us people" may speak to PO3's lack of identification with the lawyers, adding to the negative slant on the police–lawyer relationship emanating from the police, as displayed by PO4 earlier. Here in particular, there was an apprehension that lawyers could adopt and perform different roles interchangeably and nevertheless perform both objectively; the accused (as earlier) and police perspectives can highlight how the mundane reality for lawyers can be disconcerting for others. The increasing importance of developing and fostering positive relationships with the CPS was noted by BS11:

'It's important to maintain – I think, even, barristers in the past haven't appreciated that it's important to maintain a good relationship with the CPS. I think they see that now. Mainly because of the cuts in legal aid, and also because more and more solicitors, defence solicitors, are doing their own advocacy work.'

The pressures placed on the defence through cuts and stagnation to legal aid (as discussed in Chapter 5) have resulted in an increase in solicitors engaging in advocacy at the Crown Court. This meant solicitors were taking on much of the lower-end work from barristers:

'When I started in Swansea ... there were no solicitors doing real advocacy work in Swansea. So, all kind of the sentences was coming to us, all the kind of probation breaches, the bail apps, all came to us. ... The small things, the straightforward Crown Court trials. The straightforward punch-ups in the street, you know the type of case. But that, all of that is done by defence solicitors now.' (BS11)

The interconnected issues of criminal legal aid cuts and the growth of solicitor advocates in the Crown Court necessitated the maintenance of positive relationships with the CPS to guarantee work in more challenging times. Yet, maintaining this relationship was not always easy; the distance between the CPS and others (as noted earlier by DS13) was a source of frustration for barristers who also engaged in prosecution work: "I, over the last few months, have done very little [prosecution work], I'm doing something for the CPS tomorrow, but they sit in CPS tower or whatever it is and make charging decisions. There are instances certainly I've found where I think you wouldn't come and do that yourself" (BS14).

While there were concerns that some judges were difficult or harsh – which meant that "you can never have that relationship, just because of the way they are" (DS4) – there was a general acceptance of these personality differences. There was also said to be a level of professionalism and "mutual respect" (DS4) between lawyers and the judiciary, particularly when these relationships were developed over time. The general view was that barristers and judges got along well. Indeed, many of those we interviewed spoke broadly in positive terms reflecting the views of BS7 that, "I think barristers and judges tend to be pretty good, because judges tend to understand the pressures barristers are under." Chapter 5 highlighted that some barristers identified frustrations with the judiciary, including bullying and a lack of empathy regarding court listings. This therefore presents a mixed picture. We were told that the listing problem was likely to be experienced across all court centres. However, in contrast, our interviews suggested that the bullying problem had a specific south Wales element. If the problem of bullying was somehow worse, or at least had a specific local dynamic, it is worth exploring another view here in the present chapter. DS17, a solicitor with Higher Rights but who conducted "mainly" Magistrates' Court work, provided an example of one particular judge in the Crown Court:

'He's interesting – if you go in front of him, he will bully you, and a nasty piece of work he is. He's not nice to anybody … and if he can have somebody in tears, it doesn't matter who you are, the defence solicitor, the prosecutor, the defendant, he would do that. He had a couple of my clients crying, and I represented a solicitor two years ago in a drunk-drive case, and he was horrendous to him —and he's let power go to his head. And you certainly get the, you know, the "judgeitus effect", and … certain magistrates do it because it's a position where they can put "JP" [Justice of the Peace] after their name. Or you know, certain judges, because they can, because they failed at whatever, or have, maybe smaller penises, who knows!'

DS17 suggested that magistrates and judges enjoyed the status of the role and gained a sense of superiority from it.

Judges can be critical of the lawyers appearing before them. Interviews with Crown Court judges have previously identified that judges tended to think that the quality of advocacy has declined over time – largely due to underfunding of the criminal justice system, with the financial problems of solicitors' firms considered to be problematic in pushing some solicitor advocates to conduct cases they supposedly lacked the experience to undertake (Hunter et al, 2018). The professional standing of solicitors as compared with barristers was identified a common problem for solicitor advocates; it meant that they were treated with less respect by judges – mirroring Robson (2016), who has documented some of the problems of reputation that solicitor advocates have encountered.[4] However, both solicitors and barristers discussed the problems caused by a small minority of bullying judges on this circuit – a problem worsened by the circuit's diminutive size (see Chapter 4). The importance of building and maintaining relationships in small areas such as in south Wales was noted by BS15:

> 'Swansea is, is a very small court centre, and as a result you can't afford to fall out with people. You get a bad reputation that follows you around. In London, you can go to a different court every day, fall out with everyone, and nobody knows who you are … [here] there's nowhere to go. You can't hide from people.'

There was, however, a sense that an effort had to be made to maintain this relationship.

Solicitors and barristers strived to develop and maintain relationships – both between these two branches of criminal practice, and with those they worked alongside (police, prosecution and judges) – but were not always successful in doing so. The focus thus far has been on the relationships between those *working* in the criminal justice system. In the next section we explore how practitioners perceived the accused, beginning with the police but focusing predominantly on lawyers and the lawyer–client relationship.

Perceptions of the accused

In this section, we examine how practitioners viewed accused persons as suspects or clients. We will start by considering the police but give most attention to the defence lawyers, who formed the largest group of interviewees in this study.

Police perceptions of the accused were not dissimilar from previous research (McConville et al, 1991; Westmarland, 2008). Typically, the police are isolated and suspicious of 'outsiders' (Bowling et al, 2019; Dehaghani, 2019). PO1 relayed the "healthy distrust" that police officers have of the

---

[4]   Hanlon and Jackson (1999) viewed the introduction of the solicitor advocate as a neoliberal, market-led reform.

accused, explaining that many lie; they claimed that "unfortunately the reality is that having lived through that for so many years and seeing that so many times, it, it would be very hard for anybody to keep an open mind". PO4 repeatedly referred to the accused as "villains" throughout their interview (see also Dehaghani, 2017);[5] the antagonistic attitude was one of "us and them" (PO4). However, officers also pointed toward the importance of developing relationships with the suspect (see Cram, 2020). One such officer was PO2, for whom "rapport [is] probably one of the best talents you can have". PO2 expanded on this point:

> 'Police have to bend the rules to a point– I say bend the rules, not break the rules. Such as simplistic things like allowing him to smoke in the car when travelling from being arrested to the police station, you know. Things like that, you're not supposed to do but you will because it's stressful for the suspect and likewise, you want the suspect to be, not so much compliant, but have an element of trust towards how you're going to deal with him or her in the future hours of their detention.'

The building of this relationship with the suspect facilitated the police in their dealings with the suspect, making easier the role of the police officer (see also Dehaghani, 2019). However, there were also circumstances, as relayed to us, where officers were irritated by suspects. PO4 recalled the story of a young man, with no previous record, suspected of shoplifting and considered to be "quite emotional":

> 'He got under my skin a bit, I have to be honest. I don't know what it was. … He was in tears and see this is where I fell foul of PACE. He started crying, getting upset. I should be stopping the interview. I wasn't having any of that. I was giving him some grief, I was really having a go at him. Because I felt that he was nearly going to admit it … I did hammer him, I have to be honest … I really laid into him verbally trying to get to the truth, as far as I was concerned.'

He was eventually found not guilty and, for PO4, "That barrister got him off because of that tape, and that was my fault … because they [the jury] felt empathy with this kid." In circumstances where the police would generally hold negative attitudes to suspects – which can come out in examples such as

---

5   Hoyle's (1998) research on the use of language by police shows that disparaging statements can be made as something of a stress reliever, without any necessary impact on behaviour. Also, Shiner's (2010) study illustrates that what the police say works as organizational defence mechanisms, with an internal rather than external focus.

this where, in PO4's own words, "I treated him like shit in the interview" – the views and attitudes of defence lawyers are particularly important to counteract police views. Indeed, lawyers tend to hold negative views of – at least some of – their clients (see Newman, 2013a). One solicitor was concerned that the language of "regular" clients (those more experienced clients as introduced in Chapter 3) was stereotyping and little better than the language used by the police, suggesting some element of cultural overlap between defence lawyers and the police: "One of the things that I keep saying to other criminal practitioners is, 'Stop talking about "regular clients" and "good clients"; "they're regular criminals"' … which is a very bad way of talking about people who are regarded by most people as a blight on society, you know?" (DS6).

As discussed in Chapter 3, there was a distinction for most of the lawyers between 'first-timers' and the 'regular' or more experienced clients. Many lawyers adopted this framing when discussing their feelings and attitudes towards their clients. DS2, for example, offered a judgement of what they thought about their client based on a client's experience:

'Misguided, a lot of them. Duty clients – I mean, we split this up into old clients and duty clients and old clients, the regulars, they're misguided, and they need help. It's not about getting them off, it's just about helping them out. Sometimes you feel like a guidance counsellor. … Whereas the duty [clients] … they're just normal run-of-the-mill people a lot of the duties, and a lot of the duty clients have just made mistakes.'

There was, therefore, a distinction between those clients who were in need of help and those clients who had simply made a mistake, although as we note in Chapter 7, the 'regular' clients did not always receive the attention that they perhaps required. While our interview questions regarding the lawyer–client relationship were framed in general and abstract terms, that is how lawyers felt about their clients, many expressed positive feelings. Like DS2, DS8 commented that many were simply in need of support:

'I didn't expect to like crime clients. I always wanted to do crime and I couldn't tell you why, but I didn't think I would like them as much as I do. A lot of them, a lot of them you just think, "Oh, they're just down on their luck a little bit" … like 99 per cent of the clients I really get on with and you can build a good rapport with.'

Although DS8 noted that most clients were easy to get along with, DS15 pointed out that it was impossible to get along with everyone: "There are one or two, you think, 'Oh God I've got an appointment with x.' We all have clients we don't like, you know? It's the nature of things. I mean, you can't like everyone in this world. But … the majority of my clients, they're alright." Indeed, it is likely that while many individuals have colleagues who they do not like or respect, they nevertheless recognize the need to maintain professionalism within the workplace. DS8 likened criminal practice to office work:

> 'Well, I could work in an office full of a hundred people and they'd probably be one per cent that may not be my best friend, but I think that's life. But you act, with everything – you know, you act professionally. … It doesn't matter sometimes whether I like a person or not, we've got to act in their best interest.' (DS8)

DS1 expressed a similar sentiment to DS8 and DS15. For DS1, most clients were fine, but others were "not very nice":

> 'The vast majority are absolutely fine to deal with and perfectly pliant, perfectly pleasant. You know, there's a small minority that I actively like, who would always ring me and have my mobile, and then there's a small minority that I'm not that keen on. Just because they're not very nice. But you be professional with them and you still try and build a rapport with them because you've got to.'

Again, DS1 commented on the importance of building rapport; they also assessed their interactions with clients based on the client's pliancy: a client who is pliant was "fine to deal with". As Newman (2013a) has discussed, solicitors can expect clients to *take* – rather than *give* – instructions; solicitors may become frustrated when clients, for example, refused to plead guilty. The client's willingness to take instructions may result in their being liked by the solicitor, as DS4 indicated:

> 'We're not in a position where we cast moral judgement over clients. We just don't do that … some clients I like better than others, but usually it's probably because they're easier to work with, than anything else. And that's probably our criteria. If we've got a client who listens to us and gives us proper instructions, and is easy to work with, we're going to be much more inclined to like that client than the client who is difficult to work with, doesn't listen, has their own agenda. … Those type of clients we don't tend to like.'

This is perhaps unsurprising, but does raise issues regarding the power dynamics of the lawyer–client relationship (as in Chapter 4 regarding lawyer–client meetings over live-link): clients are expected to take instruction and, ostensibly, not challenge their lawyer. This may be somewhat problematic if, for example, the lawyer is not also listening to their client's account. The notion of pliancy was taken further by DS1, who explored some of the other differences between "good" and "bad" clients:

'The ones that are nice, it's generally just because they're pleasant to deal with ... Some of them are just pure innocent, you know? And you feel very sorry for them because they're being prosecuted for something they haven't done. You can get on with them well, and especially when they think that you're really fighting their corner, then they like you. And that's always a good thing. And the ones that I don't particularly like ... you've got clients who are, because of their nature, quite aggressive and confrontational. Because they're just violent people ... they've got really short fuses and at the first amount, if anybody tries to tell them what to do, or suggests that what they've done isn't right, then they go right, either on the defensive or on the attack.'

There is therefore some distinction made between the ideal client and the unsavoury client – the former is pleasant (and may also include those who are wrongfully accused) whereas the latter is someone with no remorse or someone who is combative, hostile or simply does not take instruction.[6] Thus, the lawyer may express empathy for the client based on the client's character or – perceived or actual – innocence, or frustration with clients based on the nature of their offending or their general – perceived or actual – unpleasantness. This division between the "good" clients and the "bad" clients was expressed by many of the lawyers with whom we spoke. In contrast, DS7 relayed the notion that there was "no normal or average client". This was a minority view and lawyers would often generalize about clients (see also McConville et al, 1994; Newman, 2013a).

Having established some grounding on the lawyers' sentiments regarding their clients, we now turn to consider the lawyer–client relationship in more detail.

The lawyer–client relationship

The lawyer–client relationship – and the exploration thereof – is central to this book. The lawyers in this study were unequivocal in their explanations

---

[6]   The ideal client adds to Christie's (1986) notion of how the 'ideal victim' has been constructed: a person or category awarded the complete and legitimate status of being a victim.

of how crucial this relationship was to their practice. Many of the lawyers relayed how it was vital that the client always knows someone is on their side, which somewhat conflicts with the information provided earlier (and underlines some of the frustrations reported by the accused previously in Chapter 3 and subsequently in Chapter 7). DS13 gave one such account:

> 'My experience is the most important thing is that they know that you're completely independent from the police, that you're there only for them and that it's their interests that you're concerned about and that you're representing. But the biggest thing I've picked up on is that a number of clients just want to feel like they're being listened to and that somebody is on their side, essentially, that they're not fighting the system on their own in that somebody will put up that fight for them, which a lot of them haven't had. Especially with youth cases, if you spend an hour with them ... that makes a massive difference in terms of how your relationship builds. It's just something that they're not used to.'

DS13 expressed the view that the lawyer–client relationship would generally emerge when the client was at their most desperate and fragile – at the police station (see Dehaghani, 2021) and the court (see Newman, 2013a); it was therefore important that the lawyer engenders feelings of being supported and valued. This was a sentiment shared by some of the defendants in our study. AC5, for example, was full of praise for the way their solicitor helped them feel they had an ally:

> 'She was amazing, I really can't fault her at all. And funnily enough, after I got out of all the case with her, I actually found out that she's a lesbian ... I thought, because she was a lez, she'd try and get me in more trouble. But no, she was out of this world amazing. She said, "you're not in the wrong at all, love. She's in the wrong because she provoked you. She's pushed you and pushed you and pushed you to get you like that." I said, "Yeah, granted I shouldn't have called her a dyke, but granted at the same time she shouldn't have been slagging off my dead child."'

AC5 was pleasantly surprised at the support they got from their solicitor – despite the solicitor being gay and the question of homophobic abuse at the heart of their case. The solicitor gave AC5 the confidence they needed at that moment:

> 'She explained, "N, you're not going to prison babes," she said, "I'm not letting you. Don't worry about that." She said, "We're going to get this

sorted." She said, "My job: do you know what my job is?" I said, "To stick up for me," she said "Yeah, my job is to fight in your defence."'

DS13 earlier suggested that the lawyer's purpose was to "fight the client's corner"; it was also necessary to spend time with clients to build rapport, although, as we have discussed in Chapter 4 on time pressures, this does not necessarily occur in the lawyer–client relationship under legal aid. AC5's example of their lawyer provides a positive account of the lawyer–client relationship and illustrates how important it can be for the relationship for the client to trust their lawyer. The rapport developed with clients was viewed as crucial, although this rapport was said to differ based on the "type" of client (and their level of experience): "The rapport is important, but there are so many different ways of getting that rapport, and that can vary very, very much on the type of character that you're talking about. Those repeat offenders, first-time offenders, somewhere in the middle kind of people" (DS3).

Some of the lawyers were aware of how their style, especially those adopting a more formal approach, could have varying effects on clients. BS12 considered the importance of rapport building:[7]

'You have to establish a rapport with them, because barristers – and especially with solicitors as well – there's a sort of social wall between the people you advise and the, usually, the stock of – well, not stock, but the background of people which barristers and solicitors come from, and if they don't feel that they can talk honestly to you, they may not.'

As BS12 indicated, there were challenges posed by the difference in backgrounds of barristers and solicitors as compared with the backgrounds of their clients. Some solicitors drew upon their own backgrounds, such as DS6 who felt that their background from a council estate allowed them to empathize with their clients:

'I started in it [criminal defence work] because it seemed like a good idea, because I grew up on a council estate in Barry, and it was very noticeable that people who lived in that area, in particular, didn't like to go to lawyers to help them out with their problems. ... So, when I had the opportunity I decided I'll be a solicitor and see if that changes

---

[7] It should be noted that Cram (2020) has highlighted an often hidden purpose to building a rapport in regard to the police wherein the purpose is generally nefarious. Here, it may not be, but there is certainly purpose and it is worth considering discussions of rapport in light of DS4's earlier point about valuing clients who listen to the lawyer.

minds. It didn't. But at least it meant that as a solicitor, I like to think I understood their situation.'

The challenge for DS6 was not the difference in social background, which BS12 noted earlier, but the general distrust of lawyers among some communities. DS6's background, they claimed, enabled them to understand more about their client. Class also enabled DS12 to relate to clients and build an effective rapport:

'I come from a very deprived background. I come from your one-parent family. I come from your absolute this and that … I should have a criminal record longer than most of my clients, on paper. … So it's a bit different. … And where we grew up, and who we grew up with. In the area we grew up with, that's where most of our clients come from because we've gone to school with them … we've been to our kids' parties with them. We've hung around together with them when we were kids.'

DS6 and DS12 both offer claims to have stronger relations with their clients based on class in a similar way that lawyers in Newman (2013a) had previously. DS12 indicated rapport beyond the lawyer–client relationship; they were heavily involved within the community, and this may engender trust in their clients. It was, however, suggested that there were differences in rapport between the solicitor and client as compared with the barrister and client:

'It's an entirely different world. The respect that they have for the lawyers by the time they get to the Crown Court because they're not, the solicitors that represent them in the mags [Magistrates' Court] are people that they see all the time, and so they've got a kind of like, "You're my mate" kind of relationship with them, whereas with the Crown Court, the barristers, they don't.' (BS5)

The consensus from the data was that the relationship differed based on formality, with client–solicitor relationships being the less formal of the two. The frequency of solicitor–client interactions, particularly the frequency of dealings with a particular client or the client's family, would allow for the development of positive relationships:

'Some of them are people we represent every couple of months, who come back before us quite a lot. So, we've got really good relationships with them and their families because they're the first ones who will ring us to say, "So and so just been arrested." Their brother, their mother will ring us and say, "Can you go straight to the police station." So, the families trust us. We've got some families we maybe represent a couple of siblings in the same family, you know, grandfather, son.' (DS17)

The 'regular' client then becomes known to the lawyer. DS4 discussed the development of "mutual trust" over regular contact:[8]

'I think our return clients, people we've been representing for years and years, we know pretty well. We know ... their backgrounds; we tend to know their family backgrounds; if they've got drug or alcohol issues, or mental health issues, we know about that, because we've been through all that with them before.'

As DS4 indicated, regular contact can provide the lawyer with information about the client. This may mean, then, that the lawyer does not feel that they require as much time with the 'regular' clients, as indicated in Chapter 3. The majority of lawyers explained how 'first-time' clients needed more care and attention. For DS4, spending time getting to know clients "matters to some, especially those who've never been in trouble before", explaining that, "They're the ones who particularly are most anxious to come and see ... you've got to spend a bit more time with them, just taking care of them really, because they don't have the experience." For BS12 the need to build up "trust" was most pronounced with inexperienced clients:

'For people who've been in and out of the system, you don't really have to address it with them because they know what's what. But, you know, I have defended some people ... it's their first time in trouble and it's the first time they're seeing the inside of the court and it is all, and they are petrified ... it is extremely important that practitioners remember these are human beings that are going through there, and it's not just a robotic next person off the chain, because I think that is the trap that some people can fall into.'

The danger may be that assumptions are made that more experienced clients inherently require less attention without having regard to individual needs. DS3 suggested that the more experienced clients might actually require more time with and "hand-holding" from their lawyer because "they've been in

---

[8] Nicolson and Webb (1999) highlight that trust is at the heart of professional relationships but that understanding how trust works within the lawyer–client relation is a complex matter. Here, we talk about trust in the everyday, informal sense as it was used by interviewees.

and out of prison, they've perhaps been forgotten a bit, in their life. They're in the driving seat. They're the important ones for six months because they've got a trial going on." This highlights that the purported 'first-timer'/ 'regular' dichotomy that is often presented by practitioners (as identified in Chapter 3) is not as straightforward as it might seem. Such 'regulars' may wrongly be assumed capable of moving through the process without much assistance; they may indeed experience a double-bind because they may struggle to engage with and participate in the criminal justice system *and* their difficulties may be neglected by virtue of the assumption that they are capable of moving through the process unaided (see Jacobson et al, 2016; Kemp and Hodgson, 2016; Dehaghani, 2019).

For new clients, it is important to build rapport quickly (see also Newman, 2013a). The importance of developing a connection is apparent from feelings of isolation experienced by the client and their need to see that someone is on their side, as described earlier by DS13. DS4 provided a further explanation:

'In the police station, you're their only friend. They perceive that everybody else is against them. So, they're much more likely to be amenable, to listen, to be truthful, to be honest with you … and you've got to tell them straight away, "We're acting in your best interests. We're nothing to do with the police. It's confidential, and we're independent." And you've got to give them all of that to build a bit of trust.'

In the police station, the suspect may feel weak (Dehaghani, 2021); the lawyer is crucial to providing the suspect with strength or resilience (Dehaghani and Newman, 2017). To provide this support, the lawyer must establish a positive relationship based on trust, often very quickly. Some of the lawyers explained that they needed to build up the kind of rapport that they would with anybody; this was not necessarily specific to the lawyer–client relationship. As such, it was important not to treat their clients differently to anyone else. BS15, for example, explained how their view of rapport building was universal: "It's just talking to people on a sensible, ordinary basis." BS16 expressed a similar sentiment: developing rapport was the same regardless of the person, yet they also expressed concern about how the accused was framed as "other" (even if the accused saw themself as such (as suggested in Chapter 3)):

'It is important I get a rapport with them. Sometimes it's not easy due to lack of time, but, at the end of the day it's human interaction. And, you know, defendants are no different to anyone else, apart from they just happen to be labelled "defendants". Doesn't make them any different.' (BS16)

Building rapport with anyone takes time. Communication is key and, under the 'contact hypothesis', interpersonal contact is the only way to construct successful, stable, human relationships (Allport, 1979). BS16's purported approach relates back to the issue of time pressures caused by legal aid cuts, as discussed in Chapter 5. This renders rapport development and maintenance even more challenging; it was the view of BS16, that "it can be highly pressured as your time with the client can be limited".

When we talked to the accused and family members, we were repeatedly told how frustrating and disheartening the limited time could be. These accounts echo the dissatisfaction that Newman (2013a) has previously presented when defendants did not feel that their lawyer was properly prepared for their case.[9] This was expressed by FM1 with concerns that the lawyers did not understand the case: "Forget them trying to break down something complex to us, I don't think they fully understood the case themselves because they didn't do the work." AC3 felt that the lawyer had made no effort for them:

'The barrister. Right? He knew nothing about me. He didn't want to know anything about me, he flicked through my case and made judgements with – and I had to put him right on more than one occasion. And quite frankly, when we went to court, if I could have tossed him out of court before I went into court, I would have. But it was too late.'

AC3, like several other accused individuals (as also discussed in Chapter 3), was frustrated with the inadequacy of the lawyer–client relationship as they experienced it. These negative views were much more common than the positive one of AC5 quoted earlier. The amount of time spent on a case – and thus the impact on the lawyer–client relationship – is undoubtedly adversely affected by the legal aid cuts and stagnation.[10] The ideal situation would be to meet a client early. However, lawyers were open about not being able to achieve this as often as they might have wanted. It was difficult to develop quick rapport and gain the trust of the client sufficient to be confident in

---

[9]   Newman (2013a) noted how frequently lawyers pick up cases late or at the last minute, often without any time to get to know them. He draws on Goffman (1991) and the idea of dehumanization to explore this phenomenon. Following Newman's (2013a) analysis, clients are increasingly reduced to the status of files rather than people. They are passed around from lawyer to lawyer and treated as 'numbers' of jobs on a list that need to be ticked off. This reduces their humanity and allows lawyers to excuse not taking the time to engage with or learn about the client.

[10] Although as Newman (2012) has highlighted, there are also important questions of lawyers' ethics that need to be addressed.

taking instructions, but most lawyers were clear that they were used to working around these pressures. AC10 expressed how it felt to only meet the lawyer on the day:

'He met with me in the waiting room, and we had a little chat. But it weren't even like a little chat like we're having now. He was like, writing a couple of things down, and going, "Oh I've got to go into that courtroom now". … So he didn't know anything about me, to be honest.'

Lawyers also found problems in such a 'last-minute' meeting. DS6 highlighted the pressure of only meeting the client at court from a solicitor's perspective: "I try to [see the client before court]. I have to say a lot of colleagues do wait until they're at court, and that's part of the pressure of the cost of legal aid – if you wait until then you can't be sure that you're getting the right instructions."

BS8 discussed, from a barrister's experience, how "there's the ideal and then there's what quite often happens", with the ideal being meetings in chambers and the solicitor's office before the client enters the court. The reality could differ:

'It has happened where I've turned up on the day of trial and I've met them for the first time. That happens far more often than it should. … It's the worst-case scenario for me, defending, to turn up on the day and say, "Hello my name is x, I know we've not met but I can assure you I'm fully prepared." You know, I'm already sort of on the back foot. I'm sort of apologizing about the fact that we've not met from the outset, going, "I know we've not met before but don't worry I've read all the papers … rest assured I know everything, but I need to know x."' (BS8)

There was frustration from the accused and family members regarding the lack of meetings with lawyers. When asked about the contact that their family member had with their lawyer, FM1 noted that the contact was "nothing at all, other than the visit they made to the house", the visit "to the barrister's Chambers two weeks before the trial" where "they asked him some questions", and then at trial where "they would have a little meeting every morning, and they were like, 'Oh look, we want him to speak on the stand. We want them to see who he really is and for that to come out'". From this example, the lawyers had met the client, but this was insufficient for both the accused and their family.[11] Many of the families in our study

---

[11] The significance of this can be seen when drawing on Binder et al (2004), in which lawyers are urged to focus on the client as a holistic entity and not view the legal problem

felt let down by the lawyers in their cases; there was a gap between want they wanted and what the lawyers provided.

DS8 recognized the need to try to balance managing expectations of families with building rapport for first-time accused persons in these circumstances:

'They don't necessarily understand that it's not always helpful for us trying to balance a workload, including their case, to have people ringing us constantly. And you do get some clients, and I'd say definitely it's the people that are in the first time, in the criminal justice system, they'll ring you very frequently, just to know what's going on and, you know, with the newer clients, that's how you build the rapport. But there is a line where you sort of say, "Look, if anything happens, call me. But if anything happens from outside, I'll call you." But it is nerves, and, you know, you've got to cut them a bit of slack. It's stressful.'

DS8 indicated, as with DS3 and DS4 earlier, that some clients were needier than others. It was particularly important to be responsive to the client to adequately build rapport, particularly where the client was "newer". DS8 also highlights the stress that the client experiences and the need for the lawyer to respond sympathetically. While DS8 seemed to suggest that clients can contact them personally, there were issues with 'discontinuous representation' (McConville et al, 1994; Newman, 2013a), which restricts the development of the lawyer–client relationship.[12] Solicitors noted the importance of continuity, such as DS2 who stated that, "A lot of them actually do benefit from having the same solicitor, having the same help, having an ear, having someone to talk to." DS5 explained how it worked – and why – at their firm:

'We've got about half a dozen solicitors here. Yeah, ideally some continuity is better, obviously. Equally if the case goes from the Magistrates' Court to the Crown Court, it would tend to be different people in our office who would deal with the Crown Court case.

---

in isolation. From this perspective, the lawyer–client relationship should be seen as having parallels with counselling; lawyers need to be willing to listen to clients' concerns but also move beyond that to gain a fuller understanding of who they are. From talking to the lawyers in our study, this was extremely difficult under criminal legal aid and the working practices they had developed.

[12] This is what Gilboy and Schmidt (1979) also call "horizontal representation". Clients would be seen by different lawyers at different times rather than having one consistent lawyer all through the process.

But yeah, continuity of care, the client being able to relate to you is obviously very important.'

Such a view was commonly expressed among the solicitors in this research. The barristers also affirmed that continuity was important:

'Continuity of counsel, or of any representation, I think, is massively important, because you can imagine, if you were in trouble, you would want to see the same person throughout, because you've already had this chat, rather than having to tell a different barrister the same thing twice or having got used to someone's style and having dealt with them, the trust, suddenly then you're faced with someone completely different with a different style.' (BS8)

Barristers had issues around continuity that were out of their control, often due to the listings and the time pressures that we explored in Chapter 5. They were more likely to take a firm stance against the accused seeing multiple practitioners; these challenges were a professional encumbrance for barristers who are, after all, self-employed. Solicitors were more likely to view discontinuous representation as an organizational necessity based on how their firms reacted to the problems caused by legal aid funding. It was far from perfect in terms of their work either with or for their clients. However, it was explained that this was an inevitability they had tried to manage: "And they may have seen six different faces, but it's not necessarily the six different faces that they mind. It's the fact that none of the faces knew what they'd told face number one" (DS3).

What DS3 suggests, is that it is not the practice of seeing multiple lawyers in itself that perturbs clients but, rather, having to tell the same story several times and, relatedly, the anxiety that a lawyer does not know their case well (if at all). The continuity of care, referred to by DS5 earlier, could potentially be achieved by ensuring that all solicitors were properly prepared for the clients they take on. Newman (2013a) suggests that lawyers will often take on so many clients and at such short notice that it is unlikely such knowledge will be acquired in advance of the lawyer meeting the client.

Rapport and relationships were important; it is at the heart of defence lawyers' practice (Newman, 2013a) and the lawyers in this study spoke of the centrality of rapport in their work. Yet, there were pressures on this rapport and thus on the lawyer–client relationship (many of which were presented in Chapters 3 and 5 on underfunding). However, underfunding is not the only factor undermining this relationship – although it most certainly compounds any other factors. In the following section we examine yet another pressure: the sentence discount for guilty pleas.

Pressures on accused persons

Mulcahy (1994) points to the significance of guilty pleas; Alge (2013) highlights the need for greater understanding of the phenomenon.[13] We considered this issue in Chapter 2 and it is highlighted here as integral to the lawyer–client relationship.

Lawyers in this study discussed the growing importance of sentence discount for their practice.[14] We were told that the impact of the discount differed depending on the type of case: "The more serious the case, it can become more relevant to a client" (DS7). For some clients it was said to be confusing – particularly "the new clients who've never been in trouble before" (DS15), whereas others – the "older clients who've been through" the process – seemed to grasp "the principles of credit for guilty pleas" relatively quickly (DS15). Given the passivity in the lawyer–client relationship (Tata and Stephen, 2006), it may be inevitable that lawyers believe that such a concept – and the associated permutations and calculations – are grasped quickly, even when they are not. That said, the issue of sentence discount was claimed – or accepted – to be more complicated as the potential sentence increased:

> 'I think it doesn't really cause a massive issue in the Magistrates' Court, because people tend to understand that. I think the times where it becomes an issue is where discount would be the difference between going to custody or having a community order. Or when discount's the difference between eight years and five years. Then you do see people really grappling.' (DS1)

Thus, clients faced with heavier sentences, particularly in Crown Court cases, had a more significant decision to make. Lawyers were broadly supportive of the system in principle. For DS1, it was "justifiable ... because it does encourage people to think about what they're doing when they enter a plea". However, as DS8 considered, "Some people who perhaps have committed a crime, it makes it easier for them to admit it, knowing that they're going to be deal with a bit lighter." Guilty pleas were said to be particularly prominent in conversations between barristers and their clients:

---

[13] Tata and Gormley (2016) provide the most authoritative overview of the academic research around guilty pleas and the sentence discount. Helm (2019) explores the issue of defendant vulnerability and guilty pleas (see also Peay and Player, 2018).

[14] The lawyers did not necessarily use the language of "discount"; this was the phraseology that we used in our questions. They were more likely to talk about "pleas" or "pleading"; the discount was instead rendered as a "reduction".

'Guilty pleas is always one of the first conversations that you have with a defendant ... there is definitely a role, a place in the system, for the guilty plea. ... They never want to plead guilty. They only ever plead guilty if the lawyer is saying to them, "Look, I think you're guilty and I think you should plead." So, they've got the incentive of the credit at that stage.' (BS5)

Most lawyers in this research accepted the sentence discount for early guilty pleas and their role in communicating it. As such, they reflected the views of Flynn and Freiberg (2018) that the discount was neither a benefit nor a detriment for the accused; it was a compromise between what the accused wants, what victims need and what the justice system demands. For Flynn and Freiberg (2018), this compromise shows that there is no 'perfect' outcome but, rather, a reasonably acceptable justice outcome. This is what BS5 alluded to earlier, noting that there is a role for the discount. We were also told that most of the accused simply went along with the discount. DS7 supported the general view expressed – that clients accepted the discount when it was useful for them; for DS7, "It can focus the mind."

However, a significant minority of lawyers noted problems with the system's operation and how these problems impacted the lawyer–client relationship. This mirrors the academic scholarship that frames the system of sentence discounting as coercive (Ashworth, 2006); it may also result in the innocent pleading guilty, thus resulting in miscarriages of justice (Darbyshire, 2000; Leverick, 2004). Several lawyers noted that the discount operated as part of a wider systemic pressure to plead guilty and to speed clients through:

'I think there's massive pressure from every angle to plead guilty. I think everything is geared towards early disposal these days. You've got, you know, all different, disposals at the police station other than charge, but again, it's geared towards an admission. ... And again ... defendants are told there's a cost warning if you plead not guilty; if you plead guilty you get a discount off your sentence. Everything, I think, is geared towards pressurizing defendants to ... plead guilty, and regardless of the merits of the case. It's the same warning now to everybody.' (DS9)

Accounts such as that of DS9 speak to the approach of McConville and Marsh (2014), who see the sentence discount as undermining adversarialism and encouraging trial avoidance whenever possible. Thus, the sentence discount plays into the broader systemic pressure for guilty pleas. Indeed, the criminal process has been shown to assume that guilty pleas are an inevitability (Carlen, 1976; McBarnet, 1981; Tata, 2007). Yet, BS2 indicated that the system is becoming more punitive with lesser discounts provided to the accused:

'It has become increasingly important to put your plea in, if you are going to plead guilty, early on. When I started, judges used to routinely say on the day of trial, "Well, you pleaded guilty, so I'll give you full credit." Now, that's gone. That's just a world away now. You're going to get ten per cent on the day of the trial, if you're lucky. So, you know, there has been a sea change in that.'

Another notable problem was how the accused was said to engage with and understand the impact of a guilty plea, which Tata and Gormley (2016) suggest is the least well-known effect of the sentence discount. BS2 expressed "worry and concern", indicating that the sentence discount could be "frightening" and "a significant inducement in the right case", but that "we're all conscious, in the Bar, of not having people plead guilty to things that they adamantly say they didn't do". While BS2 was concerned, they also reflected something that solicitors and barristers were conscious to emphasize – they made sure not to put pressure on their clients. BS13, for example, acknowledged that "it can be confusing" and that there was a need to "ensure we take the time to explain it properly, and to explain that … we are obliged to advise them that that is the case, but that they should only be entering a guilty plea if they are guilty". Lawyers claimed to take great care in how they managed this process:

'You have to be careful with them that they don't think you're trying to force them to plead guilty. … If you're talking about someone who has got a very serious case. Let's say it's a big drugs conspiracy, and the sentences are in the order of fourteen, fifteen, sixteen years if you get found guilty at the end of the trial. … Ultimately, it is always their choice, and that's what you have to say to them. "It's your choice. You decide what you do." But, as you can appreciate, when you talk about that moment of years, a decision of that sort is, you know, it's a huge decision. You have to be careful how you put it to them because you obviously don't want them to think that you're forcing their hand one way or the other. It's not me that's imposed this rule.' (BS1)

BS1 thus saw the need to communicate the implications carefully to the client, striking the fine balance between providing sufficient information to enable an informed choice without seemingly compelling the client to plead guilty. As AC4 indicated, the accused relies on their lawyer and, while the lawyer may be careful not to force their client's hand, they may suggest that pleading guilty is the best option:

'Obviously, you rely on your legal representative, you know? And whatever they say. Because that's what I used to say, I used to turn around to my brief and go, "What do you think?" You know, and he'd say, "Well, I can't tell you what to do, but if you go guilty," he'd kind of hint heavily that you should be pleading guilty on that one. "You'll get your time off for a guilty plea."'

The lawyer therefore has a significant role in the guilty plea system. However, as BS3 noted, communicating the sentence discount can "damage rapport" between lawyer and client:[15]

'If they don't understand what you're trying to say. Quite often … clients that are accused of something like drink-driving, or dangerous drive or something a bit more like, what we might call white-collar crime I suppose, and, and you explain it to them, you say, "Look, it's always a case of, of risk versus reward; you've got to think about, you know, pleading guilty at this stage, you know you will get a bit off your sentence, but you're going to have a criminal record, what does that mean to you?" And they're much more willing to understand that it works like that. I'd say clients with lower functioning, or who are accused of classic … blue-collar crime, that they just think it's, you know, "trying to get me to plead".'

As BS3 highlighted in the assumptions they make about clients, some clients may understand the implications of the guilty plea more than others and, in particular, the advice given by the barrister. However, BS3's quote also raises questions regarding the understanding of some clients. Undoubtedly, the time that a lawyer has with a client – as well as the lawyer's skills – may have a bearing on the lawyer's ability to explain the implications of a guilty plea in a manner that does not appear to be leading. The damage to the rapport between lawyer and client can be severe where the lawyer advises the client to plead guilty:

'This first meeting was for free. It was someone I knew. But I actually changed solicitors in the end because he told me I should plead guilty to everything. And I decided there's no way I'm pleading guilty, so I changed solicitors. And actually, when I was at the trial, I saw him again at court. He was there with someone else, and he said to me, "You know you should have pleaded guilty to everything." And I said, "Not a chance. There's no way I'm pleading guilty." I think it's because

---

[15] A counter-view, as reflected in Newman (2013a) is that rapport is a delicate balance in which the lawyer builds up enough trust to be able to persuade clients to plead guilty in cases that are not lucrative for the lawyer to pursue.

of like, they offer you a lesser sentence or something? But I mean, there's absolutely no way that I'm going to plead guilty to something I didn't do.' (AC9)

The assumption of guilt on the part of this lawyer – mirroring the routine assumption of client guilt (McConville et al, 1994) – had impacted AC9 and their relations with their lawyer. In AC9's case, so destroyed was the trust that they instructed another lawyer. While the effect on rapport, according to BS3, would vary according to the client, the pressures are enhanced for all clients given the high stakes involved, particularly in the early stages when the maximum possible discount is available. BS1 explained this point:

'It does put inordinate amount of pressure very early on, before you've got the papers. So, you have very limited information, and more or less, you're in a situation where the judge is saying– because this an old fashion phrase they use but this is the effect of it – "he [the accused] knows whether he did it or not", regardless of the fact that at that stage they don't know what the evidence is a lot of the time.'

At that early stage, most of the evidence would not have been served and, as such, the decision is a guessing game to some degree. This problem is exacerbated by the issues surrounding disclosure, which Robins (2019) has shown to have dangerous impacts for defendants (see also Chapter 2). Disclosure was a key problem for many of the lawyers, such as DS15, who, when asked about the most significant change required to the criminal justice system, replied "early disclosure". Early disclosure is thus particularly important to the issue of guilty pleas. As BS7 noted, the availability of information can either obstruct or interfere with good communication:

'I think there's quite a contradiction in the system at the moment between the push for a defendant to plead earlier and earlier. So now, obviously, they're expected to plead – get full credit if you plead at the Magistrates' Court. With the issues around disclosure? That's a contradictory position, I think. Because the pressure is on the defendant to plead earlier and earlier while the information is being delivered potentially later and later. Which just makes your job to advise the client very difficult, because you don't have all the information to hand.'

The lack of disclosure renders more difficult the task of ascertaining whether a guilty plea is the best possible option. The lack of information, as BS11 relayed, exerted additional pressure on the accused and detracted from the underfunding of the system and problems with the prosecution. The role of the lawyer, and, in particular, the potential value of the lawyer–client relationship, is undermined. The role can also be undermined by public perceptions of lawyering generated by the media as discussed in Chapter 5 when we reflected on the lawyers' concerns with their portrayal (see also The Secret Barrister, 2020). In this context, it is worth remembering DS1's comments regarding good clients and the pliancy of such clients. In contrast with BS3 earlier, DS4 explained that easily confused clients were easier to direct:

> 'If you say to them, "Listen, I've looked at all this, I think you should be pleading guilty for these reasons," and keep it at a very low level, they are much more willing to say, "Oh, all right then, if you say so, I'll do that," than your more educated client, who is much more willing or likely to be second-guessing your advice or asking questions about your advice to justify it to themselves. So, I think some of those, you know, lower-IQ clients, sometimes are actually easier to deal with, because they're more willing to take advice. As long as you pitch it at the right level for them.'

This does, however, raise serious concerns regarding the understanding of some clients of the implications of a guilty plea. This concern is particularly pertinent in relation to those considered vulnerable (see Helm, 2019; Peay and Player, 2019). Within the context of cuts and fee stagnation, lawyers have less time to spend with their clients, particularly those who are considered vulnerable (Dehaghani and Newman, 2017), with the effect that some individuals may be pleading guilty without a full and proper understanding of the implications of doing so. Thus, the guilty plea not only raises questions regarding the health of the lawyer–client relationship, but may also impact upon the accused's understanding of, and ability to participate effectively in, the criminal process (see Owusu-Bempah, 2017).

Conclusion

This chapter has explored the workings of the criminal justice system by considering key relationships. We have focused on some of the relationships that operated between practitioners, considering how lawyers felt about those with whom they worked and how lawyers felt about the accused. As Newman (2013a) has highlighted, the lawyer–client relationship is crucial to providing access to justice. Exploring how lawyers perceived their client, as we have done in this chapter, provides insight into how vital relationships are in practice. As part of this understanding, we have unpacked how the sentence discount for an early guilty plea may impact upon the lawyer–client relationship and how lawyers approached their clients. We have illustrated the awareness of the need for defending solicitors and barristers to work closely with the police, prosecution and judiciary such that they may foster professional relationships and thus perform their roles effectively. Lawyers informed us of how these relationships benefitted the client, yet McConville and Marsh (2014) caution that the danger of too close a working relationship may have led the client to perceive the lawyer as working with and for the state rather than with and for the client. It was crucial, therefore, that we explored how lawyers relayed this to the client; lawyers explained how important it was to build rapport and earn the trust of their clients. Following McConville et al (1994) and Newman (2013a), future ethnographic empirical research could assess how lawyers make use of rapport and trust and whether this always works for the benefit of the accused. Owing to legal aid pressures, discussed in Chapters 3 and 5 most notably, developing such relationships has become increasingly difficult and, as such, may serve as a threat to the lawyers' abilities to support access to justice in practice. The balancing of competing demands – and the potential risk that some duties towards clients may not be met – speaks to Tata's (2007) notion of 'ethical indeterminacy'. In this chapter, we drew out a related threat: the sentence discount. The negotiated settlement mechanism requires further consideration regarding how it may impinge upon – and undermine – the lawyer–client relationship by, in effect, co-opting the lawyer to work for the state and thus against the needs of their clients. As McConville and Marsh (2014) argue, the guilty plea culture is at the centre of the contemporary criminal justice system. The impact of sentence discount on the lawyer–client relationship merits further exploration in the form of empirical research.

Examining criminal justice relationships through a vulnerability lens allows us to detail how resilience is developed through interconnections. Relationships between different actors are inextricably linked and, to varying degrees, have some sense of reliance upon one another. This reliance is particularly marked in relation to those suspected and accused of committing criminal offences – their lawyer may help translate the complexities of the criminal law and process, enabling the client to understand the implications of their decisions. Trust and rapport are crucial; any difficulties establishing trust or rapport can potentially undermine resilience. Lawyers are also reliant upon those suspected and accused as without them they would be unable to sustain their practice. Those journeying through the criminal process rely upon their lawyer to bolster their resilience. Without their lawyer, they risk being alienated within an antagonistic, self-referential system. Lawyers must ensure positive working relationships and a strong reputation; failure to do so may spell the end of their practice. Yet, their practice is also being undermined by legal aid cuts and fee stagnation. Difficulties in developing trust and rapport may further impact upon a lawyer's resilience as they struggle with clients. The cuts are similarly undermining an accused's access to justice.

Within this chapter we have examined the generalizations made by lawyers, thus contributing to an understanding of how lawyers make sense of their work. The distinction between the 'first-timer' and the 'experienced' accused – first explored in Chapter 3 – is one such way in which lawyers made sense of the lawyer–client relationship. Lawyers also distinguished between clients based on offence type, which we have only alluded to in passing (as in quotes making assumptions about clients' capacity to understand): clients who had been accused of drug-related offences were said to have similar stances on issues such as plea and custody, while middle class clients were said to adopt a different approach to those from the working classes. The discussion of the lawyer–client relationship was inherently abstract by the nature of interview-based research and does not necessarily reflect the uniqueness of each situation a lawyer may find themself in. Certainly, there are differences between the conceptualization of *a client* in the here and now and *the client* in general (see Newman, 2013a). Again, ethnographic research would allow for an exploration of specific cases and clients and, in doing so, strengthen and deepen the analysis of the lawyer–client relationship. The generalized view of the client is easy to unpack and explore when using interview data; ethnography provides greater detail on how lawyers relate to – or are perceived to relate to – specific clients.

In Chapter 3, we established the importance of understanding the practitioners and the accused to obtain fuller insight from their criminal justice experience. This chapter has highlighted the potential of this approach by speaking to the relationships between practitioners, and between practitioners and clients, slotting these together to illustrate how the criminal justice system works in action. Establishing a firmer understanding of how these relationships work, as we have done in this chapter, will be valuable as we move forward onto our final data chapter, where we examine the experiences of those who have been subjected to the criminal justice system. As with Chapter 5, much of the focus here has been on practitioners, particularly lawyers, and how they worked to foster relationships. As Flower (2019) establishes, defence lawyers and their relationship with others in the criminal justice system play a formative role in setting the tone for the experiences of the accused. It was necessary to initially obtain their perspective as their role has the potential to shape much of the experience for accused persons and family members. In the next chapter, we will build on the practitioner insight of criminal justice relationships by considering in depth the experiences of the accused and their families, and how these compare with the accounts provided by practitioners.

7

Navigating the Criminal Justice System

Introduction

The previous chapter looked at the relationships at the heart of the criminal justice system to draw out how criminal justice works in practice. We looked at working relationships and lawyer–client relationships, and, while the accused were considered, the practitioners who mediate the accused's experiences of justice were at the fore. In this chapter, our focus switches to the accused and the family members, and their relation to the criminal justice system. Placing these voices at the forefront of the chapter gives more depth to understandings of the lawyer–client relationship and, thereon, of what it is to experience the criminal justice system.

The opportunity to combine the voices of defendants and practitioners in the criminal justice system and to analyse their experiences was a key motivation for this study. Kendall (2018), for example, has argued that suspects' voices need to be better integrated into criminal justice accounts, and Jacobson et al (2016) have presented the court process as anxiety inducing and confusing for defendants, thus highlighting the need to consider the experiences of court users. Yet, undoubtedly, in part, owing to issues of access, the accused's experience is under-researched within criminal justice studies, particularly those centred on questions of access to criminal justice. Yow (2018) has argued that research can have positive emotional impacts on interviewees, and Mitchell (2019) suggests that sharing painful stories with an 'enlightened witness' during interview can help start the healing process after a trauma. Many of the accused and their families told us how much they appreciated being listened to; it is important to our mission for us to centre their voices here.

This chapter is dedicated to exploring these often neglected individuals: those accused of committing criminal offences and those who have experienced the criminal process as family members of the accused. Our focus was not to examine satisfaction – or otherwise – with the criminal process, but instead to explore their views on their treatment during the process, their experiences of, for example, attending and appearing in court, and their interpretations of their interactions with other criminal justice actors. However, given the nature of semi-structured interviews, many interviewees did indeed comment on their dissatisfaction with outcomes. Questions of fairness seemed more important than the outcome of the case and, indeed, the fairness of treatment affected how the outcome was perceived (Sunshine and Tyler, 2003; Newman 2013a). Important too was the empathy of the lawyer (Sommerlad and Wall, 1999; Tata et al, 2004) – it was seemingly more important than legal expertise.[1]

We begin this chapter by presenting the views of the accused and, in doing so, seek to amplify these sometimes forgotten voices. We focus on whether the accused felt seen and heard and, through their narratives, elucidate some of the obstacles that they claim to have experienced. We then return to the perspective of lawyers as we consider their perceptions of the accused's experience. We draw out the issues that lawyers highlighted as making a difference to the accused. Thereafter, we explore the long-lasting impact of being subject to the criminal process. Here we are moving beyond the simplistic notion that the criminal process has a fixed beginning and end. Finally, we examine the stories of family members and the impact of the criminal process on these individuals. Indeed, the lasting effects of the process on family members urges that we broaden our understanding of what it is to be subjected to the criminal process.

This chapter builds on the theme of previous experience identified by practitioners in Chapter 3 and which emerged as a salient issue in Chapter 6. In discussing how the criminal justice system affects the accused, the practitioners' dichotomy between 'first-timer' and 'experienced', lawyers' new or 'regular' clients is drawn out. Whether through lawyers' assumptions or the examples of the accused, such a binary division has relevance across this chapter.

The accused in the criminal process

In this section, we examine what it is to be the subject of and subjected to the criminal process. The accused and family members relayed to us that they felt like passive bystanders in the process. While the accused are inherently alienated from the process (McBarnet, 1981), contemporary criminal justice reform has produced yet further marginalization (Welsh and Howard, 2018).

---

[1] An accused person or a family member may be better able to judge empathy – or their perceptions thereof – than whether the lawyer's knowledge of the law is adequate.

All the while, the accused are denied effective and meaningful participation, while also being compelled to participate in the process in a manner contrary to their own interests (Owusu-Bempah, 2017).

Undoubtedly owing to this marginalization and alienation, the accused were appreciative of the space we provided to them: AC4 stated that they "really enjoyed having [their] say" and SC3 expressed gratitude "for actually phoning back and letting me talk to you about it". Many were keen for their experiences to assist others. FM4, for example, stated, "We've been through it, the more I can help somebody else the better," and SC2 suggested that "our experience needs to get out there more". The accused and the family members impressed upon us just how ignored they felt; participation in this research led the accused and family members to feel that their narratives were worthwhile or even "real". Some felt such frustration during the criminal process, such as AC3 who was treated in a "rather flippant" manner by the judge "during the pre-trials and all the visits to the court"; AC3 felt that they were being viewed "as Walter Mitty", a fantasist. To understand how the criminal process operates, it is important to recount some of these experiences.

One of the most important messages we got from listening to these stories was that the process of criminal justice was viewed widely as mystifying by the accused in our sample.[2] Information provided at the police station was viewed as incredibly confusing (see Rock, 2007):

'She [police officer] took me in, obviously on the front desk, and they ask for all your information, don't they? Like, "Do you know why you've been arrested, blahdy blah, like sign this, sign that, pat you down, let me do it." So, I was like right, "One, I'm not signing nothing until I've seen a solicitor, because I've never been arrested before and I don't understand what I'm signing." Because their wording is in like, gobbledygook to me. It's all big words and I don't understand it.' (AC5)

This echoes findings from Clare et al (1998) on the difficulties of understanding the police caution. AC5, unlike a large number of those arrested and detained (Skinns, 2009; Kemp, 2018), insisted on speaking with a solicitor. They explained how important the solicitor was to facilitate understanding:

---

[2] Pickett et al (2015) have shown a general reliance on the media for understanding of criminal justice, which can lead to misinformation. They found that those with criminal justice experience are less likely to rely on the media. Their study was based in the United States but raises interesting issues in relation to accused and family understanding generally. Such findings also relate to the lawyers' anxieties around public attitudes to legal aid lawyers (as explored in Chapter 5).

'If I didn't have that solicitor, I would have had no one to help me understand. And then the police could have done what – and it's scary and it's sad, it's a sad world we're living in, because if it wasn't for solicitors how many people would be in prison wrongly? Wrongly accused ... who are they going to believe, do you get what I mean? There's no, without a solicitor, there's no one to defend.'

Here, the lawyer acted as a 'translator' (Cain, 1983; Newman 2013a), adopting the role of facilitator, allowing the accused – here, the suspect – and actors within the criminal justice system to communicate in a criminal justice system that has its own legal language. While many of the lawyers in this research recognized their role as facilitators, there were still instances where the accused could not effectively communicate in court and, consequently, they remained unseen and unheard. As AC5 explained, "They was hearing me, but they wasn't listening ... they was hearing what I was saying, but they wasn't understanding."

AC5 found the court process unnerving, particularly when the police were giving evidence against them.[3] They confronted a police officer giving evidence in court and asked the officer to show more respect:

'They were trying to act like the bigger man. Because I even went to one copper, I said, "Do you know when you take your uniform off?" I said, "Do you still feel like you're some kind of superhero?" He goes, "What do you mean?" I said, "Well, you're trying to act like you're better than everyone, like you're God's gift to man." Because they try to act like they're all higher up than you and they're better than you – but he wasn't better than me, I don't like when people make out that they're better than me. Because I find it rude, you're not better than me. Yeah, you've got a degree, congratulations, you know, good for you. But it doesn't make you any different. You're still a human being. So I said to him, "Would you like me to treat you the way that you're treating me?" "Yes." I goes, "So I'm going to start talking to you like you're some kind of asshole," I said, "because that's the way you're talking to me, officer."'

In contrast with their lawyer who showed them respect (as explored in the previous chapter), AC5 felt that the police were belittling them. AC5 had clearly felt they were looked down upon by the police officers in their case, thus communicating a fundamental lack of respect.[4] This reflects

---

[3] Courtroom design and usage can work against the accused (see Mulcahy, 2007; 2013).
[4] Holmberg and Christianson (2002) suggest that accused feel more confident and are able to think more clearly when police officers show them respect.

the wider view of accused and family members of the police and courts; they felt they were not understood, listened to or respected. Indeed, the importance of respect within criminal justice institutions and the need for mutuality of understanding has been highlighted by Watson (2020). Further, Skinns et al (2020) have highlighted the importance of being treated with dignity for those detained in police custody. Yet, unlike AC5, many of the accused and family members we spoke with, such as FM6, found lawyers to be disrespectful:

'They've always been very rude, very defensive, not willing to work with us or talk to us that much, and just took up an extremely defensive position. Partly because, the guy who owns the firm, his daughter was actually in the interview, so he, I think he was very protective about any criticism of her because it was his daughter, and she did nothing to protect him, whatsoever during that interview. It was appalling.'

FM6 criticized their lawyer's lack of responsivity and willingness to engage. Such experiences may undermine the lawyer–client relationship and may destroy or undermine the client's trust in the lawyer, the importance of which was discussed in Chapter 6. This may have implications for whether the client feels willing to take the lawyer's advice, which may have further implications for decision making regarding the case, such as in our Chapter 6 discussion of guilty pleas. AC2 was suspicious of lawyers and felt that they were simply liars interested only in playing legal games in the courtroom:

'A lawyer is just a liar in court. They will literally lie out their arse on the Bible – like I'm not religious … but they're, they're paid to lie. Now you go to court and lie, and you get caught for it and you'll get fucking done for it. They lie on a daily basis for their job. So how can you trust a lawyer? Do you know what I mean? Like, when they're defending you, they know you've done it, you know? They [know] full well you've done it like and they don't give a fuck because it's better for them isn't it?'

AC2, like many members of the public, may have failed to understand the purpose and role of the lawyer: although a lawyer cannot represent a guilty person as innocent, they can create a narrative that undermines the prosecution case. However, echoing Newman (2013a) and as we have explored in Chapters 5 and 6, the lawyer may not see the need or have the time to explain their role clearly and carefully to the client. Perhaps, if AC2 were informed about the role of the lawyer, they may well have adopted a different stance. Confusion over what was happening and what their role was at various points made it more difficult for those going through the system to contribute to the process. Many of the accused with whom we spoke did not understand what was happening to them until it was too late.[5] For AC9, their confusion was clear from how they "only truly understood what happened after the trial ended":

> 'Because I thought that, you know, the police are there to help you and that you can trust the police ... the police lied and they withheld evidence; they said it went missing. And then also the prosecution withheld evidence. I didn't realise until after the trial that this had actually happened because I had the one piece of evidence with me and if I'd realised at the time, I would have said, you know, "Look at this! This proves that I did not do what happened". ... So, I'd been convicted of criminal damage but there's no actual evidence to show anybody of the damage.'

AC9's experience illustrates some of the problems with criminal evidence, particularly surrounding the issue of police and prosecution disclosure, as discussed in Chapter 5. The adversarial process may be more about proof rather than truth; the 'battle' that takes place in court is a contest as to whose narrative appears more powerful and lawyers are permitted to present the evidence which best supports their case (see Finkelstein, 2011). AC9 had anticipated an experience wholly different to the reality. This highlights a misunderstanding of the process and possibly some miscommunication between the defence lawyer and the client. Had they better understood the roles of prosecution and defence, they may have appreciated what may – and may not – be presented by the prosecution and may have been able to act in a manner commensurate with a better outcome at court (that is by requesting evidence – or lack thereof – of damage and thus being able to challenge the prosecution's case). AC9 found the whole process "strange" – a word repeated frequently throughout their interview:

> 'It was very strange, okay, because lots of things changed. When I went to the police station, they said that there were two female witnesses and three men, and an independent witness. An independent witness who is a man who was walking with his dog, okay? When we went to court, that changed to one woman and all men and the independent witness went from a man walking with a dog to a man walking with his children. So, I brought that in court, I said like, "What the hell's going on here? How does this happen? This is strange!"'

---

[5]   See Jacobson et al (2016) for a discussion of defendants' understanding of the process.

It was difficult for them to follow the process or fathom what was happening –
and why – at points throughout their case, including the content of the
witness statements and the behaviour of the judge. Many of those with
whom we spoke felt inhibited from taking an active role, akin to largely
passive 'dummy players' (Carlen, 1976). AC4 expressed the difficulty of
engaging in the process:

> 'The first time, I'd never been in a room like that before in my life.
> And if I picture the Old Bailey, that I've seen on the telly, that's how
> it felt, Newport Magistrates' Court … I thought, "Wow, what an old
> building … this is kind of archaic, and … these people with these black
> robes on and stuff like that." I think I was completely confused by the
> whole [thing] – I didn't know what they were on about, you know?
> They read out your name, you confirm the charge, you confirm, you
> plead, and that's it. Everything else is over your head, especially as a
> kid, you know?'

While television representations resonated with AC4, this was not enough
for them to understand the process. It is possible that a strong lawyer–client
relationship can help ease feelings of confusion, but it is crucial for the lawyer
to spend – and have – time with the client prior to the hearing such that
these processes can be explained in detail. It is possible, however, that abstract
discussions of the process neither accurately reflect nor properly prepare the
accused for what actually happens at court. The overwhelming effects of the
courtroom and the dominance achieved through spatial arrangements – such
as the elevated seating of the magistrate or judge – has been explored in
Carlen's (1976) research. Within the court, the accused is placed the furthest
away from the judge or magistrate, with clerks, solicitors, probation officers,
social workers, press reporters and police as obstacles in between, the effect
of which can disorientate the accused and impinge upon their ability to
participate. FM1 recounted how their family member was so shocked by
the whole process of interview and investigation that they did not begin to
engage until they were in court:

> 'You actually can't believe it's happening. And all … you're doing other
> than when he went up and he had to speak, is, you're just listening.
> You're listening and listening and listening of what's being said about
> you. … Yeah, he just felt that when he was in court, when he listened
> to it all, he did feel like, he wanted to say what he wanted to say, but
> it was too late. Do you know what I mean? It was all kind of a bit too
> late then. By the time the judge read it out word for word, that was
> like a day, a day and a half before the jury went out. By then it was
> too late, and that's when the penny kind of dropped then … on the

day to sentence him, that morning, he was like, "Oh no, no, I want to speak to the judge." I'm like, "Dad, you can't." So there's that lack of understanding in that way.'

Again, as with AC9, it appears that FM1's family member had not fully understood the court process until it was too late. FM1's quote speaks to a certain naivety on behalf of the accused and, again, it may have been that the lawyer should have explained the process in more detail to ensure that the accused understood it (subject to the earlier caveat as to how difficult achieving understanding is in such circumstances). Some of the accused expressed anxieties regarding the way in which their histories and backgrounds were potentially weaponized at court. AC10 was distressed at how they were quizzed in relation to the offence in question *and* their previous life choices:

'It was really stressful ... I went to college a couple of years back, five years back, I think it was, and I done mechanical and electrical engineering. ... Yeah, the judge did say I only done that course to learn how to wire up a plug. ... It was my first ever crock, first ever criminal conviction.'

Expression and engagement were difficult beyond the courtroom. Indeed, those who had been to prison discussed the uncertainty and difficulty:

'Oh, it was hard. I went, when I first come in, I went under the Mental Health Act because I had suicidal thoughts. Because obviously you know about prison from what you see on TV, and it's always the negative and you never hear about the good stuff that happens in jail. So ... in the back of my mind, I was like, "Somebody's gonna get stabbed, or I'm going to get stabbed," or this is going to happen, and this is going to happen.' (AC10)

As with AC4 earlier, AC10 related their previous knowledge on the criminal process – and, here, more specifically, prison – to what they understood from television. AC4 outlined the initial adaptation period when first sentenced:

'That was really difficult. I remember vividly that I spent ... four months in my cell, just completely depressed. Didn't go out on association, yeah, just kind of let myself go. And I thought, "Well, that's it," you know, as far as I was concerned, life was over ... that light in the tunnel wasn't visible. I couldn't even find the tunnel. You know? That's the only way I can term it.'

Many relayed the experience of prison as one that was daunting and frightening. The interplay between prison and mental health problems was discussed frequently at interview (see Birmingham et al, 2000; Brooker and Webster, 2017; Forrester et al, 2018).[6] Indeed, the accounts relayed by the accused and family members were dominated by the difficulties they faced, with many struggling to engage with and participate in the criminal process. In the next section we examine what the lawyers in this study understood of the experience of being subjected to, and the subject of, the criminal process.

Practitioners' understandings of the accused's experience

Given the importance of the lawyer–client relationship to the accused's experience of the criminal process, it was necessary to explore how lawyers perceived their clients' experiences. While lawyers were willing to consider events from the client's perspective, many admitted to not having previously given it much, if any, thought. BS1 described a recent case of a non-English-speaking foreign national and how that had caused BS1 to reflect on their practice, particularly whether there was some degree of complacency:

'What his perception of the proceedings, or ... how I would deal with him, I think shone a light really on the fact that really over the course of twenty years, and probably less than that, how easy it is to become blasé about the experience, as far as a practitioner is concerned. So, you forget quite quickly, I think, or at least it is difficult because you're busy doing the case itself, to reflect on what the experience is for the defendant, until you come across a defendant where this is entirely alien to him in every single way. He can't understand what's going on ... it dawned on me that what the client's conception of what's happening is very different from yours. And you forget that.'

This absence of procedural knowledge was not unique to this individual; AC4, AC9 and the father of FM1 (all first-language English, UK nationals) also failed to understand the process. As BS1 highlighted, with the passage of time it may be difficult for the practitioner to appreciate the boundaries and limits of the client's knowledge. Indeed, Newman (2013a) identified that more experienced lawyers can become more detached from, and struggle to develop empathy with, their clients. Added to this, and as discussed earlier, BS1 indicated that the pressures of time prevent the lawyer from reflecting on their experience with the accused, despite the

---

[6] Mental illness has been mismanaged in prison over recent years (Coates, 2016).

fact that reflective practice is crucial to one's development as a practitioner (see Leering, 2014). Further, as BS1 explained, the process for the lawyer is very different from that of the accused. While BS1's reflections on the differences were bound up with the degree of experience that the lawyer had relative to the accused, it must also be acknowledged that the stakes for the lawyer – losing a case – and the accused – being convicted – are very different indeed. The client's anxieties can become something that the lawyer can too easily "gloss over" (BS1).

The possible disconnect between the lawyer's experience and the client's experience may derive from the type of previous interaction that the lawyer has had with the criminal process: it may be rare for lawyers to have been suspects or accused persons on previous occasions. Indeed, only two of the lawyers we spoke with had previous first-hand experience of being on the other side of the criminal justice system, and both through stop and search. This personal experience allowed them to reflect upon being drawn, even briefly, into the criminal process. DS16 discussed the potential similarities and differences between their and the client's experience:

'It feels nerve-wracking, even if, you know, you haven't got anything that you shouldn't have; it feels quite embarrassing to be stopped and searched by a police officer on the street as well ... it made me feel quite cross. ... It's sort of, "How dare you stop and search me." I imagine the feeling's quite different if you know you have something concealed upon your person that you shouldn't have! Probably feel much more frightened, apprehensive, and anxious. It's not going to be a pleasant experience.'

While the lawyer had, by their account, nothing to hide, they were nevertheless displeased, demeaned and agitated because of this encounter. None of the lawyers in this study had been arrested or been involved as an accused at any stage further along the criminal process. Thus, any thoughts about how clients found the process were based on suppositions. DS17 recounted a general lack of public understanding regarding the criminal process (building on the points made by lawyers in Chapter 5):

'Obviously, we take for granted when we're dealing with people that the average lay-person is not going to know their rights, their entitlement. I don't think they're documented well enough. Until you actually get there, and you're then told these are your rights, the average lay-person – you know, if I think of friends of mine or family members who've never experienced that, thankfully – I don't think they'd have a clue – you'd be so in shock and upset whether you've committed an offence or not. I don't think you'd really understand what your rights were – it should be documented, I think, in schools or different programmes just so you understand, and you know "this is what I'd have to do" if I got arrested.'

DS17 highlighted the need for greater public education and awareness regarding the criminal process (see Gibbs and Ratcliff, 2019). The client's understanding according to the lawyer was, however, communicated through the distinction of 'first-timer' and more experienced, the theme presented in Chapter 3 and developed further in Chapter 6. For every stage in the process – stop and search, arrest, detention and police interview, and appearance at court – almost all lawyers distinguished between those new to the process and the 'regulars' who "know the system pretty well" (DS2); despite being unaware of the "fine intricacies", the "regulars know a rough outline of it, they've been doing it long enough, probably longer than I have" (DS2). By contrast, DS2 claimed that new clients had a "lack of understanding", remarking upon the types of questions asked:

'"How long am I going to get?" "Am I going to get bail?" Two questions I hear all the time. And, with the non-regulars, it's usually, "'What happens next? What's going to happen next? What do I do? What happens next?" It's all about what happens next, they don't even think about the long-term, they just want to know what happens next. I've noticed that they never ask me, "What do you think I'm going to get for this?" Whereas the regulars always ask you that, it's like the third question. But to someone on duty who's, usually hasn't been in trouble or hasn't been in trouble that much, they never say, "What am I going to get for this?" They next say, "Well what do we do now, what's the next step?"'

Such is the apparent confusion of the 'first-timer' that they do not think beyond the short term: the process is so alien and bewildering that simply knowing the next step is all that appeared to be on the mind of the accused. The 'regular' client, by contrast, seemingly has knowledge regarding next steps and is more focused on the outcome, that is the sentence handed down at court. The repeat suspects have also been said to be less frequently discouraged to take legal advice compared with those new to the criminal process (Blackstock et al, 2014). However, we were often told that some supposedly 'regular' clients would not request a solicitor at the police station as they would frequently be made to wait and would rather get out as quickly as possible.[7] For DS10, it was "those who are in trouble regularly and have

---

[7]   For discussions of the factors affecting legal advice in police custody see Kemp, 2013; Kemp and Balmer, 2008; Skinns, 2009a; Skinns, 2009b.

become thick-skinned to … how it happens" who were most focused on leaving custody. According to some of the lawyers, these 'regulars' were keen to leave to smoke a cigarette, take drugs, or to (further) offend. That said, it was also acknowledged that even those with experience of the process found police stations unpleasant (see Skinns, 2011).

The unpleasantness of appearing in court was somewhat distinguished based on prior levels of experience:

'I mean it's dependent upon who that client is, isn't it? If it's their first time before the court it's traumatic, whether it's two hundred and fifty million pounds VAT fraud or it's a twenty-pound theft from Tesco's. For those who are regular attenders, it's their life in some ways, isn't it? But it's a system that has not changed for centuries. … Yeah, it's a very traumatic experience to appear before court … presumably you've been lucky enough not to have had it yourself, but … even as a good law-abiding citizen of course there are circumstances when you can find yourself before the court. Motoring convictions in particular, acquiring twelve penalty points or feeling strongly that you've got to contest parking on a double-yellow line even? So, we sometimes can forget it, how difficult it is, because it's commonplace for us.' (DS5)

The client's first time, regardless of offence type, was noted as particularly traumatic. Echoing BS1 earlier, DS5 acknowledged how routine involvement for lawyers can cause them to neglect the challenges for the accused when appearing in court. The consensus among lawyers was that various stages of the criminal process were especially difficult for those with no prior experience. For DS6, "The first-timers, the system is set up so that it's going to encourage them never to understand anything down at the police cells." DS13 explained:

'A lot of them don't understand what's going on … if you're there for the first time and you're obviously surrounded by other people who are withdrawing or who aren't adjusted can fuse into a really toxic atmosphere, I think, where people are getting aggressive because they don't understand what's happening most of the time.'

Indeed, the police station has been reported as an unpleasant space where the accused experience the vast array of negative mechanisms, procedures and sensory limitations (Skinns, 2011; Dehaghani, 2019; Dehaghani, 2021). These include the cold, hard slab beds, the minimal light in cells, and excesses such as the fluorescent lights in the corridors and the booking-in desk, and the banging, screaming and shouting that resonates throughout. Custody can be stressful and intimidating even for – and sometimes especially for – those with prior experience of detention (see Wooff and Skinns, 2018). DS8 acknowledged the "daunting" experience of detention in police custody:

'Sometimes you walk through custody and there's people screaming and shouting, kicking the doors. It's not a tranquil, place to be, I wouldn't say. I appreciate it's not supposed to be a tranquil place to be! But I think it is quite scary. I think scary is the main word I'm using when I'm talking about this because I think that's how a lot of people that we see feel and that's definitely how I would feel if I was in police custody!'

For DS8, the stressful nature was "obvious" and stemmed from the uncertainty associated with detention in police custody (see Hodgson, 1994; Dehaghani, 2021). As DS8 noted, "The first thing you get asked when you go to the police station is, 'When am I going to be out of here?'." The answer to that question may be "after the court appearance". The impact of being held in police custody before a court appearance was explained by DS13:

'Well I think that impacts some clients whether they're in custody or not ... from what I've been told that it's obviously a horrendous experience for them. I've been told that they don't get access to showers etc. Sometimes their medication is withheld. It's not a fit place to hold them given they expect them to be in court the next day and be able to have enough rest for them to be understanding the proceedings then ... I know if they are in custody then the journeys are quite distressing in themselves.'

Thus appearing in court could be made worse if the accused had spent the previous night in custody with all the extra stress and discomfort that might entail. Lawyers also reflected on the experience of courts in and of itself, with many discussing the Magistrates' Court as actually being potentially underwhelming for their clients. As DS13 recounted, "That's a negative experience in the Magistrates' Court, of just the chaos of the court." DS3 explained how defendants likely felt "short-changed" by the limits on the lawyer–client interaction prior to a court appearance:

'I think daunted but short-changed as well, for want of a better phrase, really. Because they are expecting a solicitor to represent them; they may or may not have made inquiries beforehand to say, "Well what can I get? What am I entitled to? How much help can I have?" And then they get to the Magistrates' Court and they get five minutes with the solicitor then and they're thrown straight into court ... I can imagine them feeling quite short-changed with the representation that they're supposed to get and what they get in the Magistrates' Court simply because of the time.'

From DS3's comments we infer that they were discussing new clients or those who see the duty solicitor. For them, while the court was still a place of intimidation, it was also a place of disappointment, with the accused preparing themselves for a "big day in court" only to see this image transformed, through the production-line approach (see Chapters 5 and 6), into a damp squib. The court process was viewed as "an alien experience" for those "who are experiencing it for the first time, or ... certainly not used to it" (BS16). This meant that it was important to "spend a bit of time with them ... trying to describe to them what's going to happen, just trying to ... put them at some ease about it" (BS16). The court process was therefore said to be demanding for those who were new(er). Yet, a handful of lawyers suggested that the process – here the police custody process – can also be difficult for the 'regulars', as DS16 reported:

'I don't think they understand the process really well or what's happening it – I mean clients who have been in the police station on a number of occasions have obviously picked up an understanding of the process. So they're going to be arrested, they're going to wait. They're going to come into the room and they're going to see a solicitor. They're going to be interviewed. They know that these things are going to happen. The understanding of the legal process and the meaningfulness of the interviews and things like that, I don't think people have a great understanding at all, even if they have been in there a number of times. I suppose because for me it's work, for them it's their whole life, you know, so maybe it doesn't go in properly, or it's difficult to some of it's difficult legal concepts! You're trying to explain to somebody petitional silence in an interview room when they've been in a police station for twenty hours and ate cereal bars. ... They haven't slept properly. So trying to then explain that kind of difficult concept is hard. ... So, I think their understanding is limited, a lot of the time in the process, and they just do as they're told.'

Although the more experienced individual may recognize the sequence of the detention process, their understanding of the legal procedures and processes – and the implications – may be limited. The experience of detention – and along with it, the uncomfortable and disrupted sleep and poor nutrition – may interfere yet further with the suspect's ability to engage (see Dehaghani, 2021). While supposedly 'regular' clients may not experience the same level of shock as the 'first-timers', and may have a greater – albeit broad – awareness of process, it should not be assumed that this equates to a full and proper understanding of the complexities – or even the simplicities – of the criminal process. The role of the lawyer was therefore key to demystifying this bewildering process. DS9, for example, found it difficult to fathom how someone could self-represent and, all the while, understand the process unfolding:

'Having seen litigants in person, I don't think that they do understand it at all. I've been qualified what, to sixteen years and I still don't quite understand all of it frankly … You've got all these government initiatives. … You can feel sorry for any defendant these days. You get next to nothing in terms of disclosure at the first hearing. You get a case summary, that's pretty much it. Without a lawyer to sort of steer you through it.'

As in the accused accounts in the earlier section, DS9 was right to see that the process was chiefly seen as confusing for the accused. DS9 also commented on "the time" concerned about how "quick" everything is now. Several solicitors highlighted problems with the speed of process in the Magistrates' Court (Newman, 2016a). For DS3 it was a "processing factory" and, for DS16, this reality made the process even more challenging for the accused to follow:

'If it's going to be dealt with in the Magistrates' Court, it's so quick. So the first hearing will probably be the last one, if it's a guilty plea, and the second hearing will be your last one if it's a trial. Things are dealt with so fast, so, I think I would struggle if I was a defendant to understand quite what was going on. I mean, it never feels like everything's been properly considered, it feels too quick for me, so I don't know how, how they would feel about that.'

For Campbell (2020), the manner in which Magistrates' Courts dispense summary justice in very short hearings means that defendants have limited opportunity to defend themselves. He believes that summary justice lacks basic due process rights in a legal process which bears a striking resemblance to what he claims passes for justice in authoritarian, non-democratic societies.

Lawyers generally thought that their clients had a better sense of what was going on at Crown Court. For DS18, Crown Court brought "more knowledgeable clients, while BS7 explained how the process in the Crown Court was "longer and "more interactive" and thus clients tended to "understand it more". Although clients were said to better follow Crown Court procedures, as compared with Magistrates' Courts procedures, there was a recognition that the atmosphere in the Crown Court was supposedly more unpleasant for clients. Further, 'law' is somewhat absent in the

Magistrates' Court, whereas the Crown Court contains more focus on legal arguments (Darbyshire, 2011).[8] BS16 referred to the Crown Court as "a much more forbidding place"; BS11 thought that Crown Court was "more formal. Most lawyers spoke of how daunting the Crown Court was:

'People who go to Crown Court … probably find it a bit more intimidating, because it's, well it's a proper court, isn't it? You get the impression, you know, you go to the Magistrates' and there are people there, it's sort of a day out. And you bring your dog, you bring your children, and it's, it's like a circus. Whereas in the Crown Court – I mean, there's still some element of, you know, this is a proper court. This is all a bit more serious than the Magistrates' Court.' (BS15)

The chaotic nature of the Magistrates' Court may sit in sharp contrast with the formality of the Crown Court. There was a widespread view among the lawyers that the accused was more likely to respect the Crown Court:

'I find it much more placid. That, I've done cases in a Magistrates' Court where the defendant has gone nuts. Screaming, shouting, should have been in contempt of court. Brought a baby in, screaming, shouting throughout, and let the baby cry. And then she had the appeal hearing in the Crown Court, legit, as in totally straight down the line. So, I think in general they're far better behaved, because it's a big sense of theatre.' (BS14)

For BS14, the enhanced formality of the Crown Court had a bearing on an accused's demeanour and behaviour (although BS14 and BS15 did not offer any indication of what a parent was supposed to do with a baby if they lacked access to childcare). Indeed, Jacobson et al (2016) found that defendants perceived the Crown Court as more professional and, as such, took it more seriously than the Magistrates' Court. Some lawyers relayed the varying impacts on clients:

'It may actually jolt people into action and say, "Oh, okay, I need to get my shit together, in a way. I need to be honest with everybody and say that

---

[8]   All the same, Darbyshire's research also highlights that it would be a mistake not to take the Magistrates' Court seriously. She notes that magistrates are generally found to be susceptible to 'case hardening' with a lack of empathy towards defendants, as reflected in verdicts and sentences. As such, the magistrates believe they have 'seen it all before', getting to know defendants by name, hearing similar stories in mitigation on many previous occasions. Thus, they are no longer receptive to the story offered by defendants, even when remorse is genuine.

this is what I did, or this is what I want to do." Or it may turn people into, you know, some of them may put their walls up. It may be very difficult to get out any information because they're very intimidated.' (BS12)

Thus, an appearance at the Crown Court can underscore the severity of the situation and thereby cause the client to 'come clean' or, conversely, become defensive. That the 'first-timer' would experience court differently was also suggested by BS6, who, while initially not considering the Magistrates' Court to be "as intimidating an environment" as the Crown Court, considered that, "Obviously if you were a first-time defendant in a case it would still be quite intimidating." They also highlighted that an appearance at the Magistrates' Court was "not in the same league as being in the Crown Court" and, as with BS12 and BS15 earlier, distinguished between the Crown Court and the Magistrates' Court based on formality: "The wigs and gowns, the judge ... the general atmosphere of it. Bigger courtrooms, certainly here obviously they're old-fashioned as well, and I would have thought that that's much more intimidating than being in a Magistrates' Court" (BS6). This apparently intimidating nature – and perhaps formality – of the Crown Court differed across south Wales:

'Of the courts that I would go to on a daily basis, Newport and Merthyr are, I think maybe sort of Sixties [build] or something? I'm not sure exactly, but they're much more modern than Cardiff Crown Court and I don't think there's quite the feel of, I don't think people would feel quite as intimidated being in those rooms as they would in Cardiff ... the rooms are bigger, there's more people, so there are things that would still be intimidating, but I don't think as much so as Cardiff.' (BS9)

The more old-fashioned courts, with their traditional grandeur, were considered to be more intimidating again than more modern, functional buildings. This gives an indication that there might also be different levels of fear and seriousness at different styles of Crown Court.

The lawyers in this study were very willing to reflect upon their clients' experiences of various stages of the criminal process. They often discussed the differences based on their judgements about the accused's level of past criminal justice experience, as well as the different experiences at various stages of, or sites within, the process. The willingness to reflect upon experiences also emanated from the accused and it is to these experiences that we now turn.

Punishment beyond the process?

The accused and family members with whom we spoke were not solely concerned with how their case unfolded, what happened in the police station, or their interactions with lawyers. In this section, we expand our account of criminal justice experiences over and beyond formal engagement with such aspects of the system. Family members and the accused highlighted the legacy of the process and the stigmatization resulting from suspicions or accusations of criminality. Stigmatization is viewed as essential within the criminal justice system to separate those who conform – and thus constitute 'the community' – from those deviant 'outsiders' (Durkheim, 1964).[9] Indeed, the 'offender' – particularly if imprisoned – is not viewed as part of the community but rather someone who must be reintegrated. The role of social stigma must be understood by locating the 'offender' within the wider community. In so doing, it helps us to see how the lives of the 'offender' and the community were entwined and impacted (Rickard, 2016). Those experiencing the process felt that those who had not themselves been accused did not understand the impact of the process: "First and foremost, I don't think people generally understand. It's a bit like when somebody's had a bereavement and people say, 'Oh I feel sorry for you, I know how you feel'. You will never know about it, unless you're in that position" (AC3).

These stories were powerful and helped us to empathize with the accused and the families. Initially, our thinking had been so much on the process itself but, once discussions were under way, we were alerted to how their experience of criminal justice went beyond the official life course of a case. This in turn generated some reflection on our part, as researchers, on what were deep and meaningful participant experiences.[10] AC3 provided more detail on punishment beyond the process:[11]

'People don't realise the consequences of not just being accused of a crime but being investigated. Not just physically, but emotionally, on you and your family and friends, right? You lose friends, you get family who disagree with you, right? I fell out with my sister ... I didn't talk to my sister for three and a half years, because she didn't understand what was going on, right? I fell out with my brother. And my brother and I were in business! We fell out and never spoke for five years, until my mum and dad died, right? I don't think people understand, even

---

[9] Mégret (2014) suggests that the individual who has gone through the criminal justice system has more agency than suggested by this account. The 'offender' retains some ability to react to the stigma and is not a passive recipient of stigma. Such analysis provides a valuable reminder not to make assumptions, but to talk to people to draw out their experiences.

[10] It was at this stage that we decided it was not appropriate to expect the interview schedules for the accused and their families to be as generalized or cover as much ground as those for practitioners; we followed the lead of what the accused and their families wanted to talk about (see Chapter 1).

[11] Here we borrow from and extend Feeley's (1979) work on the process as punishment.

the people who it happens to, genuinely don't understand what's going to happen to them until it starts happening. And they wonder where it came from, right?'

AC3 discussed the impact that criminalization has on familial relationships. The problem, as AC3 identified, is that family members may fail to truly understand the impact of being accused and investigated. AC3 likened being accused and investigated to a having a medical condition that impacts your everyday life and is impossible to ignore:

'And as things accumulate, it's a bit like me going to the doctors with a complaint. I go to the doctor's and I say to the doc, "My fingers are tingling." And they say, "Oh that's to do with your condition, diabetes." I went to the doctor's for probably four years after I was diabetic, for so many things, and all I was waiting for him to say was, "Do you know, that's new, I'd never heard of that before." Everything was down to the condition, right? It's the same when you come away from court. They say, "Don't worry, it'll get better." I don't sleep. I've not slept since 1998, when they first knocked my door. Because I live every single night this. ... You can't let it go. It's not even like a toothache. Something will jar – I'm walking down the road, and something will simply go by and I'll think, "Christ, I remember that."'

As AC3 explained, no one can understand the feeling of being accused and investigated without having been in that position before themself. They also explained the weight of the process on them and how it has disrupted their sleep ever since. The harm caused by the criminal process could affect people like a disease, a chronic illness that they cannot shift.[12] The emotional pain can endure through feelings of fear, as with AC9, who feared the police even after serving their sentence:

'I'm very scared of the police still. I'm very scared that if I do appeal, I'm going to get set-up for something and go to prison for something I didn't do. I'm very scared of all these things. I really think that the system is very, very corrupt ... my family don't want me to appeal anything, you know? They're very concerned about that. They want me never, ever to appeal. They're just so happy I'm not in prison. I am, also, ... so relieved.'

---

[12] Copson (2014) uses the zemiology approach to illustrate the merits of using the language of harm to discuss the effects of the criminal justice system. See also various contributors in Hillyard, Pantazis et al's (2004) collection.

AC9 had been left with an anxiety that the police were out to get them and that, if they provoked the police in some way, the police would be able to seek retribution (see Choongh, 1997). Despite continuing to claim their innocence – and initially telling their solicitor they wanted to appeal their conviction – they were too frightened to consider doing so. AC2 relayed that, even though they had changed (most of) their offending behaviour, they were still treated as though they were their past self by the police, mirroring the cynicism of police as regards 'offender' change reported by Cram (2018). For AC2:

> For a long, long time, the police didn't leave me alone. Even now like, there's a couple who know me from back in the day. But the police, though obviously they change areas and what not, but quite a lot of police still know me from the way I was. I was a little cunt, like!

The lasting fear of police mistreatment was expressed by several of those we interviewed. As SC1 explained, "I'm scared of the police more than anybody." SC1 considered the impact on their children of a police visit:

> 'Like, my kids, my daughter, the one day, when the police left, she was like, "Mum! That policeman stared at me straight in the face!" And she was like saying it really angrily, like, like she wanted to go mad. She was like, "He stared at me straight in the face!" And she was trying to like back me up. And my kids would comfort me as soon as the police would go.'

SC1 had been diagnosed with post-traumatic stress disorder because of their contact with the criminal justice system. They explained how this impacted them:

> 'You go over the whole event a hundred times a day … I would just jump out of my skin because I'm in my own world all the time, listening, and I'm really hypervigilant, if the door knocks, I freeze. If someone knocks the door with their fist, I literally freeze. My heart feels like it's pounding out of my chest because I think it's the police. And I literally freeze to the spot. I can't move.' (SC1)

The experience of prior criminalization stayed with SC1, and the anxiety resulting from the experience also made it difficult for SC1 to live alone:

> 'And I was so scared I gave up my house. I moved in with my dad. So I've got this flat in Grangetown [in Cardiff] that I've had for two years and never stayed there. The whole flat is brand new … and I can't

even face staying in there because I can't face the door-knocking ...
I'm too scared to stay on my own.'

SC1, like other accused persons with whom we spoke, had changed the
way in which they organized their life due to the negative effects of their
contact with the police. This is echoed by Jackson et al (2013), who found
that, when people find policing to be unfair or disrespectful, trust is lost
and legitimacy undermined. FM4 left the country to avoid the police and
concerns about a corrupt justice system that had filled them with fear:

'I've moved to France – yes! I can finally – and this is how much it
has affected me – I can finally walk out of my front door and not look
behind me. I can finally go down to the shop and ... I'm not worried
about who I'm going to bump into.'

FM9 even contemplated whether they wanted the police to investigate a
break-in to their house, so negative were their experiences. They described
what had happened and how their experience of the police shaped
their reaction:

'I would never, ever trust a police officer. It was like last night we had
police officers come to the house because young lads tried to break
into our house the night before, and do you know, they sat there, and
I was just so bitter because I thought – there wasn't only one police
officer, there were four police officers lied through their teeth on oath.
And never, ever again. I really begrudged going to them and explaining
about somebody going into the house, and it was only because my
daughter said, "Please Mum. Phone the police and let them know
and [make] them aware that somebody's tried to get into the house."
But to be honest, I wouldn't have even gone to them because I feel
so bitter and angry and I could never, ever trust the police.' (FM9)

Their negative experience of involvement with the police and criminal justice
system was such that FM9 was willing to go without help after becoming a
victim of crime, yet they had to balance their own safety and that of their
family against the antagonism they felt towards the police force. AC9 also
expressed a distrust of the police:

'I keep a hammer on my desk! Because I feel like someone's going
to break in my house, I feel like someone's going to come and attack
me. And I feel like – I actually feel like someone's going to attack me.
And that's because of this incident where I was attacked, and I wasn't
protected. I told the police, "I don't want this man knowing where

I live." A week later, he's come, and he's hammered my car. He's now got away with all of this. I've been convicted. And, I don't know what's going to happen next.'

AC9 was worried about retaliation from the person who had made a complaint against them. They did not feel protected by the police because the police had previously failed – in their eyes – to properly and fully investigate the accusations against them; they felt unable to rely on the police. SC1 noted how their social standing made it ever more difficult; they felt that others would trust the word of the police over their version of events:

'No one is going to believe what they do you or what they've done to me when I've been arrested, or they've come to my house. Nobody. It's like, I'm common … I'm from like a council estate … like my mum used to have to struggle through to feed us. I'm from, like, a run-down background, so nobody is going to believe me over two decent, honest officers. Like, they're professionals. No one is going to believe me.'

The importance of being believed ties into another of the features of AC3's account of the ongoing legacy of the criminal process described earlier: the impact that being accused or convicted of a crime can have on relationships with family and friends. FM1 recounted how they had to leave their religious community after a family member was convicted of a crime:

'They know they haven't spoken up for the truth, all the people who want to avoid you, the people who don't know where to look, the people who are worried they'd be called to court, who want to help you, and don't know how to say no so then they all just avoid you … And our tolerance has got to the end of thinking, well, if you can't help us now through this, we don't want to know … we've lost friendships of thirty, forty years.'

FM1 explained that they felt let down by their community; that nobody spoke up for their family member to avoid the moral condemnation that was being placed on them. They thus became ostracized from the community. This contact with the criminal justice system had a significant impact on their local relationships. Their friends were now drawn from those who shared their religion outside Cardiff or those within Cardiff who did not practise. In addition to the emotional impact, FM1 discussed the physical impact of the criminal process and imprisonment on the accused family member:

'In terms of how his health went and his memory went, and he was like, "I forget things." That was hard to see. And then now when you look at the size of him, it's almost like he's gone shorter as well. He's just gotten small. His shoulders have gone in, he's lost a good few stone in weight, yeah? His shoulders are hunched forward … he is like an old man.'[13]

The involvement in the 'criminal world' was also something that was said to have a long-term wearing effect:

'I'm lucky I'm still here at thirty-eight. I've technically been dead once, you know … I've seen many things I would never, ever wish my kids to ever even have a fraction of a glimpse of, do you know what I mean? I've lost three members of my family whose been killed by other people. My own family, you know? And having that, that had an impact on my life also.' (AC2)

AC2 had lost family members through criminal involvement and had worried about their own life. They also expressed concerns about a family member who had been left behind in an area where there was little choice – according to AC2 – but to be engaged in crime:

'I was lucky to get out. I didn't want my kids brought up there. I've got like cousins there, and nieces and nephews and, you know, the older drug dealers use the thirteen, fourteen-year-olds as, you know, shotters. So basically that means they're drug runners, so the guy has the phone, yeah? The kiddie has the phone, another phone, so whoever the punter is, he'll phone the phone, "Yo, I'll have two Bs and a whizz B." He'd be like, "Right, go to place X, so he's on his way there now." The main man, the drug dealer's phoned up his runner, said, "Right, yo, take two Bs and a white to my guy, he's here now." And then the youth will be off on his bike, you know? And that's how it is now.'

AC2 was glad to be out and moving on with their life. There were some positive long-term effects of contact with the criminal justice system, such as for AC2 who, when we spoke with them, was working in steady employment and was thinking of having children. AC2 discussed the changes they had made with us:

'I was in denial. I always thought I didn't have a problem, but I was bad: a crackhead, a heroin addict, you know? I was bad, even when I was still

---

[13] FM1 kept in regular contact after the interview. They had been expecting the release of their family member, but sadly this did not happen. FM1 later reported that their family member had died in prison several months after the interview.

making progress, I still had the drug habit, you know? Even though I wasn't committing crime as in theft and stuff like that, I was still dealing and that, but I was still trying to break away from it by sticking to doing this Turning Point, and I was still trying to find alternative ways, because I knew we were on a long-term solution. I just knew, even though I miss the money that's the one thing I miss is the money – but the life I don't miss. I can relax and sleep know, you know, I don't have to be like looking over my shoulders like, "Is the police going to be there? Is somebody going to be trying to jack me by here?". ... But I was lucky, I met this girl ... she's from ... a nice area, total opposite, and that's where I live now by the way. So now I'm in like two different worlds – I go back to Ely to see my family, but I had to get out of Ely to actually make the clean break, the proper break I needed.'

AC2 explained that meeting their life partner, obtaining access to steady employment, and becoming involved in a drug rehabilitation programme had helped them escape the life that they were keen to leave behind.[14] As with AC9, FM4 and SC1, AC2 explained the feeling of never being able to relax for fear of being criminalized. Like AC2, AC4 had taken part in a rehabilitation programme and had relayed to us how this enabled them to move away from crime:

'My family said, "You should go on the [12-step] rehab programme". ... So I took little bits from it, and I think the key moment for me was resentment. I can't remember what step it was, I think it was step six. And looking at my resentment and my adverse child experiences, with my mother and my step-mother, they were things that I kind of kept in my back pocket, and I used to pull that card out all the time, and say, "This is the way, this is why I am the way I am. This is why I do what I do."'

AC4 now worked in the third sector, supporting people who were in a similar position to where they had been. They relayed how they worked hard to wrestle something constructive from the criminal process – a process in which they had no faith after what had happened to them.

While the impacts of the criminal process on the accused can be deep and long lasting, there are also – often neglected – adverse impacts of criminalization on family members of the accused. Having woven some of these accounts throughout earlier chapters, given the dearth of discussion on family member perspectives in academic research, we spend more time

---

[14] For an overview of desistance literature see Best et al, 2017.

in the following section on the impact of the criminal process on the family. Although family members can provide support to the accused (as some of the earlier accounts highlight), they may nevertheless experience, vicariously and directly, the punitive impact of the criminal process (see Jardine, 2019).

The role of the family

Comfort (2016) has identified the need to pay attention to the well-being of family members, noting that, while discussions are largely focused on the effects of imprisonment, there are impacts at every stage of the criminal process that may destabilize the lives of those family members.[15] While there are studies which focus on the effects on the family (Booth, 2018; Jardine, 2019), they rarely examine necessarily how the family experience the pre-prison process. Much existing research focuses on effects of imprisonment on the family rather than the effect of court processes on the family, or the cuts to legal aid and the effects on the family.

The families we spoke with gave us an insight into prison but also these earlier stages of the criminal process. Being told that a loved one was in trouble with the criminal justice system for the first time was a dramatic, traumatic experience for many of the family members we spoke to.[16] FM4 recounted this moment:

'My solicitor at that time – because we were still using a legal aid solicitor – was told and rang me and said, "Look, I need to tell you, J is going to be charged." And it was awful because I was actually in the garage buying a new works van with my husband. So I was literally in the showroom, I answered the phone, and … it just feels like your whole world is falling apart. It's really difficult to describe it. You almost feel like your ears are ringing and the world has stopped … it's terrible. And you obviously feel sick and your mouth goes really dry and you're struggling to speak. I had to go sit in the car and cry.'

---

[15] Although this was not an issue raised in our interviews, Booth (2020) explores the familial impact for family members expected to take over care duties following imprisonment.

[16] The trauma of the criminal justice system for family members has previously been explored by Beck et al (2002–3). Their study looked at the psychological harm caused to the families of capital defendants in the United States. While their focus on capital punishment provided a very different context to our study in the criminal justice system of England and Wales – where there is no death penalty – the insight they provide on the need to involve the family members in examinations of the impact of criminal justice sets out an important principle.

FM4 described the shock of finding out that their son was being charged. From the point of charge, families had to become accustomed to the procedures, processes and judgments of the criminal process. FM9 discussed the frustration involved in supporting a family member going through the criminal process, "knowing that he's innocent, knowing what he's going through, and you're frustrated, it's just frustration". Their frustrations were not simply limited to their son's case, as they explained how "this [people being wrongfully accused or convicted] is going on all round the country, that the police are doing this, and who do you go to, who can you turn to". As with our other participants, FM9 felt that there was nowhere to turn. FM3 detailed the "overwhelming" nature of a first court appearance, exacerbated by the fact that "I've never been in trouble. I've never known him to be in trouble. So it was all like, really like, 'Oh my God, what's going on?'" FM3 felt that they "just didn't have a clue what was coming next". The overwhelming anxiety was such that "I literally cried for about a month". As with many of the accused persons discussed earlier, FM3 explained the confusion experienced; the sheer amount of activity in the courts made difficult any opportunity to follow the process. Of particular concern was the speed at which the case progressed, which made processing emotions and information somewhat challenging:

> 'Like we went into court, and then we seen the solicitor who was like, "Oh, he's looking at this much time." We're like "Okay, right. Alright." And then we go in, and they were like, "Oh, we know he had more, so he's looking at this." It was just like, really, it was really emotional.' (FM3)

FM3 was taken aback by the solicitor updating them on outcomes – agreed in private between legal professionals – before court started when they expected the changes to happen in open – accessible to the public – court. There were also concerns, particularly from FM4, about inadequate remuneration for criminal legal aid lawyers, as we discussed in Chapters 3 and 5. Of particular concern was the impact on the quality and quantity of work conducted on a case:

> 'If they're going to be competently putting maybe thousands of documents together to really fight this case for the person they're representing, my God, that is nowhere near enough money. And I can see why things, then, you know, they end up getting left … they obviously care. You know, I'm not saying they don't. But then you cannot put somebody who is going to get seven or eight grand to defend a case in the same way as somebody who is going to be paid forty, fifty, who has got all the resources, they've spent all this time

with you, you do all these things, they're emailing you at sometimes nine, ten o'clock at night. You've got the phone calls, you've got that personal thing, and everything for us was absolutely spot on ... but at the same time, I honestly think it's really, really wrong to have a two-tier system where you get what you pay for, and they've got more of a success rate, but they're able to put more into it. And why should it be fair to be based on that? That's not right.' (FM4)

The legal aid changes that have been discussed throughout this book by the lawyers had caused anxiety for FM4, who did not trust that state-funded defence would be sufficient to achieve justice. In this example, a family member was able raise the money required to pay for private legal advice. They considered remortgaging their house to pay for a private solicitor as they felt that paying more equated to a better experience and a fairer outcome. Yet, many of the accused and family members we spoke with were not in such a position. Indeed, the restrictions on criminal legal aid may cost-out a vast number of individuals, as we explained in Chapter 2. What we saw here, though, was a doubt that legal aid fees would make for competent representation. The effect was that some of the accused with whom we spoke opted not to be represented, so shattered was their faith in the system, as we looked when considering the back stories of accused persons in Chapter 3. In addition to the inadequacy of legal aid remuneration, there were also concerns that lawyers did not have an understanding of how to address a client's vulnerability (see Dehaghani and Newman, 2017; Dehaghani, 2019). FM6, for example, felt that the solicitor dealing with their son's case did not have a full enough understanding of their son's autism:

'He [the solicitor] was a really nice guy, but, in terms of autism, he didn't have a clue, and he said, "I don't know what it is. I haven't got a clue and he'll probably get a conviction." That's what he told me ... the problem was, he [the son] got pushed into, like, making a statement, when he wasn't fit to make a statement that night. And I think the solicitor was trying to make sense of things in a neurotypical way that you can't make sense of – so, you know, there were certain things he was asking him, certain questions, and certain ways and phrases and things and ways of putting things. ... So it ended up sounding like, you know, it didn't really – it wasn't really helpful. And then he had to do a no comment interview which I didn't understand the implications of that. I do now because there's good things and bad things about that. It can be very risky. But we didn't have any choice.'

For FM6's son, the consequences were such that a 'no comment' interview was given. The family, at the time, did not understand the implications of silence during police interview such as the adverse inferences that can be drawn later (see generally Quirk, 2017). Without this understanding of neurodiversity, the lawyer was unable to communicate effectively with their client. Indeed, Maras et al (2017) have identified that autistic people were largely dissatisfied by their experiences of the criminal process.[17]

In addition to being unable to fully participate in the process, some of the family members, similar to the accused discussed earlier, felt the negative impact of the criminal process on their own health. FM1 earlier discussed the negative health implications on their family member, yet also explained that "from the moment this all started, everybody's health suffered". They themself "had dizziness, vertigo, sickness all the time" to the point where they "couldn't really function normally". For FM7, the well-being of family members was too easily overlooked:

'Our health has suffered. You know, but we're not the victims and we're not seen as victims. We're just the carers, you know. Just the parents. But, actually, we're the ones, probably much more so than our son ... who've suffered psychological, emotional and health problems as a result of the aftermath of what happened. ... There should be a recognition of the emotional trauma that the parents and families have to go through, who are often the ones always there on the front line, trying to protect that person because they know they couldn't cope with what we've had to cope with.'

FM7 felt the need to "shield" their son from the fallout of his case. They felt that they were not provided with the support that they required. FM7 highlighted, very clearly, the interconnectedness between the accused and the wider familial circle. The physical and psychological health implications can be long lasting, as FM6 identified:

'I do still have a lot of flashbacks to custody, particularly; I do. I try not to think about it but every – but sometimes, especially when I'm trying to sleep, it comes back into my head a lot. About being in that room and the questions and it's hard, but sometimes it's very haunting. Because you can't, you can't process it yourself, because you don't understand it, at the time, what's happening, and so you're hardwired to try and protect, you know, your family member, or whatever, but you can't protect him, or yourself, really, because you just don't know

---

[17] Their research indicates a wider misunderstanding of neurodiversity within the criminal process, despite the fact that lawyers claimed to comprehend the difficulties experienced by autistic individuals and the adjustments suitable for supporting them.

what's going on yourself ... and, you know, try and just play the game a bit, because you feel vulnerable yourself on some level, you know. Because you just want everything to be over yourself. Like, you just want to get out of the room yourself, you know? Yeah, so, it does still haunt me a lot. ... And I can't get to a place of healing because I'm still in it.'

FM6 had attended the police station along with their son. While it has been well documented that suspects and detainees are often keen to be released from the unpleasant environment of police custody (Skinns, 2009; 2010; 2011), FM6's quote illustrates that family members also find the experience of police custody incredibly difficult and traumatic. The trauma for family members could be associated with the sense of hopeless – that they have been unable to protect their loved one from the process because they too do not have a grasp of what is going on. Losing the family member to prison custody was also difficult; FM3 discussed the sense of loss and grief associated with their loved one being imprisoned:

'His mum was worse than me, but she literally really struggled. She said, "I feel like I've lost my son, and it's not even, it's not that. But it does feel like it." And then there's no help, no information, no, like, give. It's like guess-work, and everything's really slow and what about money. Just stupid little things you just don't think about, and you're like, "Oh." So, you've got to, like, learn it? So it's hard. It's really hard.'

Again, FM3 discussed, as with FM7, the lack of support and information available to those whose loved one has been accused or convicted. Indeed, the lack of support was a consistent grievance. This was particularly the case when it came to navigating a way through the process and/or dealing with its aftermath:

'I think support, whether it be support groups which, you know, I don't know of any, because I don't think the complexity of what I've gone through, coupled with the whole community of your whole life, I don't think there's any support group out there good enough or relevant or right, at all. Being on these groups on Facebook, yeah, they're okay to an extent, but they don't understand. ... It doesn't matter where we go, it's always going to be there ... we'll never be treated normally, because the people who don't know you think, "Well, there must be some truth in it", and even though he is the one who has been imprisoned, or he is the one being accused, we're all, we're all judged. We're all sentenced on that. Forever.' (FM1)

As FM1 highlighted, the family may experience the stigma of conviction just as much as the accused person. The complexity of the experience is difficult to understand and is difficult for that person to communicate. While we may never be able to fully translate these experiences, there is great value in exploring these narratives and we would urge other criminal justice scholars to do so. In doing so, we can better understand the experiences of those within the criminal process. The impacts are broader, deeper and more long lasting than some may initially assume.

Conclusion

In this chapter we have focused on what it felt like for those drawn into the criminal justice system, a valuable addition to the experiences of practitioners, and especially lawyers, who were at the forefront of earlier chapters. We examined the ways in which the accused and their families have struggled to have their voices heard. It was also important to explore whether and how lawyers understood the experiences of accused persons and we therefore investigated the ability of lawyers to empathize with their clients. When conducting this research, it became apparent that we needed to take a broad view of criminal justice impacts and so we examined the enduring effects of being subjected to, or the subject of, the criminal process. This included the perspectives of family members to illustrate the ordeal that those accused *and* their families experience. The accused indicated that they felt a sense of invisibility, often due to their inability to fully understand what was happening in the court, with the subsequent effect of limiting their engagement in the process (see also McBarnet, 1981; Carlen, 1976). Family members felt similarly invisible and ignored, with some expressing a level of vicarious pain and anguish that their loved one was in the cell or dock; for others it was felt that the pain had been caused to them personally (see Wooff and Skinns, 2018). The strongest message to emerge from this chapter is that the impact of the criminal justice system is long lasting; the effects of the criminal process do not cease the moment that a sentence is passed or served.

Being subjected to and the subject of the criminal process can be stressful, stigmatizing and traumatic. It must be acknowledged that the faults and flaws of criminal justice, such as the drive for efficiency that pushes the accused through the process (as brought out in Chapters 5 and 6), have human consequences, and not simply for the accused person. The invisibility of the accused was one of the core messages to emerge from this research. The accused may struggle to have their voice heard, whether because of miscommunications, misunderstandings or limited interactions with criminal justice actors as discussed in Chapters 5 and 6. While our research has provided an avenue for the accused to have their stories heard, there should be more support provided to those going through the criminal process. This could be achieved by an assurance that the lawyer can spend sufficient time with their client. Perhaps more radically, this could be achieved by a move away from proof and towards truth, although this would require centuries' worth of unwiring. There are other mechanisms – such as the sentence discount for early guilty pleas discussed in Chapter 5 – that deliberately serve to prioritize efficiency over the accused having their day in court. Indeed, Bowen and Whitehead (2013: 6) have spoken of the need for 'courts which concentrate on people as well as cases'.

Vulnerability theory alerts us to the importance of recognizing the interconnectedness that comes out strongly in this chapter. Reminding us of our human frailty – and, indeed, strengths – we can appreciate that misfortune – and good fortune – could be bestowed upon any of us. We should remember that each citizen is *vulnerable* and the state could – and should – provide resilience, and yet often does not do so. The accused – and their families – may be the weaker contender within a pernicious power struggle. While the experienced accused may have relatively more resilience than the 'first-timer' (although not always), all accused persons have relatively little resilience when compared with – and battling against – the prosecuting state. Each stage of the criminal process has the potential to play on and compromise further an accused's resilience, rendering them helpless. Beyond the process, the accused may continue to feel its lasting punitive effects. Additionally, family members – who provide support and, arguably, resilience to those within the criminal process – may find their own resilience depleted. Moreover, for accused and families, adverse experiences of the criminal justice system can deplete resilience. Resilience can be provided through social and cultural capital and through rehabilitative programmes. The problem that remains is how to get people to trust the system when they feel so let down by it.

Within the five data chapters, from Chapter 3 to the current chapter, we have drawn on our interviews to give insight into the experiences of criminal justice, examining, across Chapters 3, 4, 5 and 6, aspects of the process from the perspective of those who work within it and have shaped encounters of it and thereafter, in Chapter 3 and in this chapter, exploring the lived realities of those going through the process and the often lifelong consequences of being subjected to the criminal process. This discussion provides a nuanced and detailed consideration of how aspects of the criminal process are experienced in Wales and during a period of austerity. In the following chapter, we bring together the knowledge gained from capturing these experiences and look ahead to the future by setting out policy recommendations and the possibilities for future research.

8

Doing Criminal Justice Differently

Introduction

In this chapter we draw together our findings and point towards the future for research on both criminal justice more broadly, during and after austerity, as well as, specifically, criminal justice in Wales. Thus far, we have told the story of how austerity has impacted upon individuals' experiences of criminal justice, examining thereafter the impacts on criminal defence, particularly that which is legally aided, and on other justice institutions such as the courts, the prosecution and the police. Our focus has been on how criminal justice has been experienced in Wales, and while our data is in some ways specific to south Wales, there are also many findings that can be generalized beyond Wales and to the whole of the England and Wales jurisdiction. Such findings may also be relevant to other jurisdictions that are facing difficulties in the wake of budget cuts and efficiency measures.

In Chapter 1 we explored the historical, cultural, geographic, socio-economic and legal landscapes in Wales and how they compare with England. We argued that criminal justice research must be conducted in Wales and should take account of locality given its impact on how justice is served *and* experienced. In Chapter 2 we explored the impact of austerity, and more deep-rooted neoliberalism, in England and Wales, while thereafter exploring the specific impact on Wales itself. Chapter 2 also detailed vulnerability theory – which underpins the research and will be considered again in this chapter – and the ways in which the theory prompts consideration of the implications for experiences of the criminal process and the ability of individuals to achieve justice. Across Chapters 3 to 7 we explored the narratives of those we interviewed, identifying key themes such as the underfunding faced by practitioners and accused persons' previous experience of criminal justice. We entered the research expecting to consider the role of underfunding but the importance of the 'first-timer'/'regular division is one that only came to our attention during the fieldwork. Both themes, though, emerged organically from the accounts that were provided by those we interviewed, and we followed the interviewees' leads to draw out their significance. These themes frame and inform many of the experiences that followed. We explored how the stories of practitioners and the accused underpin their experiences, examined the importance of place to criminal justice, considered the pressures that impact on criminal justice practice, assessed the state of the relationships between parties in the criminal justice system, and drew out the broader impact of criminal justice on the accused and their families.

In the discussion that follows we reflect on the core messages within our chapters, exploring the importance of vulnerability theory to our analysis of criminal justice in Wales during austerity, and stating the case for a holistic and interconnected response in criminal justice. In doing so, we present solutions that seek to improve the system to better enable access to justice. We investigate how this could be achieved in Wales as we face an important historical moment – the possible devolution of justice functions to the Welsh government. Drawing upon Fineman's vulnerability theory (2008; 2010; 2013; 2017), we also query whether and how justice can be served through a focus on the human experience, particularly the interconnectedness between each of us. This develops the application of vulnerability theory to criminal justice initiated in Dehaghani and Newman (2017). We highlight the limitations of our research sample and make suggestions for future research. We offer implications for policy and practice, both within the England and Wales jurisdiction and, more particularly, within Wales.

Connectedness in criminal justice

Our research has highlighted dissatisfaction within the criminal justice system. Many of the lawyers interviewed made an active choice to enter the criminal defence professions – and some expressed commitment to a 'social agenda' – and yet they were becoming increasingly disillusioned with, and by, their work (see also Newman, 2013a). Prior to entering the profession, they knew that criminal defence work was poorly remunerated compared with other areas of law, however they felt aggrieved by the consistent cuts and fee stagnation, by the increasing workload and by the imbalance – and thus unmanageability – between work and life. They expressed concern about the future of the profession, communicating a reluctance to encourage others to follow the path into criminal defence. The situation that legally aided criminal defence has been forced into is one which raises serious concerns regarding the future of criminal defence and, thus, the implications for access to criminal justice (see Smith and Cape, 2017).

For the accused – many of whom were engaged in the system not by choice but instead by circumstance – and their families, the various changes to the landscape of criminal justice caused by (and pursued in the name of) austerity meant that their voices were not being heard and their cases were perhaps not receiving adequate attention. Most worryingly, they felt let down, and punished, by the criminal process. The punitive nature of the criminal justice system came not simply in the form of punishment associated with the sentence handed down, but also arose because of the very nature of the system, which is punitive from start to finish (Feeley, 1979). The disposal of the case or the completion of the sentence was not the end of the road for many; rather, it seems that the trauma of involvement in the criminal process meant that lives were irreparably changed forever. For some, of course, it was 'once a criminal, always a criminal'; the label was difficult – if not impossible – to shake off (see Gordon, 2018). Further, the issue of disadvantage emerged not simply when an individual was facing the might of the criminal process: disadvantage and criminalization go hand in hand, and given the higher rates of relative deprivation and disadvantage in Wales, it is possible that the effects of criminalization and cuts have gone deeper still. The issue with criminalization is also important to how the individual experiences justice thereafter: once an individual has been brought, or forced, into this system, not only may they more readily be criminalized, they may also be assumed to know how the system works. Such individuals may therefore face even greater disadvantage by not receiving the safeguards that they might have received had they been 'first-timers'.

Among those with whom we spoke there was a sense of resignation: frustrated with how dire the criminal justice system had become, they felt unable – or were unable – to challenge the decline and deterioration. In part, this resignation came from a feeling that the challenge was too great, yet it also stemmed from exhaustion experienced by practitioners, the accused and family members. The sense was that improvements to the criminal justice system were not a key priority for the UK government: the desire to make such improvements was, and is, lacking because it pays to be 'tough on crime and tough on the causes of crime'.[1] Within political circles there seems to be an unwillingness to accept the importance of proper access to criminal justice, which is central to the functioning of a democratic society. It is clear from our interviews that action must be taken to improve the criminal process for all involved, whether by choice or by circumstance.

In Chapter 2 we examined the ill-effects of austerity and the underpinning ideology of neoliberalism on the functioning of the criminal justice system and argued for the integration of a vulnerability approach. A vulnerability analysis alerts us to the ways in which resilience is depleted and the need for a responsive state that ensures citizens are provided with such resilience. As

---

[1] Although greater focus is undoubtedly placed on the former to the detriment of the latter, if disadvantage and deprivation is what is meant by 'causes'.

we have argued previously (Dehaghani and Newman, 2017), the criminal justice system is exactly that: a system (see also Dehaghani, 2021). Within a system, there are points of interconnectedness: one cannot detach the underfunding of criminal legal aid from the ways in which individuals experience access to justice; one cannot detach the individual experience of criminalization from the effects – often deep and long lasting – on the family and the wider community; and one cannot isolate the effect of underfunding one institution from the functioning of another. The data, in Chapters 3–7, suggests that deleterious effects in one aspect of the criminal justice system can impact upon other elements of the system. The precarious nature of legal aid work can reduce the resilience of legal aid lawyers. Adverse experiences of criminal justice may deplete resilience among the accused. Moreover, the damage done by deprivation, disadvantage and criminalization can be felt beyond the accused themselves; it can affect families, and perhaps even communities, and overall trust in and respect for the criminal justice system.

A vulnerability approach urges scholars to consider the interconnectedness that exists between and among individuals and institutions. We cannot argue for better funding of the police while at the same time depleting the criminal legal aid budget (or vice versa). We also cannot argue for better funding of criminal legal aid without an assurance that the accused will receive better legal advice and assistance. Similarly, we cannot inject funding into criminal legal aid while also cutting the budgets of the police[2] and the courts. Instead, a commitment to justice must be commensurate with a commitment to all justice institutions. This commitment must mean providing resilience to all of those working within, or otherwise engaged with, the system. Applying a vulnerability analysis, this would mean providing resilience to the police, the prosecution, the courts and the defence.[3] It would mean ensuring that each of the key institutions are functioning as best they can with the ultimate goal of securing access to justice. Yet, it is not simply the institutions of criminal justice that should be of concern: we must engage more readily and more heavily with the impacts of the criminal process and criminalization more widely.

It could be queried, however, whether justice and resilience can be achieved when the criminal process places the state against the individual. The police and prosecution – as institutions of the state – are, in essence, battling the defence and defendant (Packer, 1968; Griffiths, 1970). Yet, the defence can also be coopted to work for the prosecuting state through

---

[2] It has been argued that defunding the police could resolve a number of the problems within the justice system – see Vitale (2017).

[3] There is, of course, a question about what 'resilience' means for a number of these institutions, and resilience is not always a 'good thing'.

mechanisms such as disclosure, sentence discount for early guilty pleas, and the Criminal Procedure Rules. If the criminal process is to continue to be adversarial in nature,[4] there is a clear need for the defence to work for the accused alone. Alternatively, it may be time to dismantle the notion of the criminal process as a battleground and instead to reconceptualize it as one of mutual support, where the state and the individual are not at odds with one another. The 'family model' put forward by Griffiths (1970) sees the accused or criminalized individual not as a separate species cut off from the remainder of society, but as a person deserving of respect who has committed an offence.[5] Such an approach would seek to avoid administering punishment in isolation from the rest of the relationship and would discourage labelling the individual as 'criminal' or otherwise exiling them. Instead, the state, much like a parent, would consider the individual's best interests and would perform their role 'with good faith and using [their] best judgement' (Griffiths, 1970: 380). The role of the defence would be 'cooperative, constructive, conciliatory' (Griffiths, 1970: 383), whereby energies are directed towards assisting the tribunal to arrive at the decision that meets the needs and interests of all concerned. Within such a system, punishment has an educative function whereby the nature of the process is as important as the object. While the system recognizes that conflict is inevitable and does not shy away from suppressing criminal conduct, it seeks to minimize hostility in doing so. Perhaps most importantly, by reconciling societal interests with the interests of the accused as a *person* deserving of support and respect, the accused is provided with the opportunity to learn from their mistakes while remaining part of society.

Indeed, in our sample, we were often alerted to the view that the police, the CPS and the defence needed to work together. Practitioners saw the need to help and support one another: a spirit of 'we are all in this together'. Such rhetoric has also drenched the discourse surrounding COVID-19, which has dominated our time spent writing up this research. We are told to stay home to save lives and protect our revered NHS. We have been alerted to how we must alter our lives and behaviour for the greater good. The pandemic saw the upspring of mutual aid groups across the UK, of neighbours who had lived alongside one another for years suddenly getting to know each other, with the more resilient offering help to those who lacked resilience. Writing about this (re)emerging sense of community under COVID-19, Solnit (2020) has suggested that 'the pandemic marks the end of an era and the beginning of another – one whose harshness must be mitigated by a spirit

---

[4] Although see Field and Brants (2016) on the assumptions of different criminal justice systems.

[5] Griffiths (1970) suggests that criminal activity is an expected occurrence.

of generosity'. Key to vulnerability theory is our interconnectedness and shared human frailty and ontological strengths. The pandemic has exposed our human vulnerability and the undercurrent of inequality throughout our society. Yet, it has also illustrated how through community and connection we can transform society around our vulnerability; that we can recognize the needs of others and respond with care and compassion.

It is therefore entirely possible to imagine a society where we look after one another and we recognize our interconnectedness. Of course, as our discussion suggests, the criminal justice system does not hold the same position in the public – and political – consciousness as the NHS. This is arguably, at least in part, because it is believed that criminalization will never affect us good, decent, 'law-abiding' citizens.[6] Engaging in 'criminality' is deemed to be a choice, and those who are suspected and accused of crimes are assumed to have complete agency and autonomy. Yet, people *do* become caught up in the criminal process and wider system, whether by choice or happenstance, and it is not until then that the punitive nature of the criminal process and system, its inadequate functioning,[7] and its negative impact on well-being and livelihoods become apparent.[8] A shift in public consciousness is not impossible as the pandemic has illustrated, but it would require greater empathy and understanding, and, crucially, a shift, in UK government rhetoric and action and media discourse, from punitiveness to care. This shift is precisely what is required.

And justice for all?

It is no secret that the criminal justice system is at breaking point (The Secret Barrister, 2018); our data has not only demonstrated this, but has also pointed towards the ways in which the undermining of access to criminal justice can have deep, profound and long-lasting effects on individuals and families. Our worry is that many – if not most – individuals are not able to access justice. Of particular concern is the routinization within criminal justice: in our earlier work (Newman, 2013a; Dehaghani, 2019), we witnessed how suspects' rights were being routinely breached and how lawyers – who were working within law firms employing a 'sausage factory' approach – were unable to rectify the various problems due to their excessive

---

[6] The notion of most citizens as 'law abiding' is one that could arguably be contested. Many of us have engaged in some illegal activity during our lives, even if such illegal activity is *merely* in the form of a road traffic violation or tax evasion – see Tyler (1990).

[7] One could most certainly argue that the criminal process *is* functioning, but only to produce miscarriages of justice.

[8] Unless, of course, one has knowledge of the criminal justice system through, for example, teaching, scholarship and research.

and unmanageable workloads. Newman (2013a) found that lawyers were reluctant to visit police stations owing to the paltry fees paid for this work. Dehaghani (2019) observed how police officers were aware that lawyers did not have the time to spend identifying and disputing breaches of PACE. Lawyers would either not turn up to the police station (instead favouring legal advice over the phone) or, when attending in person, would try to make their representations as quickly as possible so as not to make a loss on their time spent at the station. The police station is an important – and often the only (Jackson, 2016) – stage in the criminal process. Supposing that 'trial at the police station' becomes the norm (and we do not think that it should), it is imperative that police station work is adequately remunerated. If it is, lawyers will have the incentive and resources to mount an effective defence for their clients. Without such remuneration, many suspects may be routinely criminalized without the protection that they are entitled to by law. This, we argue, is a miscarriage of justice.

Yet miscarriages of justice do not simply emerge at the police station; they can also arise at trial, in various ways. Lawyers, without sufficient remuneration, do not have enough time to spend on their cases. They are receiving disclosure at 'the eleventh hour', and it is not until such disclosure is provided that they – lawyers argue – can obtain a full(er) understanding of their clients' cases and the viability of possible options and outcomes. They are only able to manage the bare minimum on cases, enough to ensure compliance with their regulators but not as much as the lawyer – or the client – would want. The fee structures are encouraging lawyers to 'game' the system, often to the detriment of their clients, such as in the case of the sentence discount for an early guilty plea. The limits on criminal legal aid provision at the Magistrates' and Crown Courts serve to further deplete access to criminal justice (Smith and Cape, 2017). In the former, a criminal justice institution that is chaotic and disorganized but where the overwhelming majority of cases are heard (if heard at all), the false rhetoric of simplicity, triviality and straightforwardness prevails (McBarnet, 1981; Darbyshire, 2011). Yet, it is here where the accused, owing to the restrictive means and merits tests, may fail to access criminal defence and thus access to criminal justice. The complexity of the law necessitates access to criminal defence lawyers, yet while the lower courts are dismissed as unimportant, miscarriages of justice may remain undetected.

It is also of grave concern that we are seeing fewer people entering the criminal legal profession and large numbers leaving for better-paid, and/ or less-stressful, work (see Harris et al, 2021). The worry is not simply that lawyers are unable to do their work to best serve their clients' interests but that in years to come there will be criminal defence advice deserts across large sections of the UK. With court and police station closures and cuts to criminal legal aid – and the associated issues of recruitment and retention – justice is being taken further away from communities, particularly those in rural areas, thus further hampering access to justice within these communities. We must remember that the accused, as Griffiths (1970) highlights, are *not* a separate species but instead should be recognized as an important and valued part of our communities. The process should be fair and just rather than punitive and traumatic (see Feeley, 1979); individuals who feel unfairly treated may internalize a deep distrust of and disdain for the criminal justice process (see Tyler, 1990). The drive for 'efficiency' has forced the defence to assist the prosecution yet the state still treats the defence and the accused with disdain and disregard. If the state is to require that the defence aid the prosecution, then so too must the state and prosecution assist the defence and the accused. The stripping back of access to criminal justice has gone on for far too long and there is a need to reverse the deleterious turn. Vulnerability theory, while not providing all the answers as to what can or should be done, alerts us to our inescapable interconnectedness. It is entirely possible to reimagine the criminal justice process and to engender trust through a more responsive and conciliatory system.

Doing more, doing less and doing better

While we argued against the stripping back of access to justice earlier, this is not to say that we are not in favour of any stripping back. Blair's New Labour administration introduced almost one offence for every single day it was in office (Morris, 2008). The criminal justice system has become increasingly punitive under neoliberalism, at least for adults (see Dehaghani, 2017), and prisons across England and Wales are experiencing overcrowding and dire conditions (Howard League, 2019). We recognize that there are constraints on any system, but we also believe it entirely possible for justice to be served within institutions and systems that are facing serious financial and resource shortages.

One way of doing so would be to reverse the punitive turn and to decriminalize certain types of conduct, using criminal law as a last resort (see Packer, 1968). Such an approach would ease the pressure on the system, as a point of principle, and would improve the lives of those who are already often marginalized and disadvantaged, thus alleviating much of the damage, trauma and pain that these individuals may – and do – suffer. With fewer people being brought into the system, the focus can instead be shifted towards adequately protecting those who are by guaranteeing that criminal legal aid is provided to all and ensuring that criminal defence lawyers are properly remunerated for their work. It would also ease pressure on the police and CPS, who could spend more time ensuring that cases are properly and thoroughly investigated; on the courts, where adequate time can be provided for the accused to properly set forth their case; and on prisons such that better care is afforded to those who are sentenced to custody. Resources could also be better targeted towards ensuring that the causes of crime – more often than not, disadvantage and deprivation – are genuinely and adequately addressed.

Since the 1990s there has been a move towards the curtailment of suspects' and defendants' rights, with a desire to provide greater protection of and rights for victims. Sanders et al (2010) contend that the criminal justice system should positively promote *freedom* by striking a balance between suspects' and defendants' rights on the one hand and victims' rights on the other. As the harm caused by a crime is often irreversible and the victim – supposing there is one – cannot always be restituted or compensated, the application of state power may not serve to redress the balance (Sanders et al, 2010). Sanders et al (2010) contend that society must choose whether to allow the application of state power or to restrict this such that the state may act only where the action promotes greater freedom than it erodes. They also rightly highlight that the enhancement of the freedom of victims *and* the accused is beneficial for society at large (Sanders et al, 2010). To underscore this point – and this, too, is a key consideration – they note that victims and offenders do not exist in separate categories and thus by restricting the freedom of the accused one cannot ensure that we are promoting the freedom of victims. They also emphasize the importance of recognizing just how detrimental the application of state power can be for the accused – and how this is overwhelmingly more detrimental to the accused than a crime may be to victims (supposing, again, that there is indeed a victim).

Their model requires some adjustment. It has been criticized for being utilitarian and consequentialist and thus incompatible with human rights theories – which are anti-consequentialist in nature – and for the underdeveloped – and highly contestable – nature of the term 'freedom'" (Ashworth and Redmayne, 2010); for using Packer's crime control and due process in a dichotomous manner (Henham, 1998); and for trying to adopt a freedom-based approach even where this may be incompatible with the issue at hand (Sandland, 1995). We are also concerned that freedom-centred arguments could be misused by the very neoliberal ideology we criticize as a further excuse to contract the state. Despite such caveats, we would like to see a broadly freedom-informed approach and, following Griffiths (1970), greater emphasis placed on conciliation and cooperation within the criminal justice system to the benefit of not only the accused, but also the community at large. At present we are operating under a zero-sum game where the winner is most certainly not the accused. It does not have to be this way: a state that better supports its citizens, responding to their needs, will be one that works to promote their freedom to thrive – together.

Justice in Wales

It seems that there is an appetite for change in Wales. The Commission on Justice in Wales (2019) provided the first review of justice in Wales for over 200 years. Such a review was much needed. Yet the Commissioners and those working within and on it faced many obstacles, most notably a dearth of data specific to Wales. They found data on England, or England *and* Wales, but an absence of disaggregated data on Wales. What they did find was that many of the taken-for-granted assumptions made in England did not apply squarely in Wales and, perhaps more importantly, Wales was quite different from England in many respects. While there are, of course, as we have highlighted throughout this book, similarities between and within England and Wales, there are also, crucially, very clear points of divergence. Not only should these differences be reflected within academic and policy discourse, they must also be accounted for within policy and legislative initiatives. The 'for Wales, see England' approach is indefensible when viewed in the broader frame of sovereignty, yet it is also unsuitable in practical terms when our criminal justice institutions are – and should be – deeply connected to the communities in which they operate.

The current situation of Wales lagging behind the other devolved nations of the UK is problematic in terms of fair – or even effective – policymaking. For Wyn Jones and Learner (2020: 241):

> Wales still remains out of step inasmuch as justice functions remain un-devolved, leaving the Welsh government unable to engage in any meaningful way with the fact that Wales has consistently the highest imprisonment rate in western Europe. And herein lies the rub. While the story of constitutional instability provides plenty of fodder for academic seminars and the like, in terms of progressive policymaking it can only be considered as an opportunity lost. Time and time again, when attempts have been made to develop new policy initiatives, they have run up against the limits of the Senedd's legislative competences. This was perhaps most pronounced in the first years of devolution, but it remains the case even today when devolved powers have been substantially expanded.

The time has come to remedy the ills caused by lack of justice powers for Wales.

In Chapter 1 we provided a brief overview of the Commission on Justice in Wales' (2019) recommendations in respect of the criminal justice system. A key consideration was the need for the justice system to be devolved to Wales. We agree fully with this proposal. For the Commission on Justice in Wales (2019: 16):

Only full legislative devolution, combined with executive powers, will overcome the obstacles of the current devolution scheme. It will:

- enable the proper alignment of justice policy and spending with social, health, education and economic development policies in Wales, to underpin practical long-term solutions;
- place justice at the heart of government;
- enable clearer and improved accountability;
- enable advantage to be taken of Wales' size and ability to innovate, for example by integrating legal aid and third sector advice, bringing health and justice resources together to tackle drug abuse, and providing better means of dispute resolution through ombudsmen services; and
- strengthen the constitution of the UK.

These outcomes, flowing from devolving justice and creating a Welsh legal jurisdiction, would improve access to justice for those living in Wales, allowing the Commission on Justice in Wales (2019: 32) to meet their key aim of making 'the rule of law through access to justice relevant to everyone as the means by which the right to just, equal and fair treatment in all aspects of life is realised and Wales as a nation is just, fair and prosperous'. Partitioning the England and Wales jurisdiction will allow Wales to address the access to justice crisis identified by the Commission on Justice in Wales (2019). By providing the Welsh government with justice powers, decisions can be brought closer to communities; with responsive decisions taken with consideration of these communities, experiences of criminal justice may be positively improved and fairness can be ensured. With Wales' own legal aid authority, as in Scotland, assurances could be made regarding independence from government; the agency could be located outside of its sponsoring Ministry, rather than inside the Ministry of Justice, as is currently the case in England and Wales. This is what the United Nations (2019) suggests when it states:

Legal aid authorities should be free from undue political or judicial interference, be independent of the government in decision-making related to legal aid and not be subject to the direction, control or financial intimidation of any person or authority in the performance of its functions, regardless of its administrative structure.

This could ensure principles of fairness and equality can be upheld in the face of, for example, ideological attempts to slash state support, as we have seen under neoliberal austerity in Westminster. Scotland has also shown that smaller legal aid systems can be more flexible and innovative when compared with larger systems such as in England and Wales. A smaller system can produce actual 'efficiency' while also being effective and responsive to local needs. A smaller system could also allow for increased community engagement. The devolution of justice would, more generally, allow for a better alignment across the range of already devolved areas such as education, health and housing.[9] A linkage between legal aid funding and third sector advice and assistance would also allow for a better-informed and more responsive approach to provision. The system could be premised on collaboration and transparency, part of and responsible to the communities of the country.

Some local advice providers suggest that there have been problems with previous Welsh government funding decisions for the advice sector around social welfare law, as they have tended to prioritize national bodies such as Citizens Advice over smaller, independent organizations (see Robins and Newman, 2021).[10] These providers suggest that it is the smaller, independent organizations that have the best ability to meet the local legal need, and as such argue that the Welsh government has not always recognized the importance of mixed provision of specialist legal and generalist advice providers. Such decisions have negatively impacted upon, for example, advice provision, contributing to the closure of Wales' only law centre in 2014.[11] Thus, the Welsh government's approach to access to justice is not without critique, yet, overall, the Welsh government has previously shown a willingness to promote equality and that should signal hope for the prospects of a properly functioning devolved justice system (see Owens, 2020). The promise of devolution allows us to imagine a criminal justice system better than the current situation that we have explored throughout this book. A Welsh legal jurisdiction, aligned with the principles of the Wellbeing of Future Generations Act 2015, could guarantee the promotion of social justice and thus provide greater resilience to the marginalized and disadvantaged. The principles underpinning policy and questions of justice in Wales – community, universalism, citizenship, and equality of opportunity *and* outcome – are compatible with the vulnerability theory and family model approaches we set out earlier in this chapter. It is within this frame that justice can be improved by Wales for Wales. Of course, the current devolution arrangements prevent the Welsh government from improving

---

[9] The Welsh government can create criminal offences within its areas of competency but is otherwise restricted on criminal justice matters.

[10] Such views can be gleaned from submissions of evidence to the Commission on Justice in Wales (2019) as in that from Riverside Advice or the Speakeasy Advice Centre in Cardiff.

[11] Cardiff Law Centre closed but, in 2019, the Speakeasy Advice Centre in Cardiff joined the Law Centres Network. Therefore Wales again has a Law Centre at the time of writing.

the lives of people in Wales in such ways, as keen as the government may be to make these improvements.

Evans et al (2021) have questioned the extent to which Dragonization – the development of a distinct, progressive turn – in Welsh criminal justice policy has thus far occurred. This Dragonization has become an 'empty signifier' onto which politicians' (and academics') desired Welsh values could be projected without necessarily following through in terms of real change. However, their conceptualization of Dragonization suggests that it may have value as an organizing device moving forward. For Evans et al (2021: 14):

> Dragonisation's endurance owes much to the belief that an alternative system in Wales could be possible. This prospect is one that has become more tangible in recent years as the problems within Wales' current system are laid bare. ... At a time when politicians in London and Cardiff grapple with the Commission on Justice in Wales' recommendations, a rekindling of the original spirit of Dragonisation can help to ignite a more vibrant debate over the future of Welsh criminal justice policy and its relationship to Westminster.

Subject to their caveats about the extent to which Welsh values are progressive in light of Brexit and recent votes for hard right parties in the country (the latter since cast back into the political wilderness after winning no seats in the 2021 Senedd election), the devolution of justice creates at least the potential to realize a more progressive criminal justice system, and thus, a criminal justice system more in line with the equality agenda that has characterized so much previous Welsh government policy in other areas.

Also required is further research and scholarship within and about Wales, with the aim of exposing the issues specific to Wales – and the different regions herein – and general to the entire England and Wales jurisdiction, supposing that such a jurisdiction continues to exist. Important is the recognition of differential impacts according to locality; the impact of criminal legal aid cuts has been unequally distributed throughout the England and Wales jurisdiction with rural areas suffering more greatly than urban domains. Crucially, high street firms – which still predominate in Wales – may not be able to adopt a 'sausage factory' approach to advice and representation and, further still, may not be able to sustain their practice due to issues with recruitment and retention. Courts have also closed at a much higher rate in Wales than in England; such closures present significant court access obstacles for those in rural and otherwise poorly connected areas such as the post-industrial south Wales Valleys. The investigation of the effects of policy decisions must have specific regard to, inter alia, demography and geography. While our research contributes to addressing the dearth of research on criminal justice in Wales (see also Jones, 2017; 2018; Jones and

Wyn Jones, 2019), there is much more left unexposed. In the following section, we point to further research and identify some of the challenges presented by – and limitations of – our own research.

Challenges and future research

As discussed in Chapter 1, we faced significant difficulties with regard to access to police stations and courts. Indeed, on the question of public access to courts, Twitter is replete with discussions of individuals and organizations being refused entry or asked to leave. Transparency and a willingness to engage with researchers and with the community at large is important for promoting access to justice and for engendering trust in the criminal justice system. As such, we would advocate for *more* – not less – openness to research and to public engagement and access. At the same time, we found that some practitioners, particularly lawyers, were keen to engage in this research; they hoped to expose the problems that they were facing, problems which negatively interfere with and undermine access to criminal justice for the accused. They hoped, as do we, that their stories would effect positive change within the criminal process in Wales, and we value their openness, responsivity and willingness to give of their increasingly precious and limited time. Despite being a small number relative to the other participants, we are also grateful to the police officers who gave of their time to take part in this research.

Further, while often a hard-to-reach group, we found that those who had been accused of offences were willing to discuss the – actual or perceived[12] – injustices that they had faced. Family members were also keen to have their voices heard. It is these individuals – rarely considered during discussions of the proper functioning of the system and process, *let alone* spoken with – who provide resilience and support to those experiencing the process as accused persons. It is also these individuals who often provide support to the accused, and yet they also experience trauma during this process (and thus may require their own support). Their contributions are so vitally important for understanding how justice functions and, more often than not, how it fails to function. We are incredibly grateful to these individuals for sharing their stories and bringing to light the problems encountered within the criminal justice system. We welcome more criminal justice

---

[12] We say 'perceived' as in some instances there may not actually have been an injustice (if this is taken to mean a lack of formal justice), although it is worth bearing in mind that 'justice' and the perceptions thereof are undoubtedly subjective. It is also worth acknowledging that perceptions are indeed important when considering questions of procedural justice and legitimacy (see Hough et al, 2010; Hough, 2013).

research into the experiences and stories of the accused and their families. Further, we recognize that we have barely addressed structural inequalities relating to racism, gender inequality, and disability, all of which have a significant bearing on how the criminal process and wider justice system are experienced. We acknowledge the need for further research on these structural inequalities.

Our research has illustrated the shared nature of the challenges and we thus encourage researchers to combine a range of perspectives where the research questions and methods allow. Yet we must also acknowledge the limitations of our own research: we did not engage with all of those involved in the criminal process and/or system. From the outset, owing to difficulties with access, we did not engage with the judiciary.[13] We therefore do not have any insight into how judges experience their work and their interactions with others (see Darbyshire, 2011), other than what we have gleaned from those involved in this research. Future research, dependent upon access, could explore the challenges facing the judiciary, particularly in light of the court modernization programme. Further, while we spoke with barristers engaged in prosecutorial work, we did not obtain access to the CPS staff and therefore do not know much about their experiences and views of the criminal justice process. We again rely on accounts from lawyers and the police for insight into the issues affecting the prosecution. We were also remiss not to involve those with explicit experience of the process as victims and/or witnesses as they too may be adversely affected by many of the issues raised in this book, particularly those centred on access, participation and travel. It would have been interesting to explore how they experienced the process and whether their conceptions of 'justice' and the barriers thereto were so at odds with what would benefit the accused. There has been a 'growing polarisation of the rights and interests of victims and of those accused of crime in both government rhetoric and in popular discourse' (Cape, 2004: 1), yet the interests of victims and the accused may not be irreconcilable and it is, moreover, likely that many accused have been victims and vice versa (see Sanders et al, 2010). By reframing the debate as one of shared experience – and not of irreconcilable difference – the criminal justice system could offer common protection for all.[14] Future research should therefore approach the victim/offender dichotomy more holistically, perhaps interviewing those who have been both accused and victim.

---

[13] There is a more complicated, time-consuming process for conducting social research with the judiciary.

[14] See Rethinking Crime and Justice (2005).

Summary of key findings and recommendations

In the following summary we set out our key findings and recommendations. While based on criminal justice in Wales, and specifically south Wales, there are findings and recommendations that are relevant to the entire England and Wales jurisdiction and indeed beyond, although perhaps in a broader and more general sense.

First, the austerity programme and the wider neoliberal ideology has radically altered access to criminal justice, particularly by promoting efficiency – and replacing traditional principles of justice as fairness with crude financial measures (see Mant, 2017) – and stripping the welfare state of (some of) its resources. Those who are working at the coalface of criminal justice report that the system is falling apart and requires urgent investment to avoid widespread miscarriages of justice (see also The Secret Barrister, 2018). For criminal defence lawyers, criminal legal aid cuts and continued fee stagnation have caused significant damage to their ability and willingness to 'zealously advocate' and defend. The result, for the accused, is a stifling and depletion of access to criminal justice. Solicitors and barristers alike have noted the impact of cuts on their practice: they lack the time to work to the standard they desire – or conduct the work on cases that they were once able to do. Gibbs and Ratcliffe (2019) have suggested that this problem could be addressed through the expansion of not-for-profit defence companies or the return of the public defender model; our view is that this option could – and should – be pursued. Indeed, changes to the regulation of defence services may allow those offering legal advice to access charitable income streams through a not-for-profit model. Such a model could free practitioners from the demands of profitability and, as such, offer a more holistic service akin to other social welfare-engaged third sector organizations. A Public Defender Service – introduced by New Labour, but little loved and largely unsuccessful as they introduced it largely for cost-cutting reasons[15] – may also serve to free criminal defence firms from profit motivations.[16] This would allow emphasis to be placed on the social justice requirements of the responsive state.

The criminal defence lawyers in our research also signalled the uncertain future of legally aided criminal defence practice, with both solicitors and barristers reporting recent losses to the profession due to the imbalance between remuneration and stress, a reluctance to recommend the profession

---

[15] Two of the four remaining branches of the Public Defender Service operate in Pontypridd and Swansea.

[16] Although the Public Defender Service in the US is also not unproblematic – see van Brunt (2015).

as a viable career for aspiring lawyers, and a worry that the most talented young law graduates will not go into criminal legal aid. The future of the profession should not simply be of concern to practitioners, but also raises ethical issues for legal academics who teach, guide and instruct those who wish to pursue a career in criminal defence and the higher education institutions within which these students are taught (see Harris et al, 2021). Important also to this debate is the issue of social mobility (see Young Legal Aid Lawyers, 2018). The Young Legal Aid Lawyers (2018) report notes several issues that we raise throughout this book, namely low salaries, stress and strains on – the ever elusive – work–life 'balance'. In addition, they identify issues that were not raised in our book such as the reliance on unpaid work experience (which can be exploitative), an absence of support, and high levels of debt. We echo their calls for the need for mandatory minimum salaries for trainee solicitors, and we support their charter on fair paid work experience at the real living wage, including the demand for government funds to be made available to small legal aid firms and not-for-profit organizations to assist them to properly remunerate or reimburse those undertaking work experience. In addition, we agree that there is an urgent need for improved welfare initiatives to be introduced for lawyers. Their suggestions are characteristic of the responsive state that we believe is key to promoting resilience and access to criminal justice.

The future of criminal defence is also more dismal in some areas as compared with others, to the extent that some areas are facing an absence of provision. The Law Society (2019) has highlighted the emergence of advice deserts – areas where there are no advice centres, law centres or legal aid practices – in social welfare practice, with housing law suffering most notably (see also Robins and Newman, 2021). It is very possible that criminal defence advice deserts will surge if problems with recruitment and retention remain. Rural parts of Wales are experiencing a crisis of an ageing profession, with over 60 per cent of duty solicitors above the age of 50 (Law Society, 2019). Within ten to 15 years there may be few or no criminal duty solicitors in certain rural areas, which will likely undermine the right to advice at the police station. Given that police station work is so poorly remunerated, solicitors based in urban areas may be reluctant to travel long distances to attend the remote rural police station. Even where a solicitor is willing to travel, the suspect may not be willing to wait for the solicitor to arrive and may proceed to police interview without first receiving legal advice.[17] The potential for miscarriages of justice is significant and is yet further exacerbated by the use of the police station as the de facto site of trial (see Jackson, 2016). We urge that greater attention be paid to the

---

[17] See, for example, Skinns (2009).

emergence and growth of advice deserts and recommend that incentives to practise are provided in areas with unmet need.

On the matter of community need and involvement, we must also be alert to changes within the court estate. The closure of courts across England and Wales, and particularly in the latter, may frustrate local justice, recognized by, grounded in, and working for the community. Of particular concern in our interviews was the necessity of significant travel to court – affecting also, although possibly less so, police stations – and the considerable distances between courts and from court to offices. While this issue adversely affected lawyers who were often called to attend court at short notice, it undoubtedly impacts even more adversely upon those accused reliant on public transport – particularly in Wales where such options are lacking – and those struggling to afford the rising costs of transport. This may hinder participation in the criminal process and can, for example, push the accused towards entering a guilty plea. Although not explored in this book, changes to the bail provisions were also noted as a problem for lawyers and their clients, and these merit further research and consideration (see Smith, 2020), particularly from the perspective of those with lived experience of the process. Decisions seem to be taken by those in privileged positions who have little regard for and understanding of the effects on the already marginalized, deprived and disadvantaged. These decisions also seem not to have regard for or understanding of the geography of Wales: while ten miles on a map may not look far or appear to be so for those sitting at a desk in the incredibly well-connected London, the difference is significant on the ground where a journey cuts across two different valleys. These decisions not only take criminal justice institutions away from communities, but also illustrate a failure to recognize the specific requirements of – and absence of provision within – the locale. Reversing court closures might be an ideal position but, at the very least, in situations where this is not possible, funding should be provided for the accused to attend court.

As we have argued earlier, there is great value in conducting holistic examinations of criminal justice in operation, combining the various and often complementary insights of different parties, and drawing out and making connections between these relationships. By conducting this research in one region, we were able to provide thick description and thereby offer rich, deep insight into experiences of criminal justice. We believe that there is an important role for place-based examinations of the justice system, which root the institutions of justice into the localities they serve – or used to serve as is now often the case. While investigating the interaction between local issues and wider structural trends, we also recognize that research conducted in south Wales cannot be said to speak for, or accurately represent the issues experienced in, for example, north or west Wales. We are keen to see further research in other areas of Wales, particularly those with higher levels of Welsh language usage, such as those suggested, as well as place-based research in the north of England.[18] We also think it necessary that legislators and policymakers engage with these local issues, acknowledging the similarities and differences across a jurisdiction – both between regions and within countries – relevant to how criminal justice operates in reality. Consideration of only large metropolitan areas neglects the specific experiences within smaller and more rural areas. Put simply, the issues that affect London, Birmingham and Manchester may not manifest or be experienced in the same way as in Carlisle or Cardiff or in smaller towns and rural areas.

Finally, and crucially, we also propose the need for access to justice to be reconceived as a legally enforceable right, following the recommendations of the Fabian Society (2017) and what they termed 'the right to justice'. This right could apply to Wales – if our hope of a devolved legal jurisdiction is achieved – and equally to England or, for as long as it endures, to the England and Wales jurisdiction as a whole. A Right to Justice Act would both codify existing rights to justice and establish new rights of reasonable legal assistance without unaffordable costs (Fabian Society, 2017). Constructed through the engagement with those on the front line of criminal justice and monitored by an independent body, we believe that a new legislative framework could alter how 'justice' is conceptualized. It could lead to improved public legal education, especially on issues such as the principle of access to justice and the importance of this principle within our communities. This may have the potential to dispel the notion of the anti-suspect/anti-lawyer rhetoric that has dominated for decades under neoliberalism. Justice is, we posit, an extension of the welfare state and is key to achieving our full rights as citizens. A Right to Justice Act would require responsivity of the state and, in doing so, could provide resilience to citizens. A universal right to legal advice, representation and assistance would more accurately reflect and respond to our human vulnerability. Our research has illustrated to us – and, we hope, to the readers – the need for a fundamental reshaping of how access to criminal justice is approached and achieved. Crucial to conceptualizations of 'justice' is our interconnectedness; errors in justice do not simply have an adverse effect on the accused or practitioners, they affect families too. Reshaping criminal justice, and the wider justice system, is vital. We are convinced that any changes to the justice system should recognize our shared vulnerability, differing levels of resilience, and the importance of placing communities at

---

[18] A great deal of research, particularly on criminal legal aid, tends to be focused in and around the south of England. There is, of course, research being conducted in Wales and the north of England, but this tends to examine wider structural issues rather than focusing on matters of local concern.

the heart of justice. A devolved justice system would bring decisions closer to communities and may allow for new paths of engagement with local expertise and experience. In doing so, justice may be better served by Wales for the people of and in Wales.

This book has told stories from within Wales. It can inform criminal justice debates in Wales but also across the England and Wales jurisdiction. We hope it encourages others to take Wales seriously as a site of criminal justice and we want to encourage more scholarship in Wales. While the experiences we have set out are drawn from Wales, they are intended to prompt those across England and Wales to consider how – and whether – criminal justice is working and (re)imagine how it may be improved to better serve access to justice.

Afterword

Baron Thomas of Cwmgiedd, Kt, PC

Criminal Justice has over the centuries reflected the way in which a society has tried to address infringements of the law which cause harm to others or to society. Over a long period of time it was characterized by the degree of harshness in the way it adjudged those thought to have committed a crime and the often cruel way in which it punished them, though Wales was one of the exceptions to this in the age of its Kings.

Today we generally approach the issues with a wider compass, looking at how we address the causes of crime, the way we seek to prevent it and the need for a just and fair procedure to determine guilt or innocence. For the most part, we accept there are no easy answers to the determination of punishment for those found guilty or the way in which that punishment is administered.

The attitude of society to the approach that should be taken to these issues and the money that will be provided to address them depend upon a balanced and clear understanding of the way in which criminal justice is administered. The great merit of this study, as the reader will have learnt, is that it provides such a balanced and clear understanding in relation to Wales based on careful objective research.

As has been made clear, research in relation to Wales is greatly needed. The attitude of the government in London over a long period of time, as so well summarized in the Foreword, has meant that evidence, research and statistical information that consider the distinctive position in Wales are scant; they been submerged by the far greater volume of information about England. It is the real achievement of the authors that a considerable amount of evidence has been obtained and in-depth research conducted to set out the problems as they exist in Wales.

The study makes clear why these need to be addressed by acknowledging that Wales is a different nation to England in so many respects. Some of the issues are of long standing – the most obvious being the fact that Wales is a bilingual nation, its smaller communities and its geography.

When in the early 19th century it was proposed that money be saved by amalgamating the courts for the then counties of Flint and Denbigh by combining Ruthin and Denbigh into one court, Sir James Mansfield, Chief Justice of the Court of Common Pleas, observed to a Parliamentary Committee in 1817, "Upon first view, it appears that that might be very well done, for they are but 9 miles apart; but there is a pretty good mountain between them." Despite the fact that two centuries have elapsed, attitudes and understanding have scarcely changed; Wrexham, the largest town in North Wales and the fourth-largest town in Wales, is often characterized in this decade by research commissioned in London as a rural community, a perspective entirely understandable when looked at from London.

One of the striking features of the study is the interviews which vividly set out the problems but at the same time show the great commitment of those involved in criminal justice. This reinforces the optimism that, if Wales were to have the ability to address the problems facing Wales, there would be real progress in providing better criminal justice.

Although the study concentrates on Wales, its relevance is far wider. That is because a study of criminal justice in Wales provides a manageable, across-the-board study of the way criminal justice should be approached – the effects of fiscal constraints, the need to look at costs and benefits across society, the significance of defence rights, the real contribution made by defence lawyers and the central importance of the individual.

I very much hope that the authors will continue this vital work. One area that would benefit from an in-depth study would be the branches of the state that are concerned with criminal justice – the prosecution service and the judiciary. There is much to be done for criminal justice in Wales and much benefit, as this book shows, from such work.

References

Alge, D. (2013) Negotiated Plea Agreements in Cases of Serious and Complex Fraud in England and Wales: A New Conceptualisation of Plea Bargaining? *European Journal of Current Legal Issues*, 19(1), 1–18.

Allport, G. (1979) *The Nature of Prejudice*. New York, NY: Basic Books.

Ashworth, A. (1996) Legal Aid, Human Rights and Criminal Justice. In Young, R. and Wall, D. (eds.) *Access to Criminal Justice*. London: Blackstone Press Ltd, 55–69.

Ashworth, A. (2006) Four Threats to the Presumption of Innocence. *International Journal of Evidence and Proof*, 10(4), 241–78.

Ashworth, A. and Redmayne, M. (2010) *The Criminal Process*. 4th edn. Oxford: Oxford University Press.

Baldwin, J. and McConville, M. (1977) *Negotiated Justice*. London: Martin Robertson.

Bar Council (2017) *Barristers' Working Lives 2017: Third survey of barristers' attitudes towards their working lives*. Available at: https://www.barcouncil.org.uk/uploads/assets/694001c1-7e81-4f21-8709602e7d9238ee/working-lives-2017.pdf. Accessed 06/08/2020.

Bar Council (2020) *About Barristers*. Available at: https://www.barcouncil.org.uk/about/about-the-bar/about-barristers.html. Accessed 01/08/2020.

Bar Standards Board (2016) *Women at the Bar*. London: Bar Standards Board.

Barton, A., Storey, D. and Palmer, C. (2011) A Trip in the Country? Policing Drug Use in Rural Settings. In Mawby, R. and Yarwood, R. (eds.) *Rural Policing and Policing the Rural*. Aldershot: Ashgate, 147–58.

BBC (2017) Student Liam Allan to sue after rape trial collapse. *BBC Online*, 18 December. Available at: https://www.bbc.co.uk/news/uk-england-london-42399802. Accessed 06/08/2020.

BBC (2019) Extra 300 police officers to be recruited by 2021. *BBC Online*, 9 October. Available at: https://www.bbc.co.uk/news/uk-wales-49993027. Accessed 01/08/2020.

Beck, E., Blackwell, B., Leonard, P. and Mears, M. (2002–2003) Seeking Sanctuary: Interviews with Family Members of Capital Defendants. *Cornell Law Review*, 88(2), 382–418.

Becker, H. (1963) *Outsiders: Studies in the Sociology of Deviance*. London: Free Press of Glencoe.

Bell, E. (2011) *Criminal Justice and Neoliberalism*. Basingstoke: Palgrave Macmillan.

Bennett, L. and Layard, A. (2015) Legal Geography: Becoming Spatial Detectives. *Geography Compass*, 9(7), 406–22.

Best, D., Irving, J. and Albertson, K. (2017) Recovery and Desistance: What the Emerging Recovery Movement in the Alcohol and Drug Area Can Learn from Models of Desistance from Offending. *Addiction Research and Theory*, 25(1), 1–10.

Binder, A., Bergman, P., Price, S.C. and Tremblay, P.R. (2004) *Lawyers as Counsellors: A Client-Centred Approach*. St. Paul, MN: West.

Bird, J. (2021) Why it's time for a law to protect our future generations. *The Big Issue*, 5 January. Available at: https://www.bigissue.com/opinion/why-its-time-for-a-law-to-protect-our-future-generations/. Accessed 02/06/2021.

Birmingham, L., Gray, J., Mason, D. and Grubin, D. (2000) Mental Illness at Reception into Prison. *Criminal Behaviour and Mental Health*, 10(2), 77–87.

Blackstock, J., Cape, E., Hodgson, J., Ogorodova, A. and Spronken, T. (2014) *Inside Police Custody: An Empirical Account of Suspects' Rights in Four Jurisdictions*. Cambridge: Intersentia.

Blaustone, B. (1990) To Be of Service: The Lawyer's Aware Use of the Human Skills Associated with the Perceptive Self. *Journal of the Legal Profession*, 15, 241–84.

Blyth, M. (2013) *Austerity: The History of a Dangerous Idea*. Oxford: Oxford University Press.

Blumer, H. (1969) *Symbolic Interactionism: Perspective and Method*. Los Angeles, CA: University of California Press.

Boni-Le Goff, I., Lépinard, E., Le Feuvre, N. and Mallard, G. (2020) A Case of Love and Hate: Four Faces of Alienation Among Young Lawyers in France and Switzerland. *Law and Social Inquiry*, 54(2), 279–303.

Boon, A. (2002) Ethics in Legal Education and Training: Four Reports, Three Jurisdictions and a Prospectus. *Legal Ethics*, 5(1), 34–67

Boon, A. (2005) From Public Service to Service Industry: The Impact of Socialisation and Work on the Motivation and Values of Lawyers. *International Journal of the Legal Profession*, 12(2), 229–60.

Booth, N. (2018) Family Matters: A Critical Examination of Family Visits for Imprisoned Mothers and Their Families. *Prison Service Journal*, 238, 10–15.

Booth, N. (2020) *Maternal Imprisonment and Family Life: From the Caregiver's Perspective*. Bristol: Policy Press.

Bottoms, A. (1995) The Philosophy and Politics of Punishment and Sentencing. In Clarkson, C. and Morgan, R. (eds.) *The Politics of Sentencing Reform*. Oxford: Clarendon Press, 17–49.

Bowcott, O. (2015) Legal aid fees to be cut by 8.75%, confirms Ministry of Justice. *The Guardian*, 10 June. Available at: https://www.theguardian.com/law/2015/jun/10/legal-aid-fees-to-be-cut-by-875-confirms-ministry-of-justice. Accessed 06/08/2020.

Bowcott, O. (2018) Legal aid: how has it changed in 70 years? *The Guardian*, 26 December. Available at: https://www.theguardian.com/law/2018/dec/26/legal-aid-how-has-it-changed-in-70-years. Accessed 01/08/2020.

Bowcott, O. (2020) Legal profession hits back at Johnson over 'lefty lawyers' speech. *The Guardian*, 6 October. Available at: https://www.theguardian.com/law/2020/oct/06/legal-profession-hits-back-at-boris-johnson-over-lefty-lawyers-speech. Accessed 20/10/2020.

Bowcott, O. and Duncan, P. (2019) Half of magistrates courts in England and Wales closed since 2010. *The Guardian*, 27 January. Available at: https://www.theguardian.com/law/2019/jan/27/half-of-magistrates-courts-in-england-and-wales-closed-since-tories-elected. Accessed 04/11/2020.

Bowen, P. and Whitehead, S. (2013) *Better Courts: Cutting Crime Through Court Innovation*. London: Centre for Justice Innovation.

Bowling, B., Reiner, R. and Sheptycki, J. (2019) *The Politics of the Police*. Oxford: Oxford University Press.

Boyum, K. (1979) A Perspective on Civil Delay in Trial Courts. *Justice System Journal*, 5(2), 170–85.

Braun, V. and Clarke, V. (2006) Using Thematic Analysis in Psychology. *Qualitative Research in Psychology*, 3, 77–101.

Braverman, I. (2014) Who's Afraid of Methodology? Advocating a Methodological Turn in Legal Geography. In Bravermen, I., Blomley, N., Delaney, D. and Kedar, A. (eds.) *The Expanding Spaces of Law: A Timely Legal Geography*. Stanford, CA: Stanford University Press, 120–41.

Brewster, D. and Jones, R. (2019) Distinctly Divergent or Hanging onto English Coat-tails? Drug Policy in Post-devolution Wales. *Criminology and Criminal Justice*, 19(3), 364–81.

Brogden, M. and Ellison, E. (2013) *Policing in an Age of Austerity. A Postcolonial Perspective*. Abingdon: Routledge.

Brooker, C. and Webster, R. (2017) Prison Mental Health In-reach teams, Serious Mental Illness and the Care Programme Approach in England. *Journal of Forensic and Legal Medicine*, 50, 44–8.

Brown, K. (2015) *Vulnerability and Young People: Care and Social Control in Policy and Practice*. Bristol: Policy Press.

Brown, W. (2015) *Undoing the Demos: Neoliberalism's Stealth Revolution*. Cambridge, MA: MIT Press.

Buozis, M. (2017) Giving Voice to the Accused: Serial and the Critical Potential of True Crime. *Communication and Critical/Cultural Studies*, 14(3), 254–70.

Cain, M. (1983) The General Practice Layer and the Client: Towards a Radical Conception. In Dingwall, R. and Lewis, P. (eds.) *The Sociology of the Professions*. London: Macmillan, 106–30.

Campbell, J. (2020) *Entanglements of Life with the Law: Precarity and Justice in London's Magistrates' Courts*. Cambridge: Cambridge Scholars Publishing.

Cape, E. (2004) Overview: Is Reconciliation Possible? In Cape, E. (ed.) *Reconcilable Rights? Analysing the Tension between Victims and Defendants*. London: Legal Action Group/Oxford University Press.

Cape, E. (2013) Designing Out Defence Lawyers. In Robins, J. (ed.) *No Defence: Lawyers and Miscarriages of Justice*. London: Wilmington Publishing, 14–17.

Cape, E. and Moorhead, R. (2005) *Demand Induced Supply? Identifying Cost Drivers in Criminal Defence Work*. London: Legal Services Commission.

Carlen, P. (1976) *Magistrates' Justice*. London: Martin Robertson and Co.

Chaney, P. (2009) *Equal Opportunities and Human Rights: The First Decade of Devolution in Wales*. Cardiff: Equality and Human Rights Commission. Available at: http://www.equalityhumanrights.com/wales/publication. Accessed 01/08/2020.

Choongh, S. (1997) *Policing as Social Discipline*. Oxford: Clarendon Press.

Christie, N. (1986) The Ideal Victim. In Fattah, E. (ed.) *From Crime Policy to Victim Policy*. London: Macmillan, 17–30.

Church, T. (1982) *Examining Local Legal Culture: Practitioner Attitudes in Four Criminal Courts*. Washington, DC: National Institute of Justice.

Clare, I., Gudjonsson, G.H. and Harari, P.M. (1998) Understanding of the Current Police Caution. *Journal of Community and Applied Social Psychology*, 8, 323–9.

Cloward, R. and Ohlin, L. (1960) *Delinquency and Opportunity*. New York, NY: The Free Press.

Coates, S. (2016) *Unlocking Potential: A Review of Education in Prison Mental Health In-reach Teams, Serious Mental Illness and the Care Programme Approach in England*. London: Ministry of Justice.

Cohen, A. (1955) *Delinquent Boys: The Culture of the Gang*. New York, NY: The Free Press.

Collier, R. (2005) 'Be Smart, Be Successful, Be Yourself…'?: Representations of the Training Contract and Trainee Solicitor in Advertising by Large Law Firms. *International Journal of the Legal Profession*, 12(1), 51–92.

Collier, R. (2020) Anxiety in the Legal Community – A Study of Junior Lawyers, Legal Practice, and Legal Education. In Davies, A. (ed.) *Lawyer Health and Wellbeing: How the Legal Profession Is Tackling Stress and Creating Resiliency*. London: Ark Publishing, 89–100.

Comfort, M. (2016) 'A Twenty-Hour-a-Day Job': The Impact of Frequent Low-Level Criminal Justice Involvement on Family Life. *The Annals of the American Academy of Political and Social Science*, 65(1), 63–79.

Commission on Justice in Wales (2019) *Justice in Wales for the People in Wales*. Cardiff: Welsh Government. Available at: https://gov.wales/sites/default/files/publications/2019-10/Justice%20Commission%20ENG%20DIGITAL_2.pdf. Accessed 06/08/20.

CONDEM (2014) *State of the Nation Report: Poverty, Worklessness and Welfare Dependency in the UK*. Available at: https://www.bristol.ac.uk/poverty/downloads/keyofficialdocuments/CONDEM%20-poverty-report.pdf. Accessed 03/ 08/ 2020.

Cooke, E. (2019) *The Changing Occupational Terrain of the Legal Aid Lawyer in Times of Precariousness*. PhD thesis. University of Kent.

Copson, L. (2014) Penal Populism and the Problem of Mass Incarceration: The Promise of Utopian Thinking. *The Good Society*, 23(1), 55–72.

Courts and Tribunals Judiciary (undated). Available at: https://www.judiciary.uk/you-and-the-judiciary/going-to-court/magistrates-court/#:~:text=Virtually%20all%20criminal%20court%20cases%20start%20in%20a,jury.%20Magistrates%20deal%20with%20three%20kinds%20of%20cases%3A. Accessed 01/08/2020.

Cram, F. (2020) The 'Carrot' and 'Stick' of Integrated Offender Management: Implications for Police Culture. *Policing and Society*, 30(4), 378–95.

Crockett, N. (2017) Cardiff Bay: What has 30 years of development achieved? *BBC*, 13 August. Available at: https://www.bbc.co.uk/news/uk-wales-40681940. Accessed 02/12/2020.

Cullen, F.T., Jonson, C.L. and Nagin, D.S. (2011) Prisons Do Not Reduce Recidivism: The High Cost of Ignoring Science. *The Prison Journal*, 91(3), 48S–65S.

Currie, E. (1985) *Confronting Crime: An American Challenge*. New York, NY: Pantheon.

Darbyshire, P. (2000) The Mischief of Plea Bargaining and Sentencing Rewards. *Criminal Law Review*, November, 895–910.

Darbyshire, P. (2011) *Sitting in Judgment: The Working Lives of Judges*. Oxford: Hart Publishing.

Davies, J. (2007) *Hanes Cymru*. London: Penguin.

Davies, R., Jones, M., Parhi, M., Taylor, C., Drinkwater, S. et al. (2011) *An Anatomy of Economic Inequality in Wales*. Wales Institute of Social and Economic Research and Data. Available at: https://wiserd.ac.uk/research/research-projects/anatomy-economic-inequality-wales. Accessed 01/08/2020.

Daw, C. (2020) *Justice on Trial: Radical Solutions for a System at Breaking Point*. London: Bloomsbury.

Dearden, L. (2018) UK's 'creaking' criminal justice system needs urgent funding increase, outgoing CPS head Alison Saunders says. *The Independent*, 28 October. Available at: https://www.independent.co.uk/news/uk/crime/crime-prosecutions-uk-police-cps-budget-cuts-criminal-justice-system-alison-saunders-a8605276.html. Accessed 01/08/2020.

Dehaghani, R. (2017) 'Vulnerable by Law but Not by Nature': Examining Child and Youth Vulnerability in the Context of Police Custody. *Journal of Social Welfare and Family Law*, 39(4), 454–72.

Dehaghani, R. (2019) *Vulnerability in Police Custody: Police Decision-making and the Appropriate Adult Safeguard*. Abingdon: Routledge.

Dehaghani, R. (2021) Interrogating Vulnerability: Reframing the Vulnerable Suspect in Police Custody. *Social and Legal Studies*, 24(4), 417–40.

Dehaghani, R. and Newman, D. (2017) 'We're Vulnerable Too': An (Alternative) Analysis of Vulnerability within English Criminal Legal Aid and Police Custody. *Oñati Socio-Legal Series*, 7(6), 1199–228.

Dehaghani, R. and Newman, D. (2021a) The Crisis in Legally Aided Criminal Defence in Wales: Bringing Wales into Discussions of England and Wales. *Legal Studies*, 41(2), 234–51.

Dehaghani, R. and Newman, D. (2021b) Criminal Legal Aid and Access to Justice: An Empirical Account of a Reduction in Resilience, *International Journal of the Legal Profession*, DOI: 10.1080/09695958.2020.1868474.

Dehaghani, R. and White, A. (2020) Police Outsourcing and Labour Force Vulnerability. In Phillips, J., Albertson, K. and Corcoran, M. (eds.) *Marketisation and Privatisation in Criminal Justice*. Bristol: Policy Press, 107–18.

Denscombe, M. (2002) *Ground Rules for Good Research: A 10 Point Guide for Social Researchers*. Buckingham: Open University Press.

Devereux, A., Tucker, J., Moorhead, R. and Cape, E. (2009) *Quality Assurance for Advocates*. London: Legal Services Commission.

Dickins, S. (2017) What happens next with Wales' EU funding? *BBC Online*, 2 June. Available at: https://www.bbc.co.uk/news/uk-wales-40105919. Accessed 20/07/2020.

Dixey, R. and Woodall, J. (2012) The Significance of 'the Visit' in an English Category-B Prison: Views from Prisoners, Prisoners' Families and Prison Staff. *Community, Work and Family*, 15(1), 29–47.

Dixon, D. (1997) *Law in Policing: Legal Regulation and Police Practices*. Oxford: Clarendon Press.

Dodd, V. (2017) Britain's police budgets to lose £700m by 2020, amid rising crime. *The Guardian*, 9 November. Available at: https://www.theguardian.com/uk-news/2017/nov/09/britains-police-budgets-to-lose-700m-by-2020-amid-rising. Accessed 01/08/2020.

Dodd, V. (2018) Policing at 'tipping point' over budget cuts, warns police chief. *The Guardian*, 10 October. Available at: https://www.theguardian.com/uk-news/2018/oct/10/policing-at-tipping-point-over-budget-cuts-warns-police-chief. Accessed 01/08/2020.

Donnermeyer, J., Barclay, E. and Mears, D. (2011) Policing Agricultural Crime. In Mawby, R. and Yarwood, R. (eds.) *Rural Policing and Policing the Rural*. Aldershot: Ashgate, 193–204.

Donnermeyer, J., Scott, J. and Barclay, E. (2013) How Rural Criminology Informs Critical Thinking in Criminology. *International Journal for Crime, Justice and Social Democracy*, 2(3), 69–91.

Dugan, E (2019) This Leaked Report Says Moving Justice Online Might Lead to Innocent People Pleading Guilty. *BuzzFeed*, 18 January. Available at: https://www.buzzfeed.com/emilydugan/leaked-report-says-moving-justice-online-could-lead-to. Accessed 01/08/2020.

Duggan, M. (2018) Victim Hierarchies in the Domestic Violence Disclosure Scheme. *International Review of Victimology*, 24, 199–217.

Duggan, M. and Grace, J. (2018) Assessing Vulnerabilities in the Domestic Violence Disclosure Scheme. *Child and Family Law Quarterly*, 30, 145–66.

Durkheim, E. (1964) *The Division of Labour in Society*. Glencoe: The Free Press.

Economides, K., Blacksell, M. and Watkins, C. (1986) The Spatial Analysis of Legal Systems: Towards a Geography of Law? *Journal of Law and Society*, 13(2), 161–81.

Edmondson, C. (1996) Rural Courts, the Rural Community and the Challenge of Change. In McDonald, T., Wood, R. and Pflug, M. (eds.) *Rural Criminal Justice: Conditions, Constraints and Challenges*. Salem, WI: Sheffield Publishing Company, 93–111.

Eisenstein, J. (1982) Research on Rural Criminal Justice: A Summary. In Green, R., Jankovic, J. and Cronk, S. (eds.) *Criminal Justice in Rural America*. Washington, DC: National Institute of Justice, 105–43.

Elliott-Davies, M., Donnelly, J., Boag-Munroe, F. and Van Mechelen, D. (2016) 'Getting a Battering': The Perceived Impact of Demand and Capacity Imbalance within the Police Service of England and Wales: A Qualitative Review. *The Police Journal*, 89(2), 93–116.

Equality and Human Rights Commission (2011) *How Fair is Wales? Equality, Human Rights and Good Relations*. Available at: https://www.equalityhumanrights.com/en/publication-download/how-fair-wales-2011-equality-human-rights-and-good-relations. Accessed 01/08/2020.

Evans, J., Jones, R. and Haines, K. (2017) The Criminal Justice System in Wales. In Case, S., Johnson, P., Manlow, D., Smith, R. and Williams, K. (eds.) *Criminology*. Oxford: Oxford University Press, 2–19.

Evans, J., Jones, R. and Musgrove, N. (2021) 'Dragonisation' Revisited: A Progressive Criminal Justice Policy in Wales? *Criminology and Criminal Justice*, forthcoming, 1–18.

Fabian Society (2017) *The Right to Justice: The Final Report of the Bach Commission*. London: Fabian Society.

Fahnestock, K. and Geiger, M. (1993) We All Get Along Here: Caseflow in Rural Courts. *Judicature*, 76(5), 258–63.

Farnsworth, K. and Irving, Z. (2015) Introduction: Social Policy in the Age of Austerity. In Farnsworth, K. and Irving, Z. (eds.) *Social Policy in Times of Austerity: Global Economic Crisis and the New Politics of Welfare*. Bristol: Policy Press, 1–8.

Farnsworth, K. and Irving, Z. (2018) Austerity: Neoliberal Dreams Come True? *Critical Social Policy*, 38(3), 461–81.

Farrington, D. (1995) The Development of Offending and Antisocial Behaviour from Childhood: Key Findings from the Cambridge Study in Delinquent Development. *Journal of Child Psychology and Psychiatry*, 36(6), 929–64.

Feeley, M.M. (1979) *The Process Is the Punishment: Handling Cases in a Lower Criminal Court*. New York, NY: Russell Sage Foundation.

Fenn, P., Gray, A. and Rickman, N. (2007) Standard Fees for Legal Aid: An Empirical Analysis of Incentives and Contracts. *Oxford Economic Papers*, 12 June.

Field, S. and Brants, C. (2016) Truth-finding, Procedural Traditions and Cultural Trust in the Netherlands and England and Wales: When Strengths Become Weaknesses. *International Journal of Evidence and Proof*, 20(4), 266–88.

Findley, K.A. and Scott, M.S. (2006) The Multiple Dimensions of Tunnel Vision in Criminal Cases. *Wisconsin Law Review*, 2, 291–397.

Fineman, M.A. (2008) The Vulnerable Subject: Anchoring Equality in the Human Condition. *Yale Journal of Law and Feminism*, 20(1), 1–24.

Fineman, M.A. (2010) The Vulnerable Subject and the Responsive State. *Emory Law Journal*, 60, 1–41.

Fineman, M.A. (2013) Equality, Autonomy, and the Vulnerable Subject in Law and Politics. In Fineman, M.A. and Grear, A. (eds.) *Vulnerability: Reflections on a New Ethical Foundation for Law and Politics*. Farnham: Ashgate, 12–28.

Fineman, M.A. (2017) Vulnerability and Inevitable Inequality. *Oslo Law Review*, 4(3), 133–49.

Finkelstein, R. (2011) The Adversarial System and the Search for Truth. *Monash University Law Review*, 37(1), 135–43.

Flower, L. (2018) Doing Loyalty: Defense Lawyers' Subtle Dramas in the Courtroom. *Journal of Contemporary Ethnography*, 47(2), 226–54.

Flower, L. (2019) *Interactional Justice: The Role of Emotions in the Performance of Loyalty*. Abingdon: Routledge.

Flynn, A. and Freiberg, A. (2018) *Plea Negotiations: Pragmatic Justice in an Imperfect World*. London: Palgrave Macmillan.

Forrester, A., Till, A., Simpson, A. and Shaw, J. (2018) Mental Illness and the Provision of Mental Health Services in Prisons. *British Medical Bulletin*, 127(1), 101–9.

Forstenlechner, I. and Lettice, F. (2008) Well Paid but Undervalued and Overworked: The High and Lows of Being a Junior Lawyer in a Leading Law Firm. *Employee Relations*, 30(6), 640–52.

Fouzder, M. (2019) Falconer: my 'regret' over Labour's effort to curb legal aid budget. *Law Society Gazette*, 31 May. Available at: https://www.lawgazette.co.uk/news/falconer-my-regret-over-labours-effort-to-curb-legal-aid-budget/5070458.article. Accessed 20/07/2020.

Fouzder, M. (2020) 'Woefully inadequate': profession reacts to £50m criminal legal aid offer. *Law Society Gazette*, 28 February. Available at: https://www.lawgazette.co.uk/news/woefully-inadequate-profession-reacts-to-50m-criminal-legal-aid-offer/5103273.article. Accessed 20/10/2020.

Francis, A. and Sommerlad, H. (2009) Access to Legal Work Experience and Its Role in the (Re)production of Legal Professional Identity. *International Journal of the Legal Profession*, 16(1), 63–86.

Francis, R. and Fleck, J. (2021) *Vicarious Trauma in the Legal Profession: A Practical Guide to Trauma, Burnout and Collective Care*. London: Legal Action Group.

Franklin, A. and Lee, R. (2007) The Embedded Nature of Rural Legal Services: Sustaining Service Provision in Wales. *Journal of Law and Society*, 34(2), 218–43.

Fyfe, N. and Reeves, A. (2011) The Thin Green Line? Police Perceptions of the Challenges of Policing Wildlife Crime in Scotland. In Mawby, R. and Yarwood, R. (eds.) *Rural Policing and Policing the Rural*. Aldershot: Ashgate, 169–82.

Garland, D. (2001) *The Culture of Control: Crime and Social Order in Contemporary Society*. Oxford: Oxford University Press.

Geertz, C. (1973) *The Interpretation of Culture*. New York, NY: Basic Books.

Gibbs, P. (2016) *Justice Denied? The Experience of Unrepresented Defendants in the Criminal Courts*. London: Transform Justice.

Gibbs, P. (2017) *Defendants on Video: Conveyor Belt Justice or a Revolution in Access?* London: Transform Justice.

Gibbs, P. and Ratcliffe, F. (2019) *Criminal Defence in an Age of Austerity: Zealous Advocate or Cog in a Machine?* London: Transform Justice.

Gilboy, J. and Schmidt, J. (1979) Replacing Lawyers: A Case Study of Sequential Representation of Criminal Defendants. *Journal of Criminal Law and Criminology*, 70, 1–26.

Goffman, E. (1990) *The Presentation of Self in Everyday Life*. London: Penguin.

Goffman, E. (1991) *Asylums*. London: Penguin Books.

Gordon, F. (2018) *Children, Young People and the Press in a Transitioning Society: Representations, Reactions and Criminalisation.* London: Palgrave Macmillan.

Gordon-Bouvier, E. (2020) *Relational Vulnerability: Theory, Law and the Private Family.* London: Palgrave Macmillan.

Goriely, T. (1996) The Development of Criminal Legal Aid in England and Wales. In Young, R. and Wall, D. (eds.) *Access to Criminal Justice.* London: Blackstone Press Ltd, 26–54.

Grant, H. (2020) Home secretary's 'dangerous' rhetoric 'putting lawyers at risk'. *The Guardian*, 6 October. Available at: https://www.theguardian.com/global-development/2020/oct/06/home-secretarys-dangerous-rhetoric-putting-lawyers-at-risk. Accessed 20/10/2020.

Gray, A., Fenn, P. and Rickman, N. (1996) Controlling Lawyers' Costs through Standard Fees: An Economic Analysis. In Young, R. and Wall, D. (eds.) *Access to Criminal Justice.* London: Blackstone Press Ltd, 192–216.

Griffiths, J. (1970) Ideology in Criminal Procedure or A Third 'Model' of the Criminal Process. *Yale Law Journal*, 79, 359–417.

Haines, K. and Case, S. (2008) The Rhetoric and Reality of the 'Risk Factor Prevention Paradigm' Approach to Preventing and Reducing Youth Offending. *Youth Justice*, 8(1), 5–20.

Hall, S. (2011) 'The Neo-Liberal Revolution'. *Cultural Studies*, 25(6), 705–28.

Hanlon, G. and Jackson, J. (1999) Last Orders at the Bar? Competition, Choice and Justice for All – The Impact of Solicitor-Advocacy. *Oxford Journal of Legal Studies*, 19(4), 555–82.

Harris, N., Dehaghani, R. and Newman, D. (2021) Vulnerability, the Future of the Criminal Defence Profession, and the Implications for Teaching and Learning. *The Law Teacher*, 55(1), 57–67.

Harvey, D. (2006) *A Brief History of Neoliberalism.* Oxford: Oxford University Press.

Helm, R.K. (2019) Constrained Waiver of Trial Rights? Incentives to Plead Guilty and the Right to a Fair Trial. *Journal of Law and Society*, 46(3), 423–47.

Henham, R. (1998) Human Rights, Due Process and Sentencing. *British Journal of Criminology*, 38(4), 592–610.

Hester, R. (1999) Policing New Age Travellers: Conflict and Control in the Countryside. In Dingwall, G. and Moody, S. (eds.) *Crime and Conflict in the Countryside.* Cardiff: University of Wales Press, 130–45.

Heumann, M. (1978) *Plea Bargaining.* Chicago, IL: University of Chicago Press.

Hillyard, P., Pantazis, C., Tombs, S. and Gordon, D. (eds.) (2004) *Beyond Criminology: Taking Harm Seriously.* London: Pluto Press.

Hillyard, P., Sim, J., Tombs, S. and Whyte, D. (2004) Leaving a 'Stain Upon the Silence': Contemporary Criminology and the Politics of Dissent. *British Journal of Criminology*, 44(3), 369–90.

Hodgetts, C. and MacParthólan, C. (2021) An Evolution in Devolution? Welsh Criminal Justice and the Commission on Justice in Wales. *Criminal Law Review*, 1, 34–55.

Hodgson, J. (1994) Adding Injury to Injustice: The Suspect at the Police Station. *Journal of Law and Society*, 21, 85–101.

Hoggett, P. (1996) New Modes of Control in the Public Service. *Public Administration*, 74(1), 9–32.

Holder, J. and Harrison, C. (2003) *Law and Geography*. Oxford: Oxford University Press.

Holmberg, U. and Christianson, S. (2002) Murderers' and Sexual Offenders' Experiences of Police Interviews and Their Inclination to Admit or Deny Crimes. *Behavioural Sciences and the Law*, 20(1–2), 31–45.

Home Office (2019) *Home Office announces first wave of 20,000 police officer uplift*. Available at: https://www.gov.uk/government/news/home-office-announces-first-wave-of-20000-police-officer-uplift. Accessed 01/08/2020.

Hough, M. (2013) Procedural Justice and Professional Policing in Times of Austerity. *Criminology & Criminal Justice*, 13(2), 181–97.

Hough, M., Jackson, J., Bradford, B., Myhill, A. and Quinton, P. (2010) Procedural Justice, Trust and Institutional Legitimacy. *Policing: A Journal of Policy and Practice*, 4(3), 203–10.

Howard League (2019) *Revealed: The Scale of Prison Overcrowding in England and Wales*. Available at: https://howardleague.org/news/revealed-the-scale-of-prison-overcrowding-in-england-and-wales/. Accessed 05/08/2020.

Howells, C. (2019) Cyfraith Howell (The Laws of Hywel Dda), c. 940. In Rackley, E. and Auchmuty, R. (eds.) *Women's Legal Landmarks: Celebrating the History of Women and Law in the UK and Ireland*. Oxford: Hart Publishing, 25–32.

Hoyle, C. (1998) *Negotiating Domestic Violence*. Oxford: Oxford University Press.

Hunter, G., Jacobson, J. and Kirby, A. (2018) *Judicial Perceptions of the Quality of Criminal Advocacy*. London: Institute for Criminal Policy Research.

Hynes, J., Gill, N. and Tomlinson, J. (2020) In Defence of the Hearing? Emerging Geographies of Publicness, Materiality, Access and Communication in Court Settings. *Geography Compass*, 14(9), e12499.

Hynes, S. and Robins, J. (2009) *The Justice Gap*. London: Legal Action Group.

Inman, P. (2019) Number of Europe's poorest regions in UK 'more than doubles'. *The Guardian*, 10 December. Available at: https://www.theguardian.com/business/2019/dec/10/number-of-europes-poorest-regions-in-uk-more-than-doubles. Accessed 30/07/2020.

Inspector Gadget (2008) *Perverting the Course of Justice: The Hilarious and Shocking Inside Story of British Policing.* Cheltenham: Monday Books.

Ipsos MORI (2017) *Veracity Index 2017.* Available at: https://www.ipsos.com/sites/default/files/ct/news/documents/2017-11/trust-in-professions-veracity-index-2017-slides.pdf. Accessed 06/08/20.

Ipsos MORI (2018) *Veracity Index 2018.* Available at: https://www.ipsos.com/sites/default/files/ct/news/documents/2018-11/veracity_index_2018_v1_161118_public.pdf. Accessed 06/08/20.

Jackson, J. (2016) Responses to Salduz: Procedural Tradition, Change and the Need for Effective Defence. *Modern Law Review,* 79(6), 987–1018.

Jackson, J., Bradford, B., Stanko, B. and Hohl, K. (2013) *Just Authority? Trust in the Police in England and Wales.* Abingdon: Routledge.

Jacobson, J., Hunter, G. and Kirby, A. (2016) *Inside Crown Court: Personal Experiences and Questions of Legitimacy.* Bristol: Policy Press.

Jardine, C. (2019) *Families, Imprisonment and Legitimacy: The Cost of Custodial Penalties.* Abingdon: Routledge.

Johnson, E. (1980) Lawyer's Choice: A Theoretical Appraisal of Litigation Investment Decisions. *Law and Society Review,* 15(3), 567–610.

Johnston, E. (2020) The Adversarial Defence Lawyer: Myths, Disclosure and Efficiency – A Contemporary Analysis of the Role in the Era of the Criminal Procedure Rules. *The International Journal of Evidence & Proof,* 24(1), 35–58.

Johnston, E. and Smith, T. (2017) The Early Guilty Plea Scheme and the Rising Wave of Managerialism. *Criminal Law and Justice Weekly,* 181, 210–12.

Johnson, J. and Heaney, P. (2015) Miscarriage of justice warning over CPS funding cuts. *BBC Online,* 5 February. Available at: https://www.bbc.co.uk/news/uk-wales-35496012. Accessed 01/08/2020.

Jones, E., Graffin, N., Samra, R. and Lucassen, M. (2020) *Mental Health and Wellbeing in the Legal Profession.* Bristol: Bristol University Press.

Jones, R. (2013) A Welsh Criminological Imaginary: The State of Criminology in Wales. *Contemporary Wales,* 26, 99–120.

Jones, R. (2017) *The Hybrid System: Imprisonment and Devolution in Wales.* PhD thesis. Cardiff University.

Jones, R. (2018) *Imprisonment in Wales: A Factfile. Project Report.* Cardiff: Wales Governance Centre at Cardiff University.

Jones, R., Series, L. and Dehaghani, R. (2019) *International Covenant on Civil and Political Rights: Conditions of Detention in Wales.* Technical Report. Cardiff: Cardiff University.

Jones, R. and Wyn Jones, R. (2019) *Justice at the Jagged Edge in Wales.* Cardiff: Cardiff University.

Jones-Evans, S. and Barry, S. (2019) Wales is no longer the poorest part of the UK. *Business Live*, 23 December. Available at: https://www.business-live.co.uk/opinion-analysis/wales-no-longer-poorest-part-17465667. Accessed 30/07/2020.

Joseph Rowntree Foundation (2020) *Briefing: Poverty in Wales 2020.* York: Joseph Rowntree Foundation. Available at: file:///Users/dannewman/Downloads/poverty_in_wales_2020_0.pdf. Accessed 02/11/2020.

Junior Lawyers Division (2019) *Resilience and Wellbeing Survey 2019: Survey Report.* London: Law Society.

Kemp, V. (2018) *Effective Police Station Legal Advice: Country Report 2: England and Wales.* Nottingham: University of Nottingham.

Kemp, V. and Hodgson, J. (2016) England and Wales: Empirical Findings. In Vanderhallen M., van Oosterhout M., Panzavolta M. and de Vocht, D. (eds.) *Interrogating Young Suspects II: Procedural Safeguards from an Empirical Perspective.* Antwerp: Intersentia, 127–81.

Kendall, J. (2018) *Regulating Police Detention: Voices from Behind Closed Doors.* Bristol: Policy Press.

Kinghan, J. (2021) *Lawyers, Networks and Progressive Social Change: Lawyers Changing Lives.* Oxford: Hart Publishing.

Koffman, L. (1999) Crime in Rural Wales. In Dingwall, G. and Moody, S. (eds.) *Crime and Conflict in the Countryside.* Cardiff: University of Wales Press, 60–75.

Kohn, N. (2014) Vulnerability Theory and the Role of Government. *Yale Journal of Law and Feminism*, 26, 1–27.

Lacey, N. (1994) Introduction: Making Sense of Criminal Justice. In Lacey, N. (ed.) *A Reader on Criminal Justice.* Oxford: Oxford University Press, 28–34.

Law Society (2018) *Criminal Duty Solicitors: A Looming Crisis.* London: Law Society.

Law Society (2019) *Justice on Trial 2019: Fixing our Criminal Justice system.* London: Law Society.

Lawthom, J. (2018) Law Society warns duty solicitors could become extinct. *BBC Online*, 17 November. Available at: https://www.bbc.co.uk/news/uk-wales-46127118. Accessed 05/08/2020.

Lea, J. and Young, J. (1984) *What Is to Be Done about Law and Order.* Harmondsworth: Penguin.

Leering, M. (2014) Conceptualizing Reflective Practice for Legal Professionals. *Journal of Law and Social Policy*, 23, 83–106.

Legal Aid Agency (2018) *Crown Court Fee Guidance.* Available at: https://assets.publishing.service.gov.uk/government/uploads/system/uploads/attachment_data/file/745068/Crown_Court_Fee_Guidance_-_v.1.7A_.pdf. Accessed 01/08/2020.

Legal Aid Agency (2020) *Guidance: Criminal Legal Aid: Means Testing*. Available at: https://www.gov.uk/guidance/criminal-legal-aid-means-testing. Accessed 01/08/2020.

Leo, J. and Reuss-Ianni, E. (2017) *Two Cultures of Policing: Street Cops and Management Cops*. New York, NY: Routledge.

Leverick, F. (2004) Tensions and Balances, Costs and Rewards: The Sentence Discount in Scotland. *Edinburgh Law Review*, 8(3), 360–88.

Leveson, B. (2015) *Review of Efficiency in Criminal Proceedings*. Judiciary of England and Wales.

Lord Chancellor's Department (1998) *Modernising Justice*. London: Martin Pearce Associates.

Mant, J. (2017) Neoliberalism, Family Law and the Cost of Access to Justice. *Journal of Social Welfare and Family Law*, 39(2), 246–58.

Maras, K., Crane, L., Mulcahy, S., Hawken, T., Cooper, P., Wurtzel, D. and Memon, A. (2017) Autism in the Courtroom: Experiences of Legal Professionals and the Autism Community. *Journal of Autism and Developmental Disorders*, 47(8), 2610–20.

Marsden, T.K. and Franklin, A. (2013) Replacing Neoliberalism: Theoretical Implications of the Rise of Local Food Movements. *Local Environment*, 18(5), 636–41.

Massey, D. (2005) *For Space*. London: Sage.

May, T. (2016) Theresa May's keynote speech at Tory conference in full. *The Independent*, 5 October. Available at: https://www.independent.co.uk/news/uk/politics/theresa-may-speech-tory-conference-2016-in-full-transcript-a7346171.html. Accessed 06/08/2020.

McAra, L. and McVie, S. (2010) Youth Crime and Justice: Key Messages from the Edinburgh Study of Youth Transitions and Crime. *Criminology and Criminal Justice*, 10(2), 179–209.

McBarnet, D.J. (1981) *Conviction: The Law, the State and the Construction of Justice*. London: Macmillan.

McConville, M., Hodgson, J., Bridges, L. and Pavlovic, A. (1994) *Standing Accused: The Organization and Practices of Criminal Defence Lawyers in Britain*. Oxford: Clarendon Press.

McConville, M. and Marsh, L. (2014) *Criminal Judges: Legitimacy, Courts and State-induced Guilty Pleas in Britain*. Cheltenham: Edward Elgar.

McConville, M. and Mirsky, C. (2005) *Jury Trials and Plea Bargaining: A True History*. Oxford: Hart Publishing.

McConville, M., Sanders, A. and Leng, R. (1991) *The Case for the Prosecution: Police Suspects and the Construction of Criminality*. London: Routledge.

McKay, C. (2015) Video Links from Prison: Court 'Appearance' within Carceral Space. *Law, Culture and the Humanities*, 14(2), 242–62.

McKay, C. (2017) Video Links from Prison: Permeability and the Carceral World. *International Journal for Crime, Justice and Social Democracy*, 5(1), 21–37.

McKenzie, L. (2013) The Stigmatised and De-valued Working Class: The State of a Council Estate Class Inequality. In Atkinson, W., Roberts, S. and Savage, M. (eds.) *Austerity Britain*. London: Palgrave Macmillan, 128–44.

Mégret, F. (2014) Practices of Stigmatization. *Law and Contemporary Problems*, 76, 287–318.

Melville, A. and Laing, K. (2007) 'I Just Drifted into It': Constraints Faced by Publicly Funded Family Lawyers. *International Journal of the Legal Profession*, 14(3), 281–300.

Miller, J. and Glassner, B. (2011) The 'Inside' and the 'Outside': Finding Realities in Interviews. In Silverman, D. (ed.) *Qualitative Research: Theory, Method and Practice*. London: Sage, 99–112.

Ministry of Justice (2012) *Swift and Sure Justice: The Government's Plans for Reform of the Criminal Justice System*. Available at: https://assets.publishing.service.gov.uk/government/uploads/system/uploads/attachment_data/file/217328/swift-and-sure-justice.pdf. Accessed 06/08/2020.

Ministry of Justice (2018) *Government Announces Changes to Court Estate*. Available at: https://www.gov.uk/government/news/government-announces-changes-to-court-estate. Accessed 01/08/2020.

Misztal, B. (2011) *The Challenges of Vulnerability: In Search of Strategies for a Less Vulnerable Social Life*. Basingstoke: Palgrave Macmillan.

Mitchell, D. (2019) Oral Histories and Enlightened Witnessing. In Moruzi, K., Musgrove, N. and Pascoe Leahy, C. (eds.) *Children's Voices from the Past: New Historical and Interdisciplinary Perspectives*. London: Palgrave Macmillan, 211–31.

Moody, S. (1999) Rural Neglect: The Case Against Criminology. In Dingwall, G. and Moody, S. (eds.) *Crime and Conflict in the Countryside*. Cardiff: University of Wales Press, 8–28.

Moorhead, R. (2004) Legal Aid and the Decline of Private Practice: Blue Murder or Toxic Job? *International Journal of the Legal Profession*, 11(3), 160–90.

Morgan, R. (2002) *Clear Red Water*. Speech at National Centre for Public Policy, Swansea, 11 December. Available at: https://www.sochealth.co.uk/the-socialist-health-association/sha-country-and-branch-organization/sha-wales/clear-red-water/. Accessed 06/08/20.

Morris, N. (2008) More than 3,600 new offences under Labour. *The Independent*, 4 September. Available at: https://www.independent.co.uk/news/uk/home-news/more-than-3600-new-offences-under-labour-918053.html. Accessed 05/08/2020.

Morrison, J. and Leith, P. (1992) *The Barristers World and the Nature of Law*. Maidenhead: Open University Press.

Mueller, B. (2019) What Is Austerity and How Has It Effected British Society? *New York Times*, 24 February. Available at: https://www.nytimes.com/ 2019/02/24/world/europe/britain-austerity-may-budget.html. Accessed 09/12/2020.

Mulcahy, A. (1994) The Justifications of Justice. *British Journal of Criminology*, 34(4), 411–30.

Mulcahy, L. (2007) Architects of Justice: The Politics of Courtroom Design. *Social and Legal Studies*, 16(3), 383–403.

Mulcahy, L. (2013) Putting the Defendant in Their Place: Why Do We Still Use the Dock in Criminal Proceedings? *The British Journal of Criminology*, 53(6), 1139–56.

Muncie, J. (2006) Governing Young People: Coherence and Contradiction in Contemporary Youth Justice. *Critical Social Policy*, 26(4), 770–93.

Mungham, G. and Thomas, P. (1979) Advocacy and the Solicitor-Advocate in Magistrates' Courts in England and Wales. *International Journal of the Sociology of Law*, 7(2), 169–96.

Munro, V.E. and Scoular J. (2012) Abusing Vulnerability? Contemporary Law and Policy Responses to Sex Work in the UK. *Feminist Legal Studies*, 20(3), 189–206.

Nason, S. and Pritchard, H. (2020) Administrative Justice in Wales. *Journal of Law and Society*, 47(S2), S262–S281.

National Audit Office (2009) *The Procurement of Criminal Legal Aid in England and Wales by the Legal Services Commission*. London: The Stationary Office. Available at: https://www.nao.org.uk/report/the-procurement-of-criminal-legal-aid-in-england-and-wales-by-the-legal-services-commission/. Accessed 06/08/2020.

National Audit Office (2015) *Financial Sustainability of Police Forces in England and Wales*. Home Office. London: National Audit Office. Available at: https://www.nao.org.uk/report/financial-sustainability-of-police-forces-in-england-and-wales/. Accessed 06/08/2020.

National Audit Office (2018a) *Financial Sustainability of Police Forces in England and Wales 2018*. Home Office. London: National Audit Office. Available at: https://www.nao.org.uk/wp-content/uploads/2018/09/Financial-sustainability-of-police-forces-in-England-and-Wales-2018.pdf#page=9. Accessed 30/07/2020.

National Audit Office (2018b) *Early Progress in Transforming Courts and Tribunals*. HM Courts & Tribunals Service. London: National Audit Office. Available at: https://www.nao.org.uk/wp-content/uploads/2018/05/Early-progess-in-transforming-courts-and-tribunals.pdf. Accessed 30/07/2020.

Naughton, M. (2013) *The Innocent and the Criminal Justice System: A Sociological Analysis of Miscarriages of Justice*. London: Palgrave Macmillan.

Newman, D. (2012) Still Standing Accused: Addressing the Gap Between Work and Talk in Firms of Criminal Defence Lawyers. *International Journal of the Legal Profession*, (19)1, 3–27.

Newman, D. (2013a) *Legal Aid Lawyers and the Quest for Justice*. Oxford: Hart Publishing.

Newman, D. (2013b) More than Money. In Robins, J. (ed.) *No Defence: Lawyers and Miscarriages of Justice*. London: Wilmington Publishing, 40–3.

Newman, D. (2016a) Attitudes to Justice in a Rural Community. *Legal Studies*, 36(4), 591–612.

Newman, D. (2016b) Are Lawyers Alienated Workers? *European Journal of Current Legal Issues*, 22(3).

Newman, D. (2018) Are Lawyers Neurotic? *International Journal of the Legal Profession*, 25(1), 3–29.

Newman, D. and Ugwudike, P. (2013) Defence Lawyers and Probation Officers: Offenders' Allies or Adversaries? *International Journal of the Legal Profession*, 20(2), 183–207.

Newman, D. and Welsh, L. (2019) The Practices of Modern Criminal Defence Lawyers: Alienation and Its Implications for Access to Justice. *Common Law World Review*, 48(1–2), 64–89.

New Statesman (2015) From the archive: Tony Blair is tough on crime, tough on the causes of crime. *New Statesman*, 28 December. Available at: https://www.newstatesman.com/2015/12/archive-tony-blair-tough-crime-tough-causes-crime. Accessed 30/07/2020.

Nicklas-Carter, C. (2019) *Efficiency of The English Criminal Courts in a Time of Austerity. Exploring Courtroom Lawyers' Assessment of Government Policy (2010–2017)*. PhD thesis. Keele University.

Nicolson, D. and Webb, J. (1999) *Professional Legal Ethics*. Oxford: Oxford University Press.

Oakley, E. and Vaughan, S. (2019) In Dependence: The Paradox of Professional Independence and Taking Seriously the Vulnerabilities of Lawyers in Large Corporate Law Firms. *Journal of Law and Society*, 46(1), 83–111.

Office for National Statistics (2015) *Nearly one in five people had some form of disability in England and Wales*. Available at: https://www.ons.gov.uk/peoplepopulationandcommunity/healthandsocialcare/disability/articles/nearlyoneinfivepeoplehadsomeformofdisabilityinenglandandwales/2015-07-13. Accessed 06/08/2020.

Office for National Statistics (2019) *Population estimates for the UK, England and Wales, Scotland and Northern Ireland: mid-2018*. Available at: https://www.ons.gov.uk/peoplepopulationandcommunity/populationandmigration/populationestimates/bulletins/annualmidyearpopulationestimates/mid2018. Accessed 29/07/2020.

Organ, J. and Sigafoos, J. (2018) *The Impact of LASPO on routes to Justice.* Equality and Human Rights Commission Report 118. Available at: https://www.equalityhumanrights.com/en/publication-download/impact-laspo-routes-justice. Accessed 06/08/2020.

Owens, A. (2020) *Access to Justice: Does the Legal Problem and Resolution Survey 2014–15 Accurately Depict Accessibility Levels for Wales?* MA dissertation. Cardiff University.

Owusu-Bempah, A. (2017) *Defendant Participation in the Criminal Process.* Abingdon: Routledge.

Packer, H.L. (1968) *The Limits of the Criminal Sanction.* Stanford, CA: Stanford University Press.

Palmer, E., Cornford, T., Guinchard, A. and Marique, Y. (eds.) (2016) Access to Justice: Beyond the Policies and Politics of Austerity. Oxford: Hart Publishing.

Papp, J., Campbell, C., Onifade, E., Anderson, V., Davidson, W. and Foster, D. (2016) Youth Drug Offenders: An Examination of Criminogenic Risk and Juvenile Recidivism. *Policy, Practice and Research*, 1(4), 229–45.

Peay, J. and Player, E. (2018) Pleading Guilty: Why Vulnerability Matters. *Modern Law Review*, 81(6), 929–57.

Phelps, C.S. (2019) 'They look at us like we're foreigners': the stories of gentrification in Cardiff. *Nation Cymru*, 13 June. Available at: https://nation.cymru/news/they-look-at-us-like-were-foreigners-the-stories-of-gentrification-in-cardiff/. Accessed 03/12/2020.

Phillips, J., Albertson, K. and Corcoran, M. (eds.) (2020) *Privatisation and Criminal Justice: Recent Experience in England and Wales.* Bristol: Policy Press.

Phoenix, J. and Kelly, L. (2013) 'You Have to Do It for Yourself': Responsibilization in Youth Justice and Young People's Situated Knowledge of Youth Justice Practice. *British Journal of Criminology*, 53(3), 419–37.

Pickett, J., Mancini, C., Mears, D. and Gertz, M. (2015) Public (Mis) Understanding of Crime Policy: The Effects of Criminal Justice Experience and Media Reliance. *Criminal Justice Police Review*, 26(5), 500–22.

Pivaty, A. (2020) *Criminal Defence at Police Stations: A Comparative and Empirical Study.* Abingdon: Routledge.

Pleasence, P., Balmer, N. and Sandefur, R. (2013) *Paths to Justice – Past, Present and Future Roadmap.* UCL Centre for Empirical Legal Studies. Available at: http://www.nuffieldfoundation.org/sites/default/files/files/PTJ%20Roadmap%20NUFFIELD%20Published.pdf. Accessed 06/08/2020.

Plehwe, D., Walpen, B. and Neunhoffer, G. (2006) Introduction. In Plehwe, D., Walpen, B. and Neunhoffer, G. (eds.) *Neoliberal Hegemony: A Global Critique.* Abingdon: Routledge, 1–24.

Pollock, I. (2019) Child poverty: Wales is the only UK nation to see increase. *BBC Online*, 15 May. Available at: https://www.bbc.co.uk/news/uk-wales-48259327. Accessed 29/07/20.

Pratt, A. (2019) *Police Stations: Are They a Thing of the Past?* London: House of Commons Library. Available at: https://commonslibrary.parliament.uk/home-affairs/communities/police-stations-are-they-a-thing-of-the-past/. Accessed 01/08/2020.

Pratt, J. (2007) *Penal Populism*. Abingdon: Routledge.

Quirk, H. (2006) The Significance of Culture in Criminal Procedure Reform: Why the Revised Disclosure Scheme Cannot Work. *Journal of Evidence and Proof*, 10(1), 42–59.

Quirk, H. (2017) *The Rise and Fall of the Right of Silence*. Abingdon: Routledge.

Rees, A., Staples, E. and Maxwell, N. (2017) *Final report June 2017: Evaluation of Visiting Mum Scheme*. Cardiff: CASCADE at Cardiff University. Available at: https://sites.cardiff.ac.uk/cascade/files/2017/09/Final-PACT-report-Final-version.-12.7.17.pdf. Accessed 06/08/20.

Rethinking Crime and Punishment (2005) *Victims and Defendants' Rights: Can They Be Reconciled?* London: Esmee Fairbairn Foundation.

Rhoades, K., Leve, L., Eddy, M. and Chamberlain, P. (2016) Predicting the Transition From Juvenile Delinquency to Adult Criminality: Gender Specific Influences in Two High-risk Samples. *Criminal Behaviour and Mental Health*, 26(5), 336–51.

Rhode, D. (2004) *Access to Justice*. Oxford: Oxford University Press.

Rickard, D. (2016) *Sex Offenders, Stigma, and Social Control*. New Brunswick, NJ: Rutgers University Press.

Robins, J. (2019) Justice gap: the towns where there's no access to free legal advice. *The Guardian*, 27 March. Available at: https://www.theguardian.com/society/2019/mar/27/justice-gap-towns-no-access-to-legal-aid-wales-england. Accessed 30/07/2020.

Robins, J. and Newman, D. (2021) *Justice in a Time of Austerity: Stories From a System in Crisis*. Bristol: Bristol University Press.

Robson, J. (2016) Gove's Nonsense: Barristers vs Solicitor Advocates. *Solicitors Journal*, December.

Rock, F. (2007) *Communicating Rights: The Language of Arrest and Detention*. Basingstoke: Palgrave.

Ruthston, P. and Donovan, C. (2018) Introduction. In Rushton, P. and Donovan, C. (eds.) *Austerity Policies: Bad Ideas in Practice*. London: Palgrave Macmillan.

Ryan, F. (2015) Conservatives promised to protect the 'most vulnerable'. How's that going? *The Guardian*, 10 August. Available at: https://www.theguardian.com/commentisfree/2015/aug/10/conservatives-most-vulnerable-iain-duncan-smith-george-osborne-reforms. Accessed 06/08/2020.

Sandefur, R. (2001) Work and Honor in the Law: Prestige and the Division of Lawyers' Labor. *American Sociological Review*, 66(3), 382–403.

Sanders, A., Young, R. and Burton, M. (2010) *Criminal Justice*. Oxford: Oxford University Press.

Sandland, R. (1995) Review of Criminal Process: An Evaluative Study. *Criminal Law Review*, 42, 679–80.

Satchwell, G. (2016) *An Inspector Recalls*. Cheltenham: The History Press.

Save the Children (2012) *Child Poverty Snapshots: The Local Picture in Wales*. Cardiff: Save the Children. Available at: https://www.savethechildren.org.uk/content/dam/global/reports/hunger-and-livelihoods/Child-Poverty-Snapshots-English.pdf. Accessed 29/07/20.

Scoular, J. and O'Neill, M. (2007) Regulating Prostitution: Social Inclusion, Responsibilization and the Politics of Prostitution Reform. *British Journal of Criminology*, 47(5), 764–78.

Scraton, P. (2007) *Power, Conflict and Criminalisation*. London: Routledge.

The Secret Barrister (2018) *Stories of the Law and How It's Broken*. Basingstoke: Pan Macmillan.

The Secret Barrister (2020) *Fake Law: The Truth About Justice in an Age of Lies*. Basingstoke: Pan Macmillan.

Secretary of State for Justice (2019) *Companies: Written question – 227146*. UK Parliament. Available at: https://www.parliament.uk/business/publications/written-questions-answers-statements/written-question/Commons/2019-02-28/227146/. Accessed 01/06/2020.

Sentencing Council Guidelines (2017) *Reduction in sentence for a guilty plea - first hearing on or after 1 June 2017*. Sentencing Council. Available at: https://www.sentencingcouncil.org.uk/overarching-guides/magistrates-court/item/reduction-in-sentence-for-a-guilty-plea-first-hearing-on-or-after-1-june-2017/. Accessed 06/08/2020.

Sherr, A. (2000) The Value of Experience in Legal Competence. *International Journal of the Legal Profession*, 7(2), 95–124.

Shiner, M. (2010) Post-Lawrence Policing in England and Wales: Guilty, Innocence and the Defence of Organizational Ego. *British Journal of Criminology*, 50(5), 935–53.

Silk Commission (2014) *Empowerment and Responsibility: Legislative Powers to Strengthen Wales*. Second Report of Commission on Devolution in Wales. Available at: https://assets.publishing.service.gov.uk/government/uploads/system/uploads/attachment_data/file/310571/CDW-Wales_Report-final_Full_WEB_310114.pdf. Accessed 06/08/2020.

Simson Caird, J. (2016) Court and tribunal closures: Briefing Paper CBP 7346 21 March 2016. London: House of Commons Library. Available at: https://researchbriefings.files.parliament.uk/documents/CBP-7346/CBP-7346.pdf. Accessed 30/07/2020.

Skinns, L. (2009) 'Let's Get It Over With': Early Findings on the Factors Affecting Detainees' Access to Custodial Legal Advice. *Policing and Society*, 19(1), 58–78.

Skinns, L. (2011) *Police Custody: Governance, Legitimacy and Reform in the Criminal Justice Process*. Oxford: Willan.

Skinns, L., Sorsby, A. and Rice, L. (2020) 'Treat Them as a Human Being': Dignity in Police Detention and Its Implications for 'Good' Police Custody. *British Journal of Criminology*, 60(6), 1667–88,

Skinns, L., Sprawson, A., Sorsby, A., Smith, R. and Wooff, A. (2017) Police Custody Delivery in the Twenty-first Century in England and Wales: Current Arrangements and Their Implications for Patterns of Policing. *European Journal of Policing Studies*, 4(3), 325–48.

Skinns, L., Wooff, A. and Sprawson, A. (2017) Preliminary Findings on Police Custody Delivery in the Twenty-first Century: Is It 'Good' Enough? *Policing and Society*, 27(4), 358–71.

Smith, T. (2013) The 'Quiet Revolution' in Criminal Defence: How the Zealous Advocate Slipped into the Shadow'. *International Journal of the Legal Profession*, 20(1), 111–37.

Smith, T. (2018) The 'Near Miss' of Liam Allan: Critical Problems in Police Disclosure, Investigation Culture and the Resourcing of Criminal Justice. *Criminal Law Review*, 9, 711–31.

Smith, T. (2020) 'Rushing Remand'? Pretrial Detention and Bail Decision Making in England and Wales. *The Howard Journal of Crime and Justice*, 60(1) 46–74.

Smith, T. and Cape, E. (2017) The Rise and Decline of Criminal Legal Aid in England and Wales. In Flynn, A. and Hodgson, J. (eds.) *Access to Justice and Legal Aid: Comparative Perspectives on Unmet Legal Need*. Oxford: Hart Publishing, 63–86.

Social Mobility Commission (2019) *State of the Nation 2018–19: Social Mobility in Great Britain*. Available at: https://assets.publishing.service.gov.uk/government/uploads/system/uploads/attachment_data/file/798404/SMC_State_of_the_Nation_Report_2018-19.pdf. Accessed 06/08/2020.

Solnit, R. (2020) 'The way we get through this is together': the rise of mutual aid under coronavirus. *The Guardian*, 14 May. Available at: https://www.theguardian.com/world/2020/may/14/mutual-aid-coronavirus-pandemic-rebecca-solnit. Accessed 06/08/2020.

Sommerlad, H. (1995) Managerialism and the Legal Profession: A New Professional Paradigm. *International Journal of the Legal Profession*, 2(2–3), 159–85.

Sommerlad, H. (1996) Criminal Legal Aid Reforms and the Restructuring of Legal Professionalism. In Young, R. and Wall, D. (eds.) *Access to Criminal Legal Aid: Legal Aid, Lawyers and the Defence of Liberty*. London: Blackstone Press Ltd, 282–312.

Sommerlad, H. (1999) The Implementation of Quality Initiatives and the New Public Management in the Legal Aid Sector in England and Wales: Bureaucratisation, Stratification and Surveillance. *International Journal of the Legal Profession*, 6(3), 311–43.

Sommerlad, H. (2001) 'I've Lost the Plot': An Everyday Story of Legal Aid Lawyers. *Journal of Law and Society*, 28(3), 335–60.

Sommerlad, H. (2012) Minorities, Merit and Misrecognition in the Globalized Legal Profession. *Fordham Law Review*, 80(6), 2418–512.

Sommerlad, H. and Wall, D. (1999) *Legally Aided Clients and their Solicitors: Qualitative Perspectives on Quality and Legal Aid*. London: Law Society.

Soubise, L. (2017) Prosecuting in the Magistrates' Courts in a Time of Austerity. *Criminal Law Review*, 11, 847–59.

South Wales Police (2015) *Freedom of Information Request 508/15: Response date 6th July 2015*. Available at: http://swplive.blob.core.windows.net/wordpress-uploads/Response-508_15.pdf. Accessed 06/08/2020.

Squire, G. and Gill, A. (2011) 'It's Not All Heartbeat You Know': Policing Domestic Violence in Rural Areas. In Mawby, R. and Yarwood, R. (eds.) *Rural Policing and Policing the Rural*. Aldershot: Ashgate, 159–67.

Stahl, G. (2017) The Practice of 'Othering' in Reaffirming White Working-class Boys' Conceptions of Normative Identities. *Journal of Youth Studies*, 20(3), 283–300.

Statistics for Wales (2019) *Welsh Index of Multiple Deprivation (WIMD) 2019 Results report*. Available at: https://gov.wales/sites/default/files/statistics-and-research/2019-11/welsh-index-multiple-deprivation-2019-results-report-024.pdf. Accessed 06/08/2020.

Stephen, F. and Tata, C. (2006) *Impact of the Introduction of Fixed Payments into Summary Legal Aid: Report of an Independent Study*. Edinburgh: Scottish Executive.

Sugarman, D. (2015) From Legal Biography to Legal Life Writing: Broadening Conceptions of Legal History and Socio-legal Scholarship. *Journal of Law and Society*, 42(1), 7–33.

Sunshine, S. and Tyler, T. (2003) The Role of Procedural Justice and Legitimacy in Shaping Public Support for Policing. *Law and Society Review*, 37(3), 513–48.

Tague, P. (2007) Guilty Pleas and Barristers' Incentives: Lessons from England. *Georgetown Journal of Legal Ethics*, 20, 287–320.

Tata, C. (2007) In the Interests of Clients or Commerce? Legal Aid, Supply, Demand and 'Ethical Indeterminacy' in Criminal Defence Work. *Journal of Law and Society*, 34(4), 489–519.

Tata, C., Goriely, T., McCrone, P., Duff, P., Knapp, M., Henry, A., Lancaster, B. and Sherr, A. (2004) Does Mode of Delivery Make a Difference to Criminal Case Outcomes and Clients' Satisfaction? The Public Defence Solicitor Experiment. *Criminal Law Review*, February, 120–36.

Tata, C. and Gormley, J. (2016) Sentencing and Plea Bargaining: Guilty Pleas Versus Trial Verdicts. In Tonry, M. (ed.) *Criminology & Criminal Justice*. Oxford: Oxford Handbooks Online. Available at: https://www.oxfordhandbooks.com/view/10.1093/oxfordhb/9780199935383.001.0001/oxfordhb-9780199935383-e-40. Accessed 06/08/2020.

Tata, C. and Stephen, F. (2006) 'Swings and Roundabouts': Do Changes to the Structure of Legal Aid Remuneration Make a Real Difference to Criminal Case Managements and Case Outcomes? *Criminal Law Review*, 8, 722–41.

Thomson, M.A. (2018) Bioethics and Vulnerability: Recasting the Objects of Ethical Concern. *Emory Law Journal*, 67(6), 1207–33.

Thornton, J. (2019) The Way in Which Fee Reductions Influence Legal Aid Criminal Defence Lawyer Work: Insights from a Qualitative Study. *Journal of Law and Society*, 46(4), 559–85.

Thornton, J. (2020) Is Publicly Funded Criminal Defence Sustainable? Legal Aid Cuts, Morale, Retention and Recruitment in the English Criminal Law Professions. *Legal Studies*, 40(2), 230–51.

Travers, M. (1997a) Preaching to the Converted? Improving the Persuasiveness of Criminal Justice Research. *British Journal of Criminology*, 37(3), 359–77.

Travers, M. (1997b) *The Reality of Law: Work and Talk in a Firm of Criminal Lawyers*. Aldershot: Dartmouth.

Travis, A. (2017) Public services face real-terms spending cuts of up to 40% in decade to 2020. *The Guardian*, 22 November. Available at: https://www.theguardian.com/uk-news/2017/nov/22/public-services-face-real-terms-spending-cuts-of-up-to-40-in-decade-to-2020. Accessed 06/08/2020.

Tyler, I. (2013) The Riots of the Underclass? Stigmatisation, Mediation and the Government of Poverty and Disadvantage in Neoliberal Britain. *Sociological Research Online*, 18(4), 25–35.

Tyler, T. (1990) *Why People Obey the Law*. New Haven, CT: Yale University Press.

Ungoed-Thomas, J., Harper, T. and Shveda, K. (2018) 600 police stations shut in eight years. *The Times*, 2 September. Available at: https://www.thetimes.co.uk/article/600-police-stations-shut-in-eight-years-nvjdjwmwj. Accessed 01/08/2020.

UNISON (2017) *Policing by Numbers*. 8 May. Available at: https://www.unison.org.uk/news/article/2017/05/policing-by-numbers/. Accessed 01/08/2020.

United Nations (2019) *Crime Prevention and Criminal Justice*. United Nations University Module Series. Available at: https://www.unodc.org/e4j/en/tertiary/criminal-justice.html. Accessed 06/08/2020.

van Brunt, A. (2015) Poor people rely on public defenders who are too overworked to defend them. *The Guardian*, 17 June. Available at: https://www.theguardian.com/commentisfree/2015/jun/17/poor-rely-public-defenders-too-overworked. Accessed 05/08/2020.

Vitale, A. (2017) *The End of Policing*. London: Verso.

Wacquant, L. (2009) *Prisons of Poverty*. Minneapolis, MN: University of Minnesota Press.

Watson, G. (2020) *Respect and Criminal Justice*. Oxford: Oxford University Press.

Weis, L. (2004) *Class Reunion: The Remaking of the American White Working Class*. New York, NY: Routledge/Falmer.

Welsh, L. (2013) Does Tendering Create Travesties of Justice? *Criminal Justice Matters*, 93(1), 28–9.

Welsh, L. (2016) *Magistrates, Managerialism and Marginalisation: Neoliberalism and Access to Justice*. PhD thesis. University of Kent.

Welsh, L. (2017) The Effects of Changes to Legal Aid on Lawyers' Professional Identity and Behaviour in Summary Criminal Cases: A Case Study. *Journal of Law and Society*, 44(4), 559–85.

Welsh, L. (2022) *Access to Justice in Magistrates' Courts: A Study of Defendant Marginalisation*. Oxford: Hart Publishing (forthcoming).

Welsh, L. and Howard, M. (2018) Standardization and the Production of Justice in Summary Criminal Courts: A Post-Human Analysis. *Social and Legal Studies*, 28(6), 774–93.

Welsh Government (2013) *Advice Services Review: Final Research Report*. Available at: https://gov.wales/sites/default/files/statistics-and-research/2019-08/130515-advice-services-review-en.pdf. Accessed 06/08/2020.

Welsh Government (2018a) *Commission on Justice in Wales comes to Butetown*. Available at: https://gov.wales/commission-justice-wales-comes-butetown. Accessed 06/08/2020.

Welsh Government (2018b) *Equality: Annual Report 2017 to 2018 and Welsh Ministers' Report*. Available at: https://gov.wales/equality-annual-report-2017-2018-and-welsh-ministers-report-2018. Accessed 06/08/2020.

Welsh Government (2019a) *Summary statistics for Welsh economic regions: North Wales*. Available at: https://gov.wales/sites/default/files/statistics-and-research/2019-08/summary-statistics-for-welsh-economic-regions-wales-north-wales.pdf. Accessed 06/08/2020.

Welsh Government (2019b) *Summary statistics for Welsh economic regions: Mid and South West Wales*. Available at: https://gov.wales/sites/default/files/statistics-and-research/2019-08/summary-statistics-for-welsh-economic-regions-mid-and-south-west-wales.pdf. Accessed 06/08/2020.

Welsh Government (2019c) *Summary statistics for Welsh economic regions: South East Wales*. Available at: https://gov.wales/sites/default/files/statistics-and-research/2019-08/summary-statistics-for-welsh-economic-regions-wales-south-east-wales.pdf. Accessed 06/08/2020.

Welsh Government (2019d) *Statistical Bulletin: Welsh language results: Annual Population Survey, 2001–2018*. Available at: https://gov.wales/sites/default/files/statistics-and-research/2019-05/welsh-language-results-annual-population-survey-2001-to-2018.pdf. Accessed 06/08/2020.

Welsh Government (2020) *A More Equal Wales – Commencing the Socio-Economic Duty: Factsheet*. Cardiff: Welsh Government. Available at: https://gov.wales/sites/default/files/consultations/2019-11/a-more-equal-wales-commencing-the-socio-economic-duty.pdf. Accessed 06/08/2020.

Westmarland, L. (2008) *Police Cultures*. Cullompton: Willan.

White, A. (2014a) Post-crisis Policing and Public–Private Partnerships: The Case of Lincolnshire Police and G4S. *British Journal of Criminology*, 54(6), 1002–22.

White, A. (2014b) The Politics of Police 'Privatization': A Multiple Streams Approach. *Criminology and Criminal Justice*, 15(3), 283–99.

White, M.D., Cooper, J.A., Saunders, J. and Raganella, A.J. (2010) Motivations for Becoming a Police Officer: Re-assessing Officer Attitudes and Job Satisfaction After Six Years on the Street. *Journal of Criminal Justice*, 38(4), 520–30.

Winckler, V. (2009) *Equality Issues in Wales: A Research Review*. Tredegar: Bevan Foundation/Equality and Human Rights Commission for Wales. Available at: https://www.bevanfoundation.org/publications/equality-issues-in-wales-a-research-review/. Accessed 06/08/2020.

Wooff, A. and Skinns, L. (2018) The Role of Emotion, Space and Place in Police Custody in England: Towards a Geography of Police Custody. *Punishment and Society*, 20(5), 562–79.

Worrall, A. and Mawby, R. (2014) Probation Worker Cultures and Relationships with Offenders. *Probation Journal*, 61(4), 346–57.

Wyn Jones, R. and Learner, J. (2020) Progressive Home Rule? *Progressive Review*, 27(3), 235–245.

Young, R. (2013) Exploring the Boundaries of the Criminal Courtroom Workgroup. *Common Law World Review*, 42(3), 203–39.

Young Legal Aid Lawyers (2018) *Young Legal Aid Lawyers: Social Mobility in a Time of Austerity*. Available at: http://www.younglegalaidlawyers.org/sites/default/files/Soc%20Mob%20Report%20-%20edited.pdf. Accessed 06/08/2020.

Young, R. and Sanders, A. (2004) The Ethics of Prosecution Lawyers. *Legal Ethics*, 7(2), 190–209.

Yow, V. (2018) What Can Oral Historians Learn from Psychotherapists? *Oral History*, 46, 33–41.

Legislation

Access to Justice Act 1999.
Crime and Disorder Act 1998.
Criminal Defence Service Act 2006.
Criminal Justice Act 2003.
Criminal Justice and Public Order Act 1994.
Equality Act 2010 (Specific Duties) Regulations 2011.
European Convention on Human Rights.
Human Rights Act 1998.
Legal Aid Sentencing and Punishment of Offenders Act 2012.
Police and Criminal Evidence Act 1984.
Social Services and Well-being (Wales) Act 2014.
Well-being of Future Generations (Wales) Act 2015.
Welsh Language Act 1993.

Case law

Salduz v Turkey 49 EHRR 19 (2009).
Teixeira de Castro v Portugal 28 EHRR 101 (1998).

Index

References to figures appear in *italic* type; those
in **bold** type refer to tables. References to footnotes show both
the page number and the note number (34n18).

www.ingramcontent.com/pod-product-compliance
Lightning Source LLC
Chambersburg PA
CBHW070916030426
42336CB00014BA/2437